Andy Bull was born in 1956 in _____ _____
Kent. He has a degree in Englis____ _____
University of Lancaster. He has b____ _____ ____ 1977, and
joined the *Independent* upon its launch in 1986. He has been
Deputy Features Editor and Weekend Editor, and his travel writing
for the newspaper won him a commendation in the British Press
Awards. He is currently Picture Editor. He is married, has two
young children and lives in Ealing, west London.

COAST TO COAST
A rock fan's U.S. tour

Andy Bull

BLACK SWAN

COAST TO COAST
A ROCK FAN'S U.S. TOUR
A BLACK SWAN BOOK 0 552 99493 6

First publication in Great Britain

PRINTING HISTORY
Black Swan edition published 1993

Copyright © Andy Bull 1993

Set in 11/12½pt Linotype Melior by
County Typesetters, Margate, Kent

Black Swan Books are published by Transworld Publishers Ltd,
61–63 Uxbridge Road, Ealing, London W5 5SA,
in Australia by Transworld Publishers (Australia) Pty Ltd,
15–25 Helles Avenue, Moorebank, NSW 2170,
and in New Zealand by Transworld Publishers (NZ) Ltd,
3 William Pickering Drive, Albany, Auckland.

Made and printed in Great Britain by
Cox & Wyman Ltd, Reading, Berks.

*For my young son Fred
the little bopper*

Acknowledgements

I am indebted to everyone who helped me on my journey and to all those who took the time to share their stories with me.

Grateful thanks are extended to the copyright holders of the following songs for their permission to quote from the lyrics:

'Peggy Sue' (Petty/Allison/Holly) copyright 1957 MPL Communications Inc., Peermusic (UK) Ltd, 8, Denmark Street, London WC2. Reproduced by permission.

'(Get Your Kicks On) Route 66' by Bobby Troup. Reproduced by permission of Chappell Morris Ltd, London W1Y 3FA.

'Only The Lonely.' Composed by Roy Orbison and Joe Melson, copyright Acuff-Rose Publications Inc. by kind permission of Acuff-Rose Opryland Music Ltd.

'Chelsea Hotel II' and 'Suzanne' by Leonard Cohen. Copyright MAM Music Publishing/Chrysalis Music Ltd. Reproduced by permission.

'Chelsea Morning' by Joni Mitchell. Copyright Westminster Music Ltd. Reproduced by permission.

'Sara' and 'Sad-Eyed Lady Of The Lowlands' by Bob Dylan. Copyright Sony Music Publishing. Reproduced by permission.

'New York City' (Lennon, John). Copyright ATV Music Ltd. All rights controlled and administered by MCA Music Ltd, under licence from ATV Music Ltd.

'Waiting For The Man' by Lou Reed. Copyright 1967

Contents

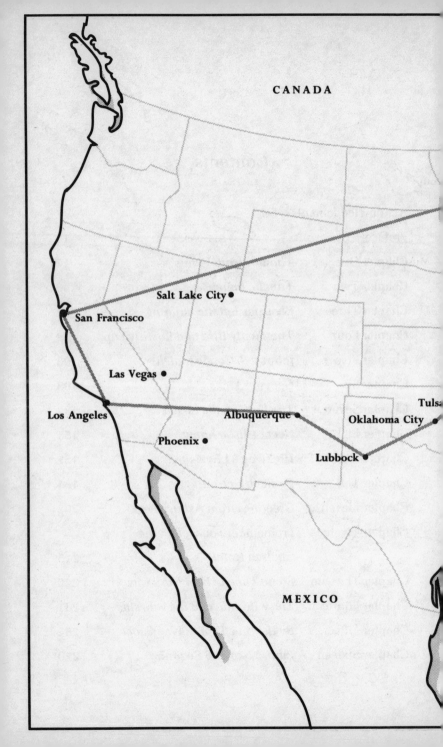

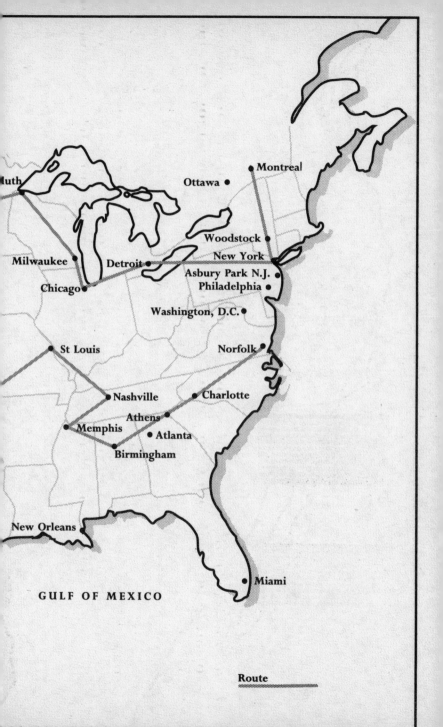

Duluth

Montreal

Ottawa •

Woodstock

Milwaukee

Detroit

New York

Chicago

Asbury Park N.J.

Philadelphia

Washington, D.C. •

St Louis

Norfolk •

Nashville

Charlotte

Athens

Memphis

Atlanta

Birmingham

New Orleans

Miami

GULF OF MEXICO

Route

Preface

I was in Memphis, talking to Elvis's psychic about my dead father. Not that I had planned to. Not that I wanted to.

I had come to talk to the woman who put Elvis in touch with his mother in the afterlife and who has kept up a psychic correspondence with him since his death in 1977. I had come to build up my stock of dead Elvis jokes. And I got what I came for. Elvis is an entertainer on the other side, Dolores Cunningham told me. She has heard him singing 'Teddy Bear'. He looks well, like he did when he was about thirty-two, before he became bloated from drugs and junk food. Like he did the last time he was happy on earth.

I had expected this conversation to be a bit of fun. Real Elvis kitsch. Chatting with a batty old bird about her conversations with the dead King. But it wasn't like that once she turned the tables and started talking about me and my father. This was meant to be the trip of a lifetime, a fun thing. For the best part of a year I had arranged to travel in a great loop around the United States, exploring not the tourist landscape of America but the landscape of pop music, visiting the places my favourite stars were from, where the songs that meant the most to me were set, talking to the people who were in those songs, who appeared on those album covers, and to those who knew the stars before they became stars and shut themselves off from the real world.

It was to be a real fan's trip. And so it turned out to be, but Dolores Cunningham, the psychic, taught me something early on: that I could not divorce myself from what I was seeing.

It had struck me that pop music and the landscape of America – its dreams, aspirations and the love of travel – were inseparable. In pop culture the car and the popular song go hand in hand, but the pop landscape of America is largely unmapped. This seemed curious, when you think of the huge fame of some of the people and the fascinating places that inspired their music. Novelists get a blue plaque and a museum dedicated to them. What had Bob Dylan been awarded? Nothing. My aim on this journey would be to go out and find those places, find the people, draw the pop-music map of America in the pages of this book.

There had already been surprises along the way, right from the start, in Athens, Georgia, the small-town home of R.E.M. I was amazed to find that the members of just about the biggest rock band in America hang around the town, drinking in the bars, getting up to jam with amateur bands in the clubs, positively refusing to allow fame to cut them off from ordinary life and thus making it possible for a stranger like me to wander in and become a part of their social circle for a few days.

In Memphis I had spent a night with Elvis's buddies, who still sit around reminiscing about the time they were in the Court of the Corpulent King. After Memphis I would go on to the schlock horror of Nashville, home of music so sugared and stars so exploitative of their fame that it made me want to retch. I would go on to St Louis and a fleeting meeting with Chuck Berry. I would get my kicks on the old Route 66, which inspired the great song. In Texas I would meet the woman who is Peggy Sue, subject of the Buddy Holly song, and sit in the spot where Roy Orbison wrote 'Only The Lonely'. In Los Angeles I would find that the mythic California created by Brian Wilson, the land of surfing, cruising, girls and sun, was rooted very much in geographic reality, that the hamburger stand in 'Fun Fun Fun' to which the teenage girl drives her daddy's T bird really existed, and is still there.

I would meet a man befriended at the age of twelve by Jim Morrison of the Doors. I would visit the Haight-Ashbury district of San Francisco which, in the summer of 1967, the Summer Of Love, was the one place to be in all the world. I would share Bob Dylan's horror of small-town life in Hibbing, Minnesota and learn about the significance for him of the road that inspired his song 'Highway 61 Revisited'. I would eat rock candy with the woman who appeared with Dylan on the cover of *Bringing It All Back Home*, and find the former café owner who gave him a secret upstairs hideaway in which he wrote two albums. I would drink margueritas, a lot of margueritas, with the woman who talked Paul Simon through his first acid trip.

But this was just the beginning. Or rather, not quite the beginning. This weird journey actually began in Athens, Georgia, so let me take you there.

Chapter One

Thomas from Venus

I was sitting in the Grit when Michael Stipe walked in.

And I thought, this is funny. A couple of days ago I was at home in London, in the bathroom, brushing my teeth and listening to Radio Four, and Michael Stipe came on. R.E.M., the band of which he is singer, lyricist and spokesman, had won three Grammy Awards and Stipe was saying not 'Gee, thank you, we love you all', but 'Register to vote' and 'We must spend on AIDS research'.

And now I was in Athens, Georgia, in the wholefood restaurant on Prince that he owns (motto: We grind your beans) and here he was, one of the most famous rock stars in the world, in person. Hi Michael, glad to meet you.

In Athens itself people are pretty laid-back about R.E.M. You would be hard-pressed here to discover that they are any bigger than other local talent like the Chickasaw Mudd Puppies, Love Tractor or Dreams So Real. That week's local paper had given them a spot on the front page, slotting them in there along with the dull tales of local politics, market prices for livestock and auto wrecks. 'This year marked the first time R.E.M. had been nominated for a Grammy Award,' read the report. '"Out Of Time" was also the band's first number one single . . . The awards and fame have not gotten in the way of productivity for R.E.M. The band is taking a short vacation right now but has already begun work on their next album.'

Michael sat down at the next table. There were only the two of us in the place. I caught his eye. I said hi and he nodded. Wooh! The big time.

I was having a Grit Special, large size – which the menu told me would give me all my beans and rice – with cheese and onion and optional black bean chilli. The room was high and large, with a black and white checkerboard floor and an ornately patterned tin ceiling, dark wood bar, and large, colourful, abstract paintings on the rough plaster walls.

When Michael Stipe appeared I was reading an interview with him in *Rolling Stone*. Before he arrived I had run my eye down the 1992 Music Awards and seen R.E.M. had been chosen by the magazine's readers as Artist of the Year. *Out Of Time* had been selected as the Best Album, 'Losing My Religion' as the Best Single, R.E.M. had been named the Best Band, Michael Stipe as the Best Male Singer. Perversely, *Out Of Time* also appeared in the shortlist for Worst Album.

I had the magazine spread out on the table beyond my plate at page 47, a Stipe interview, and there was a picture of Michael, sporting two days' stubble, a peaked cap pushed well back on his head, a double looped earring in his left ear.

Glancing up from an article and seeing the subject of it approaching you is a pretty weird experience. I felt as if he had caught me peering through his window. I turned to another page.

I'd been reading how in ten years he had gone from being an underground rock singer to a major pop celebrity, but I wasn't really sure what the article taught me. It said he was guarded about his personal life. He wouldn't even discuss his background, except to say he had a very happy childhood and is still close to his family. I suppose the subtext was, 'Look, a rock star must be an enigma. If I put myself across as the uncomplicated boy next door everyone will lose interest.'

The article quoted him as saying that he had got fed up with giving interviews and trying to explain things and having them misunderstood and misquoted, so he had seen the power and sense of the sound bite. You figure out what you want to say and then you condense it. This sounded reasonable.

But I just couldn't get used to the fact that I was sitting in an empty restaurant in a small town with one of the biggest rock stars in the world. He didn't look like a rock star. It was as if he had listed all the things that would make him look like one and then done the opposite. He wore a shapeless, colourless jacket, some old hat, wore his straggly hair in no style at all. He used to have a lot of curls and a cleft chin that put him somewhere down the league table in gorgeousness from Jim Morrison. Now he looked gaunt and haunted. He reminded me of the character in the TV series *Taxi* who seemed to suffer from acid flashbacks and was always clapping his palm to his forehead and going 'Woooooooh!'

Michael Stipe didn't look at a menu and I didn't hear him order anything, but after a few minutes, while he sat with a book held up in front of his face, the waitress brought a plate of mush that looked pretty similar to mine.

You won't find a much bigger band in the world than R.E.M., and you're unlikely to get a much smaller, more homely and laid-back southern town than Athens, Georgia. Its 50,000 population is augmented by 20,000 students attending the University of Georgia, which has a reputation as the place to come if you aim for a double first in drinking and fucking. It's a party town. Downtown is a grid of about six roads this way, six roads that, and the students keep the bars and the

19

cafés and the music clubs full and the little place alive.

And R.E.M., who came here either as art-college students or because the place is renowned for its fun, have chosen to stay. As everyone tells you as soon as you ask about them, they don't hide away. They are very visible, using the bars and the clubs, living in houses in the Boulevard area not far from downtown. They produce, record and play with promising local bands. They are heavily involved in the local community, politics, the environment, urban renewal, preservation of buildings, sheltering the homeless. They fought for the election of a liberal mayor, Gwen O'Looney, in place of all the good ole boy southern Baptists who, they felt, were allowing the town to be destroyed. Barrie Berry, wife of Bill, R.E.M.'s drummer, runs the 40 Watt Club, the town's premier music venue. In almost every way they are archetypal small-town businessmen and pillars of the community, except that they also happen to sell millions of records.

So you could add another sound bite to the ones I had heard while I was brushing my teeth, and it would go as well for the other three members of R.E.M. – Berry, Peter Buck and Mike Mills – as for Michael Stipe: Athens is my Home. I will not be driven out.

I was wary of approaching Michael. I had been warned that, as part of their determination to live as ordinary people in an ordinary town, the band would happily talk on an informal basis but that if I tried to conduct a formal interview they would back off. But as Michael was here and I'd come a long way, it seemed ridiculous not to talk to him. In any case, I wasn't interested in cranking out the tired old questions of the *Rolling Stone* interview. I didn't really want to know about the pressures of success, the meaning of his songs, his environmental concerns.

20

I was much more interested in feeling a part of the place R.E.M.'s music came from, music that for me was the very best to have been written in the eighties and early nineties. It was almost enough to go cruising around town with favourite songs on the car stereo like 'Radio Free Europe' from the *Murmur* album, 'Seven Chinese Brothers' and 'Pretty Persuasion' from *Reckoning* and 'Orange Crush' from *Green*, and think: 'This is where these great songs were made.' I wanted to talk to R.E.M. not as a writer, but as someone who was passing through town and would be hanging out for a while in the places where they hang out. As, for want of a better word, a fan.

I'd talked to a friend of a friend about Athens before I flew over. A Scot now living in Manhattan, Jack had told me about his weekend visit here. He'd said R.E.M. are everywhere, you will bump into them all the time, 'Try the Georgia Bar, or Rocky's Pizzeria', and that the town was the friendliest place he had ever been. Jack was right.

I had tried the formal approach from London, telephoning Jefferson Holt, the band's manager, and asking if I could meet them. 'Well, "no", I guess is the answer,' he said. 'They aren't doing any interviews, Michael is all talked out, they won't do anything now until after the next album is out. When you are here they will be really busy, they may not even be here. No, I'm a lousy interview, I don't want to talk. No, all the stuff about what they do in the town, that's well documented, I don't think there is anything new to say on any of that.'

So I tried the informal approach on Michael Stipe. I said something like, 'I'm just in from England, heard you on the radio, really pleased for you,' etc etc, and he, having glanced up, a little startled, didn't look at my face again but kept his head down, nodded a few

21

times jerkily and said, 'Oh, OK' twice. And then I said see you around, and left.

I'd been in town a couple of days, and the party atmosphere was rubbing off on me. It seemed to take only one drink before I'd feel smashed. One small joke would have me weak with laughter. My limbs felt heavy. But it put me in the right mood for hanging out and meeting people. I mentioned this state to one of the guys I bumped into, Mark Cline, who, like most people in the bars, seemed to be in a band. His was called Love Tractor. Catchy little name. He nodded and grinned when I was telling him about my smashed condition. 'I dunno,' he said, 'some say it's LSD in the water,' and sniggered. 'This is a big drug town. Ecstasy has never caught on, it's still acid around here.' I had been warned.

I was telling Mark and the bunch of people he was with why I was in town and he latched on to the idea immediately, offering to give me a musical history tour of Athens. He'd done this before, and annoyed Michael Stipe in the process.

'Michael got really pissed with me one time,' he said. 'There was this contest on MTV to win a trip to Athens and I was supposed to be your host when you got here. He cornered me at a party at his sister's house and was sooo pissed about it! I thought get real girl, everybody knows where you live.

'I've become oblivious to their fame. Around here they are not perceived as stars, everyone knows them.

'In spring break all the kookie kids from colleges around the country show up, they come to hunt down their favourite band, but they come and they go. And each fall you get five thousand new students and they go crazy for a time seeing these rock stars walking around town, but they quieten down when they realize they are going to see those people every day.

'It is really weird to think that R.E.M. are so famous. The other night I turned on TV and watched them receive three Grammies. I mean, these are the boys I went to school with. Shocking!'

The first place we went to was the spire of a demolished church on Oconee Street, a road which swoops down from the town towards the railroad tracks. That was where it all began for R.E.M. On 5 April 1980 the as-yet-unnamed group played its first gig here.

Mark explained to me that in those days the whole Athens scene, which was very lively, was based on parties rather than public places like bars or clubs. Part of the redundant old episcopal church had been converted into flats. Dan Wall, one of the tenants, discovered a huge empty space behind a bedroom wall, which was perfect for large parties or rehearsing a band. Dan was part of the music scene and when Peter Buck and Michael Stipe dropped by, the three would jam.

The day of the first gig, 5 April, was the birthday of Kathleen O'Brien, one of Dan's flatmates, and the cavernous unused area of the church was set up for the party. Three bands played that night and the last was the still-to-be-named R.E.M. They went down a storm and were promised a gig at a coffee bar in town, if they got a name. Mark remembers suggestions being chalked up on the church walls: Cans of Piss and Slut Bank were two of the less likely. In the end they settled on R.E.M., which might stand for Rapid Eye Movement, the visible indication that a sleeping person is dreaming, or it might not.

Mark remembers the party, but not that well: 'Oh, boy,' he said when I asked him, 'what a night. The place was jumping, there must have been 500 people there. I was on quaaludes!'

For a few months after the party all four members of

R.E.M. lived in the church. Today all that is left is the ugly, stunted Victorian spire standing beside the road. It has been given a thick all-over coat of some kind of protective paint of a purply-brown colour. Where the body of the church stood is now a parking lot for a new three-storey development of mock colonial apartments in pale grey and white, called Steeple Chase.

In the concrete of the sidewalk someone had traced with a finger:

'I am the poetry of the Street
speak to me only with your feet'.

'I heard that when they were going to demolish the place a couple of years ago R.E.M. were asked if they wanted to save it,' said Mark, 'and Peter Buck said hell no, that place was full of rats.

'I don't think it was saved because it is the R.E.M. church but now that it has been it has become a landmark, everyone knows its significance in the R.E.M. story.'

As we drove back through town Mark told me how he had come to Athens in '77 to go to art school. 'I grew up in Atlanta, I came here and I never left. There was so much going on then, all centred around the art school. The B52s [Athens' second most famous band] were just beginning. The band, particularly Cindy Wilson and her brother Ricky, and Keith Strickland, were party animals. They wore garish outfits, amazing great wigs and gatecrashed the parties, which were really wild, bacchanalian blowouts.'

Out on Prince, on the other side of town, we came across the Potter's House thrift store on the corner of Barber Street. This was where the B52s used to buy their clothes. It was a big place with plate glass windows, like a disused supermarket. No rock stars stopped by while I was there, just a few old ladies picking over the cast-off clothes, broken kitchen utensils and plastic toys. A nasty little fibreboard and

24

laminate table was marked: 'From our antique department'.

Barber is the entrance to Rock Star Boulevard. 'This is where all the bands lived,' said Mark as we drove past. 'It used to be just these two blocks on Barber, but then it sort of fanned out to take in Grady and Boulevard, and the area's gotten known as Boulevard. At one time on these two blocks you had everyone in R.E.M., plus Pylon, Love Tractor, the Method Actors and the Side Effects. In fact when the sidewalk was laid here in 1980 someone went and listed down it all the people in the bands. In this house the guys from Pylon lived upstairs and Mike Mills and Bill Berry from R.E.M. lived next door.

'Everyone still lives in the same sort of area because we were all in college together and then these places, which are lovely neo-colonial places now, were all really run down. We used to say, "God, wouldn't it be great to have the money to buy these homes" so when we could we did. We could rent them then for absolutely nothing because they were dumps.'

We moved on.

'This is Grady, this is (gasp) Michael Stipe's street, his is the house with all the bamboo in front of it.' Michael's house was much more modest than those around it, not much more than a little clapboard bungalow, the bamboo growing right up against the front windows in an impenetrable belt of jungle through which you could not squeeze or even see. A garden overgrown to such an extent usually telegraphs the fact that the occupant is either old and helpless or pretty eccentric. Here it was the equivalent to a big neon sign saying: 'Look! Very famous rock star in hiding!'

I hopped out of the car to take some pictures. I went up a drive at the side to get a shot of the house without the foliage, and a face appeared at a window. Oh shit, I thought, if being seen by Michael Stipe reading about him in a magazine felt like being caught peering through his window, being caught by Michael peering through his window felt like being copped stealing his underwear off the washing line. I retreated.

The tour went on, taking us out on Prince to Normaltown (yes, honestly) where, in a rough redneck bar called Allen's, renowned locally for its generous interpretation of the licensing laws, Peter Buck has a Wednesday night residency with a countryish band called the Normaltown Flyers.

We crossed Prince into a neighbourhood called Cobham, where there were more wide, tree-lined streets and grand houses. Athens seemed a strange mix of the wild and the refined. The town was founded in the 1780s and the university in 1785, which gave it a sense of establishment that I was not used to discovering in America.

On Cobb Street we came to Peter Buck's house, which really is a mansion. I recognized it from magazine photos, a substantial white affair with the shingles painted pale grey. A broad verandah surrounds the ground floor and the first floor is topped with a tower room.

'And of course Peter is in there watching TV as usual,' said Mark as we crawled past. 'Watching away, always got the tube on. I lived in that house throughout college. It looked like the house out of the Addams Family when I lived there, it was falling in, but Peter has redone it. It's still sort of a monstrosity though.'

Mark was telling me how he formed his band, how Pylon was getting together at the same time, and that his band and Pylon and maybe some of R.E.M. would sit around jamming and get together to play at parties, where instruments would often be set up for use by anyone in the mood. I decided I had better buy some of these other outfits' tapes and find out what they sounded like. At present I was busking it, claiming a vague awareness of who Love Tractor, Pylon and Dream So Real were. But I risked having my total ignorance uncovered at any moment.

Next day I went to the town record store, Wuxtry, where Peter Buck once worked and where he and Michael Stipe first met, in 1978. I put the tapes I bought at Wuxtry on in the car as I cruised around town. *Pylon Hits* featured a lot of predictable New Wave thrash and a girl singer with a thin voice who shouted a lot. *Feast On My Heart* had a nice bass line but that was about it. R.E.M. have credited Pylon as being a big influence on them, and because of their endorsement the band, which had split up, got together again for a while in the early nineties, but they had split again before my visit. 'It was just a joke,' said Mark. 'The girl singer had ballooned out to about three hundred pounds and she was in these tights. It was a sight.'

'Rubenesque?' I asked.

'Squared,' he replied.

I bought a double tape of Love Tractor, which started promisingly, a good chunky beat moving along, but it didn't get anywhere. The next track was an instrumental too. They all were. After one side I had to give up. The whole thing was lame instrumentals. But when I checked the credits all four band members got a name check for vocals. It seemed my tape was missing the vocal tracks. I had another tape too, which I thought from the cover art was called *Thomas From Venus* but turned out to be *Themes From Venus*. That was really pretty good.

I spent ten very laid-back days in Athens. I covered the scene. I tested the story that you would bump into the members of R.E.M. all over the place. It was true. I went to the Georgia Bar and met Bill Berry and Peter Buck, saw Peter again one Wednesday out at Allen's, met Michael Stipe walking down Clayton Street.

I went to Rocky's Pizzeria, where I didn't meet R.E.M. but got talking to half a dozen members of the other bands I had just been listening to for the first time. It was a Sunday, when Athens is dry, and the big glass-fronted cool chests stacked with beer were kept locked. One of the party was compensating by wearing a T-shirt which read: 'Beer nation – we're drunk, we're here, get used to us'. Strange how not being allowed to have a drink can make you crave one.

Athens had the feel of any university town as far as liveliness and tolerance of weirdness goes. There was a wig shop eagerly perused, I was told, by the large minority of locals who like to dress in drag. Next to it was a sex shop with a large bed at the back on which you could pose for a professional photographer, wearing as little as you liked. Down the street I fell into a dark basement café where the waiter told me that for ideological reasons I really ought to have a thing which he called a Colonel Mustard but which to me looked and tasted like a lentil sandwich.

The chef came out when I was halfway through it, stirring a big tin pot of something. 'How ya like ya Colonel?' he asked me. Speech was difficult with a mouth full of the thing, so I just nodded. 'This is it in its raw state,' he went on, stirring vigorously, and launched into the ideological justification for eating this unappetizing gunge. 'Cuba eradicated starvation with the lentil. In the Soviet Union they have hunger. I figured the lentil is the answer, all it needs is to make them palatable. So I came up with this recipe. I sent it to the Russians. They printed it in one of their magazines there.'

At the other end of the culinary scale I went to a vintage fast-food place the size of a school, called the

Varsity. It was a wonderfully old-fashioned place, all fifties cream and red plastic seats with a chrome counter stretching to the horizon. The menu was simple: dogs and burgers. French fries were listed under specialities. And they did fried pies for dessert. Why fry a pie, I wondered? I was still wondering as I bit into the hot sandwich of crunchy pastry and scalding peach fluid. From the counter you take your food into one of half a dozen dining rooms, each with a TV tuned to a different channel. I ate my cheeseburger to *I Love Lucy*, and my pie to basketball.

I went to the 40 Watt Club, situated in a corner of downtown that seemed to be secondhand-furniture city, and itself beneath the Furniture Mart at 285 West Washington. Among the ads for musicians on the board outside – sound man required and vocalists and percussionist needed – was a bill for an appearance that night for something called the Roach Clips. In fact it was the Black Crowes, heavy southern rockers, playing incognito.

I asked Mark if he was going but he said no, there would be nasty redneck types there. I just found nine hundred college kids and felt very old. It was too crowded, too hot and too noisy. And I had that funny smashed feeling again. Maybe there *was* acid in the water. My ears were still buzzing the next day.

There is always a chance that R.E.M. will get up on stage with any band visiting Athens, but not that night. Terry Allen, another guy I met in a bar, told me how they gave Athens a sneak preview of the album *Out Of Time* just before it was released. 'Bill Berry, Stipe and Michael Mills got up at the end of a show by a band called Driving and Crying and played three songs from the new album. They did "Losing My Religion" and a couple of others. It was a big thrill locally.'

Terry is a photographer, and has a large collection of photographs he took of R.E.M. in their early days. He also manages Dreams So Real, in which his brother Trent is the bass guitarist. I wondered if R.E.M.'s fame caused any resentment among the also-rans?

'Considering how much money, success and fame they have,' Terry said, 'they deserve an award for it not changing any of them: their personalities and the way they act when they see you in the street and so on. And they are willing to help – Pete Buck still will go and help any band that he likes no matter how bad they are, jam with them or produce them, and the other guys too. And politically R.E.M. is a focus, they have made liberal opinion more respectable.'

In the next street from the 40 Watt and almost backing on to it is R.E.M.'s office. The headquarters of R.E.M./Athens Ltd is an anonymous dark wood building without sign or number, next to a music store called Chick Piano which had a 'Do not play the drums' sign on a pearly blue kit set up in the window. There was some graffiti nearby, ranging from 'War is good business: Invest your son' to 'R.E.M. Sux'.

I decided to pop in and say hello, but the only person there was a girl called Brooke Johnston. I ran my eye over the piles of awards, the gold and platinum discs, the statuettes from MTV's award ceremony, the Earth Day 1990 award for environmentally responsible businesses, the Athens-Clarke Heritage Foundation Inc. award for support of historic preservation in Athens. There was also a letter from a soldier fighting in the Gulf War of 1991 who said he had come to the desert with just one cassette, R.E.M.'s *Murmur*, and thanked them for entertaining him through 'this political bullshit prep war'.

I'd been reading an interview with Brooke Johnston in *Flagpole*, the local free paper for kids, in which she raved about working for R.E.M.: 'I could not do this for David Lee Roth or even someone like the Beach Boys, they're nice but R.E.M. – they're exciting, I've

30

learned so much from them, they're very genuine, they're good people . . . I have never been exposed to any kind of filth.' Brooke even gets a credit on the inner sleeve of *Out Of Time*, and the band's manager and accountant are down there as members of the group.

Absolutely everyone had a good word to say for R.E.M. And I didn't doubt any of it. To become so famous but still to retain a normal life in an ordinary town, and to be able to use your fame to do good, locally, nationally and internationally, seemed to me to be a pretty classy thing to pull off. And they have.

Another of the things I wanted to do on my tour of America was to meet some of the people who had inspired the songs that I loved. I asked everyone I met for clues, but it seemed that as far as R.E.M. were concerned, the material's roots were more abstract than that. In other towns it would prove to be a different story.

Someone told me that 'Don't Go Back to Rockville' from 1984's *Reckoning* was about Ingrid Schorr, a good-looking new girl in town who was planning to return to Maryland for the summer. Someone else vaguely remembered hearing that 'Seven Chinese Brothers', 'So. Central Rain' and 'Camera' from the same album were written about Carol Levy, an Athens photographer who died in a car crash.

I did make one discovery though, while driving out to a town called Gainesville, forty minutes north on the shores of Lake Sidney Lanier. I drove past a used-car lot with a large sign naming the owner, Wendell Gee. The name is also the title of a track from the album *Fables Of The Reconstruction*. I stopped and went over. A guy came out of the office and looked at the big fat purple Mercury Sable I was driving with some relish, presumably thinking I'd buy something even bigger and uglier without too much persuasion. He was disappointed when he heard I was trying to trace the subject of a song. 'No,' he said, 'I ain't Wendell Gee. I ain't a Gee at all. Wish I was. Wish I had their money.' He told me that the Gees had a string of businesses locally and were very well-known, and then he spotted a genuine customer and my conversation was over.

I was headed to Gainsville because of an R.E.M. video. It accompanied the whole of the first side of *Reckoning* and was taped at R.A. Miller's Whirligig Gardens. Miller is a folk artist who makes weather vanes out of tin, which he paints in primary colours and embellishes with slogans. 'You really should go and buy some of his stuff,' I was told in Athens. 'People from New York and Washington are starting to snap it up.'

The garden was hard to find. In the end I spotted a bank on the highway, just past Starvin' Marvin's grocery, that was covered in whirling objects. In the middle of the garden was a two-room wooden shack. On the back porch in deep shadow behind a bench, an old man in a hat and plastic ear mufflers like parts of a prehistoric Walkman was slapping household paint from a run-streaked red tin on to a sheet of metal. I said hello and just when I thought he wasn't going to answer Bill Miller said, 'Hi, I can't see you today.' I thought he meant he was too busy to talk, but he added, 'My eyes are not too good today.'

I wandered over the half-acre, looking at the weather vanes on their eight- or nine-foot poles. Sometimes they consisted of bits of tin on a bicycle wheel painted red and yellow and green and blue. Some had slogans on them: 'The Lord love you' was common. There was a large red and yellow cross bearing the same words. A lot of the whirligigs had Valentine messages on them, although 14 February was weeks past.

There were strips of tin too, decorated with cats and pigs, the pigs with both eyes on one side of their snouts and long black eyelashes. Long thin strips of tin had snakes on them, and there were whisky bottles painted green and blue with the same three creatures. Bill Miller was painting away, adding to his stock, but I couldn't imagine taking any of these things out of this setting, where they seemed to belong.

Just driving through the countryside set up echoes of R.E.M. The trees, telegraph poles, barns and abandoned houses were draped in a grey ghostly film like thick cobwebs or some kind of ectoplasm from a horror movie. The film crawls over and covers any neglected area of ground too, and hangs down from the telegraph wires in ragged grey sheets. I was told it was called kudzu, and I remembered it from the picture on the cover of the album *Murmur*. Later in the season it would sprout leaves and appear less alien, but in spring it looked strange and sinister.

The night before I was to move on I met up with Mark Cline again for a bar crawl. We started in a smart corner place called the Globe but then descended, in more ways than one, to a dark and crowded hole down the street. This was a really camp place. A guy in demin shorts, cowboy boots and a silk shirt, his short sandy hair combed straight forward and sprayed, his lips coated in gloss, was strutting backwards and forwards giving Mark the eye and then tossing his head. 'He's dressed down tonight,' Mark said. 'He usually wears a dress.'

At the bar were two girls who, while they had their backs to me, I was convinced were men in drag. They had powerful, muscular legs and tight Lycra skirts that stopped several inches above the tops of their fishnet stockings. They were knocking back shorts in one swallow in some kind of drinking contest.

33

The guy in the cowboy boots came strutting over to us and Mark screamed out, 'Git back in da house!' The guy tossed his head and turned away.

'He and his set are like what the B52s were in the late seventies,' said Mark. 'The first time I saw one of the men in that band he was in a massive purple wig. Dressing up here is a big thing still. Have you seen the wig shop down the street? We have an annual drag ball and the drag queens are quite amazing.'

Mark has tried on the odd frock himself. He complained that the only picture of him in one of the two books written about the Athens music scene shows him in a dress. That did not please him. 'I mean thanks for that,' he said, 'hi Mother, buy the book! We didn't like the guy who wrote it in school and this was his way of paying us back.'

I had had several more than the one beer it seemed to take me to get smashed in this place, and the scene in the bar struck me as the funniest thing on earth. There was a group of women sitting beside us and they appeared to find it nothing short of hilarious too.

The girl to my left and a black guy sitting across from me were trading poses with the boy in the cowboy boots. They put their hands on their hips, clenched their teeth and twisted their lips into a square pout. Mark added regular cries of, 'Umm UMM! Git back in da house!'

When the girl beside me, who said her name was Rachel, heard my English accent she wanted to know what I was doing in Athens. She was a stranger too, it turned out, though I would have imagined she had known the rest of the group all her life. She was from New York, and was visiting Athens to see friends. Mark knew New York and all its clubs from the five years Love Tractor spent on the road. He and Rachel started trading names of people they both knew who had AIDS. They didn't put it like that, they used a euphemism. 'Oh, is he ill?' one would ask. 'I had no idea.'

They knew someone called John Sex who used to dance with a python called Delilah in Manhattan clubs. 'One day the snake escaped,' said Mark, 'and was found in the back yard of a woman from Queens. And the newspaper carried a story about it and there was a quote from John: "That's Delilah, I'd know her anywhere, we dance together."'

Rachel asked Mark what he did and he replied, 'Oh, I'm in a band,' and she said, wide-eyed, 'Oh rilly, what's the name?'

'Love Tractor.'

She giggled. 'Are you serious?'

Mark said sure, he was.

'It makes me think of her over there,' said Rachel, and pointed to one of the muscular shorts drinkers at the bar. 'I bet she's a Love Tractor,' she said and, turning to me, asked, 'don't you?' I said, 'What?' a little nervously and she put her lips close to my ear and repeated the phrase in a mock southern drawl so it came out, 'Leurve Trac-tour. Get her motor runnin', honey, and you won't *never* shut it off!'

Then she sat back and asked where I was going next. When I told her she said, 'Oh rilly, that's rilly bizarre, 'coz I'm going to Memphis tomorrow too. I gotta see my mother, she lives there with my stepfather now.'

So how was I going?

I said I had a rental car.

And that's how I got saddled with the hitchhiker.

Chapter Two

Tupelo, honey?

'You can listen to Buddy Holly when you are alone, but Chuck Berry? You have to be out on the highway.'

Bob Dylan

Next morning I drove through town to the Greyhound station, where I had arranged to pick up Rachel. She was standing at the kerb with a giant suitcase, tall and skinny and instantly recognizable by her bleached white hair with the inch-wide band of mouse at the crown. I pulled up beside her but she made no move to get in, and kept looking down the street in the direction I had come from. I hooted and she bent down to peer in.

'My Gad,' she said, 'I didn't recognize you. What is this thing?' She meant the car.

'It's a Mercury Sable.'

'Um *um*. Sable's a big lady. I reckon she's *your* love tractor.'

I told her there had been a mix-up at Atlanta. I was supposed to get a compact but they had me down for this and it was late at night and I hadn't been able to sort it out, but I had called them and I would get a much smaller and cheaper car for the drive to Memphis.

Her suitcase stowed, she got in but sat looking uneasy.

'Gad, it looks like we stole it. Or like it's your daddy's car or something.' She looked around at the

36

expanse of maroon imitation leather, the maroon velour seats, maroon rugs and door trims.

I was already regretting letting her come along.

She started riffling through the tapes in the glove compartment.

'All you have is R.E.M.,' she complained. 'And what's this? Chuck Berry? Don't you have anything a little more contemporary?'

I explained that it was Chuck Berry that I wanted to listen to on this part of the trip, just as it was R.E.M. I had wanted to listen to in Athens, because they were why I was there.

'Oh right,' she said, fanning the tapes out in her hands, 'these are your soundtrack. You think you're makin' a movie or something?'

She clearly thought I and my whole enterprise were mad.

'OK, I can understand you came to Athens because of R.E.M., but how does Chuck Berry make you want to drive to Memphis?'

I tried to explain that there were two factors involved in my trip around America. The first was my plan to visit the towns that groups or individuals were from, the places that influenced them, that they sang about. I hoped to meet the people in the songs, and people who knew the stars. My other intention on this trip was to travel on the roads that had inspired songs, such as Bob Dylan's album *Highway 61 Revisited*. Almost everybody had at one time sung Bobby Troup's 'Route 66'. And Chuck Berry had written a song in 1963 called 'Promised Land', about a trip by a 'poor boy' on Greyhound bus, train and plane from Norfolk, Virginia across the continent to California.

I told her he had written it while in prison and had had to ask for a map to work out the route, making the guards worry that he was planning an escape. The song was very specific. Berry sang about the bus

37

taking his character from Norfolk to Raleigh, on across Carolina, stopping in Charlotte, bypassing Rockhill. He was ninety miles out of Atlanta by sundown and leaving the state of Georgia. But then the bus got motor trouble halfway across Alabama and finally broke down in downtown Birmingham.

I put the Chuck Berry tape on and made Rachel listen to the song. 'I don't even need a road map,' I said, 'I can just follow the lyrics. You can do that with Route 66 too. I could almost throw away my Rand McNally and use music to navigate.'

As the song went on she said, 'Yeah but he's on a train now, he's going across Mississippi to New Orleans. Then he's in Houston, right, and he gets a plane. He's singing about waking up over Albuquerque on a jet taking him to the Promised Land. But you go wrong after Birmingham. Memphis isn't in the song.'

I explained that I was only following part of the route, that from Birmingham I would make the short trip north to Tupelo, where Elvis Presley was born. From there I could follow Highway 87, which has become known as the Elvis Presley Highway, to Memphis. Then I would use planes to hop to Nashville and then St Louis. And from there I could follow Route 66 to Los Angeles.

She sat quiet for a few minutes and then said, 'You know something, this is a great idea. You go all around the country, you visit all the places your heroes are from. I'd love to do that. Who else do you have?'

I told her that after Elvis it would be Nashville, where, among others, there was Roy Orbison. Then there would be St Louis for some more Chuck Berry, because he is from there and still lives just outside town. Then down to Texas for Buddy Holly, then across to Los Angeles, on Route 66, for the Beach Boys and the Doors. I explained that there was a chronology to it, too. In the south, apart from R.E.M., I would explore the landscape of the birth of rock and roll during the fifties; in Los Angeles the Beach Boys would take me into the first half of the sixties, the Doors into the latter. Then I'd go north on Highway 1 – the road the Beach Boys sang about in a three-song cycle on the album *Holland* – to San Francisco, again late sixties, flower power and all that.

Then it would be back east and up to the far north for Hibbing, Minnesota where Bob Dylan was from, and Highway 61. Further east I'd visit Detroit and Motown, the other big piece in the sixties pop-music jigsaw. Back on the east coast I would drive to New Jersey for Bruce Springsteen. This brought me right up to date again, I pointed out, because I could sense Rachel thought this was all ancient history.

But she was becoming quite enthusiastic. 'And he had roads, didn't he?' she chipped in. 'Highway Nine, right?'

Yeah, and then there was the New Jersey Turnpike up to New York City, and Springsteen, Paul Simon, Chuck Berry and who knows how many others had written about that.

In New York there was Bob Dylan again, and Paul Simon, Lou Reed, John Lennon and a rock and roll hotel called the Chelsea which both Dylan and Leonard Cohen had mentioned in songs.

'OK, OK, so then where?'

'North to Woodstock. More Dylan.'

'Oh no,' she said, 'too much Dylan.'

'But I've listened to more Dylan in my life than every other singer or band put together. And in any case, this has to be my journey. Yours would be different, so would anybody else's probably.'

'Yeah,' she said. 'I'd have Prince in Minneapolis, and Madonna. Where is she from?'

I told her Rochester, Michigan.

My journey would end in Montreal, across the

39

border in Canada, where Leonard Cohen is from, and where John Lennon and Yoko Ono stayed in bed for a week, for peace, in 1969. I would spend my last night sleeping in the room they used, which is now called the John Lennon Suite.

'Well,' she said, 'I think you have to be a little mad to do what you're doing.'

The grey concrete of the Interstate wound beneath us. It would take more than the thought of the Promised Land to make the drive interesting. There wasn't much to look at, except the traffic, the signs reading 'Let's keep Georgia peachy clean' and the dead animals on the hard shoulder.

The hitchhiker was spotting fatalities, and identifying them in a mock southern drawl: 'Dawg,' she would go, 'racoon. 'Nuther dawg. Sperm way-ul. Iddy bidda fluff.'

It was funny at first, but she kept it up all day. I only got her once, when in a small town in Mississippi I spotted a sign pinned to a roadside tree which said: 'Lost. Arctic Fox.'

'Arctic fawx,' I intoned. 'Headed nawth.'

To try and keep the conversation off dead animals I did my tour-guide bit for her. I told her there was more than just music to my journey, because the music had come out of social movements, great shifts in population, the breakdown of the divisions between the races. The journey from Atlanta to Memphis mirrored the life of Martin Luther King Jr, the most powerful force for black Civil Rights. He was born in Atlanta. On Auburn Avenue, the cradle of black business, is the Ebenezer Baptist Church where both he and his father were preachers. He was assassinated in Memphis, on the balcony of his room in the Lorraine Motel, which is now a Civil Rights museum.

Within a couple of blocks of the Ebenezer Baptist

Church is the Royal Peacock Club, a major venue for black people, and the first place Chuck Berry saw his name in lights. Remember the line, I asked, in 'Johnny B. Goode'? She did. I was surprised.

And if that was too old-fashioned for her, Atlanta was also one of the gigs on the Sex Pistols' 1978 tour of America. I had learned in Athens that Bill Berry had had to gatecrash because of a mix-up over his ticket and got thrown out by bouncers. Mark Cline told me he had been there too, and been galvanized, as had a whole generation, at the energy and, what no-one over twenty-five could see at the time, the fun of it all. What a relief punk was after the fat and mellow early seventies. Athens got a shot in the arm from the Sex Pistols.

'You know something,' she said, 'they're ancient history too.'

We drove south through Atlanta to the airport to change the car. I suggested Rachel wait outside with the bags but she came in too.

Just as the clerk and I were sorting things she asked, 'Do you have any convertibles?'

'Sure, we have two just in.'

'We don't want a convertible,' I said.

'Sure we do.'

I turned to her and said through clenched teeth, 'Are you paying for this car? I can't afford a convertible.'

'Oh honey,' she said, slipping her arm through mine as I leant on the counter. She put her head on my shoulder and said to the woman, 'It's our honeymoon.'

I felt sick. The girl was a lunatic. She'd probably slit my throat on the road.

'Oh, really!' said the clerk, beaming indulgently at us now. 'Congratulations. You wait one second while I make a call.'

She came back to say we could have the convertible for the price of a compact. And congratulations to us once again. Would we like it in silver or white?

'You choose, honey,' said Rachel.

There was not enough room for our luggage in the tiny boot, so we drove with the hood down and her giant suitcase wedged in the well behind our seats. We took Interstate 20 for the 150 miles from Atlanta to Birmingham.

I was mad about the performance at the airport.

'Are we supposed to be some sort of comedy double act?' I asked. 'Do you think I'm your straight man?'

'Cummon,' she said, 'lighten up. I got you a convertible, didn't I?'

And then she pointed out a huge flashing electric sign above a building beside the road.

'Ridco
Bug of the month:
Swarming termites.'

And I had to laugh.

She asked me about the array of buttons on the steering wheel. I told her it was for cruise control, there was on and off, and this one made the car accelerate.

'And what's this one, coast?'

'Oh,' I said, 'If I push that it takes me to California.'

'Hey, you made a joke. What about resume?'

'You mean resumé,' I said. 'That prints out your CV.'

'That was another joke, right?'

I was beginning to collect crazy roadside signs. There was one on a water tower: 'Jesus is Lord over Pell City'.

Birmingham appeared as a long low dark stain on the grey countryside to the south, with a handful of tower blocks suggesting some sort of modern downtown. We headed for them, but found we were out the other side and climbing into the better suburbs before we had hit anything approximating to a town centre. We turned and retraced our steps but there was hardly anything to Birmingham. The railway cut right through the centre and the place seemed to have fanned out from it. It is a steel town, a purely functional place. The railway was the centre of town. There was no embellishment. Athens had been a city with a heart – I couldn't see anything in Birmingham worth a second look.

And, particularly after Athens, where I hardly saw a black face, this was a very black town.

The state of Alabama has not shaken off a reputation for racial bigotry. Only thirty years ago there was still segregation, separate drinking fountains for whites and blacks in the Sears department store, and more frightening manifestations of intolerance.

In October 1962 the Motown Revue came to town. The black-owned company was making some of the most popular music, and styling itself the Sound of Young America. Its principal artists – the Supremes, Marvin Gaye, Martha Reeves and the Vandellas – were touring the country. In Birmingham, as elsewhere, they took the then radical step of playing to a racially mixed crowd. As the performers were getting back on their bus, shots rang out. They piled on board and fled under gunfire. As Mary Wells said at the time: 'Me in my little Motown star bubble. All of a sudden everything kind of crushes.'

If I had been Chuck Berry's poor boy, stranded by a broken-down Greyhound, I would have got out of town as fast as I could.

We stopped for petrol and then moved on. While I filled the tank Rachel said she would pay, and disappeared inside the garage. She came out insisting I just had to go in there and see Joyce. Joyce was a real live love tractor, I had to go look, I'd be impressed.

So I went in. Joyce was certainly a big lady; she wore a grey shirt with her name embroidered on the left pocket, grey trousers with the crease sewn into them and a grey bellboy cap. She had a tiny red bow tie on a piece of elastic around her neck like a stripper's nipple tassle. The tube on her stool disappeared up under her – there was no sign of any seat.

I bought some gum as my excuse for being there and said have a nice day.

And she replied, 'Missing you already,' which struck me as a great rejoinder to that meaningless pleasantry. I decided I would use it whenever I could.

From Birmingham to Memphis is 230 miles up Route 78, but it didn't look like we would make it that day. We would make Tupelo, which was 100 miles closer. The road was much quieter than the Interstate, and once in Mississippi the scenery changed dramatically. The state was so much greener. These four lanes seemed inhabited only by trucks, and all the stores beside the road appeared to cater for them.

There was Hubcap Heaven, promising everything for the trucker. Garages quoted the price of truck oil changes, and there was entertainment, too. 'The Boobie Trap. Topless dancers. Rig park in back. I bet Joyce has a rig park in back.'

'Truckers.' The hitchhiker was disdainful. 'I worked on a porno magazine once, doing page layout. They ran a lot of stories about truckers getting lucky. They were always shooting their loads.'

'Like they might do if they took a corner too fast,' I said, eyeing the big rig in front which was weaving around and farting black smoke out of its skyward-pointing stack. I could imagine him shooting his load of logs all over the bonnet of the convertible. Earlier I had seen a bumper sticker on a truck which read: 'How's my driving? We aim for courtesy and consideration. How am I doing? Call . . .' and there was a 1800 number.

This one had a slightly different sticker: 'How's my driving? Dial 1-800-eat-shit.'

We were passing through wooded country. I saw

signs to Verona and then Guntown. Such a mishmash of names made me feel someone had invented this whole place. This whole country, probably, and not that long ago, either.

We made Tupelo in the late afternoon and found a motel. This time I had the hitchhiker stay in the car while I went in to book two singles. I didn't want her stage-whispering to the puzzled clerk, 'Mah husband has no co-lahn, our relations are at an end.'

Then we went to eat. There was plenty of choice, and almost none at the same time. Tupelo seemed to be the fast-food crossroads of the world. Every chain in America was represented here on two wide streets that crossed near the railway at downtown. But there was nowhere that was likely to sell lentils, or promised to give me all my beans. The first non-identikit place we saw was called the Catfish Galley. The menu was brief. They had catfish. You could have two catfish, three catfish or four catfish. And they had a special of the day. 'As many catfish as you can eat: $6.95.' Later I discovered the graffito in the men's room read: 'I love catfish'.

It was a fifties kind of place with blue plastic seats and a nautical air. The waitress, whose badge identified her as Veronica, plonked down a plastic basket with some kind of fried balls in it. We asked what they were. 'Hush puppies,' she said.

And what were they?

'It's corn and a little bit of onion and oil fried. I'm not from the south either,' she confided, as we bit into them suspiciously. They tasted sweet.

So the hitchhiker had to know where she was from (Colorado), and why she was here (because it was her boyfriend's home).

'Wooh,' said the hitchhiker. 'I moved for love once. Forget it!'

I couldn't help thinking that if she moved for me, I'd move on myself pretty fast.

When the food came, the fish had been coated in flour and deep-fried so comprehensively they were like leather. They came with a little pile of coleslaw and half a red onion. Not sliced or chopped or anything, just half an onion plonked on the plate.

Then we went looking for a drink, to be told that the bars were closed until Thursday. Thursday! Today was Tuesday. We had to go to a place called Bogart's in the Ramada Inn where groups of guys in business suits drank beer from the bottle and looked around for something to lay.

There wasn't much to Tupelo apart from the fast food. Downtown, I discovered next morning, was a cluster of elegant, chamois-coloured buildings. There was the courthouse square, a domed city hall and a Confederate war memorial inspired by Nelson's Column. The only building downtown with an Elvis connection was Tupelo Hardware, where he bought his first guitar. It was open at 7.30, a deep, cluttered store that had overflowed into the shop next door, filled with chainsaws, wheelbarrows, shovels, cast-iron kitchen utensils and every nail, screw, nut and bolt that anybody was likely to need. But no guitars. If Elvis were growing up in Tupelo today he'd be out of luck. Have another catfish, son.

There was a long counter by the till where five or six square-built men, in blue dungarees and caps advertising tractors and livestock feed, were standing and mumbling to each other. I thought they were just looking at us because we were strangers, but the hitchhiker was convinced she was the source of their interest.

'This must be the shortest skirt in Tupelo this year,' she said to me, but loud enough for them to hear. I glanced at it. She was probably right.

There was a guy behind the counter, so I approached him with the three-foot wooden ruler I had found, inscribed 'Tupelo Hardware Company Inc. Where Elvis bought his first guitar'. He was counting screws from his palm into a little brown cardboard box. He shook his head silently at me. I thought maybe he was deaf and dumb but he said, 'Ah don' work here.'

'Why are you behind the counter then?' asked Rachel. 'You special or something?'

Another man came over and asked if he could help us. I offered him the ruler.

'Just this?' he asked.

I said yes, that was all.

'Oh, in that case you don't owe us nothing,' he said.

I thanked him but Rachel was still seething.

'You see this thing goes up to thirty-six?' she asked, grabbing the ruler. 'That's so's it can measure the IQs of the assholes you get in here.'

Oh God! As I walked quickly out I could imagine guns aimed at the small of my back. I seriously thought about dumping her. I could drive off, stop a few hundred yards up the road, sling her bag out, and take off before someone in one of these places decided to shoot me to teach me to keep ma wummun in lahn.

We drove to East Tupelo, a couple of miles away on the wrong side of the railroad tracks, where the two-room white-painted wooden shack where Elvis was born is now a museum. Vernon and Gladys Presley lived here for three years, among the poor whites and the even poorer blacks, while he tried to farm and she slaved away in a shirt factory. There is a swing seat on the small porch from which the door opens straight into the first room, which has a bed, a picture of a very young Elvis with his parents – a good-looking family – and a framed print of Kipling's 'If'. The back room

47

is the kitchen. The house is sparsely furnished to echo the Depression of the 1930s.

'Not even a pot to piss in,' said Rachel as she looked around.

When Elvis was thirteen the family gave up on Tupelo and moved to Memphis, and six more years of poverty, before their white trash son somehow, miraculously, became the king of rock and roll. But I didn't feel that this place told me very much, really. There is no life in a museum.

The gift store had a visitors' book with some good entries in it, though. They ranged from, 'If there were more people like Elvis the world would be perfect' to personal boasts like 'I was in the Army with Elvis' to disaffected jibes such as 'The man is as dead as a door nail' and the anguished 'I'm only here because of my mother'.

In the gift shop I bought a Memphis paper published on the day Elvis died.

'Do you know what you were doing when Elvis died?' the hitchhiker asked me.

'I was working in an onion-pickling factory in Holland. How about you?'

'I was eating bagels and cream cheese with my friend Shaun. I have a *New York Times* of when he died.' She paused. 'Unless we threw it out with the bagels.'

We took a late breakfast at a Waffle House before moving on to Memphis. The place had an elaborate code which disguised all the things they could do to potatoes. They could be scattered and smothered. They could be scattered, smothered and covered. Or scattered, smothered, covered and chunked, or even scattered, smothered, covered, chunked and topped.

I asked the hitchhiker, whose idea this place was, to translate.

'Scattered is just on a grill. Smothered is with

onions. Covered is with melted cheese. Chunked is with ham, topped is with chilli.'

She was decisive when the waitress came over; 'Can I have them scattered and covered but not smothered?'

To my great relief she could.

The Waffle House had the weirdest juke-box selection I had ever seen. There was Kate Smith singing 'God Bless America' and 'The Star-Spangled Banner', and a whole selection devoted to songs about waffles. There was 'Waffle House Home', 'I'm Cookin' At The Waffle House' and 'Waffle Doo Wop'.

The waitress was having fun at the expense of a fat perspiring boy who seemed to be a trainee short-order cook. The hitchhiker started to embellish her jibes.

'Hey, Vernon, I want some chicken and I want it fast. Oh boy, you got that ay-crilic shirt on again. Vernon, don't go near no nekkid flame in that thing, you gonna go up like a gas tank.'

I had to get her out of there.

Back in the car, my head was light and I felt smashed again. The hitchhiker had a theory. 'Have you ever thought it's all the coffee you drink?'

I hadn't, but, as she pointed out, I had had three with breakfast, and I'd had one earlier when we stopped for gas. Yep, I was a caffeine junkie.

The road from Tupelo to Memphis is through a series of dirt-poor villages, with little dirt farm roads leading off through the woods. On the stretches through the Holly Springs National Forest some of the roadside farms had Elvis souvenirs, T-shirts and garish rugs hanging out on the fence alongside the road. In Potts Camp we stopped and admired some tea towels inscribed with a verse:

'Can it be true –
That this Christmas when he sings
"Mama liked the roses"

he will be in Heaven with his Moma
singing the song to her?'

I followed a self-drive truck from a company called Taj-me-haul through the forest, the trees crowding in from either side, the convertible sliding through a cool green tunnel.

At Memphis it proved easy to lose the hitchhiker. I dropped her at her parents' house, then followed the signs south for Graceland. Across the street I found what I was looking for in the Memory Lane Motel. The sign boasted:

Guitar Shaped Pool
24 Hour Elvis Movies FREE in room
Weekend Special $49.95 plus tax.

I checked in and switched on the TV. There was Elvis. It was like coming home.

Chapter Three

Elvis has left the building

'Come on in,' said Elvis's big buddy as I hesitated at the door, 'this ain't no private party.'

George Kline was right. It was more like a revivalist meeting. A little gathering of the faithful. Those who feed the eternal flame of Elvis. Former friends and employees of the King getting together to keep the memory burning bright.

I was in an Irish bar and steakhouse called Malone's, just a couple of blocks south of Graceland, Presley's former home. Its green neon clover-leaf logo lit up Elvis Presley Boulevard with a bilious hue.

Every Thursday night they gather here, in the terrace bar. They are distinct from the multitude, the 700,000 who make their pilgrimages to Graceland each year. Punters, having paid, are whizzed through the shrine with the utmost efficiency. It is a clinical experience. Here at Malone's you don't just get a packaged memory of the King. At Malone's you meet the disciples.

George Kline is a skinny little guy with a permed rug and a permanent tan. He was dressed in white slacks and a white sweatshirt with a pig pink picture of Elvis on it. His short collar stood straight up from beneath it, and around his neck was a gold TCB medallion, a personal gift from Elvis, he told us. George is a disc jockey, and was a long-standing buddy of the King. He had a disco set up just inside the door, facing the dozen tables at which thirty people

51

sat, and was pretending that he was broadcasting a live radio programme.

As I found my way to a table he got on with his show. He was talking about the Elvis stamp, a subject of hot debate in America at the time. The US Mail had decided to honour the King. But what likeness should they use? Should the stamp depict the young Elvis, or the old Elvis? George was asking his sidekick, a toweringly tall man called Richard Davies, who had been Elvis's valet.

Young or old? 'What do you think, Richie?'

'Hum haw.'

'It's hard for us to say,' said George, interpreting Richard's indecision for the benefit of those who had never been intimates of the King. 'It's hard for us to be objective.'

A couple of people gave their views. First there was Darnell, from Lubbock, Texas, dressed in red shirt, red jeans, red shoes and socks. He favoured the middle-period Elvis, the King in the black leather outfit he wore for the 1968 TV special.

Then it was Betty Broom's turn. I'd been watching Betty, a middle-aged matron who was knocking back the cocktails, smiling and winking at all around her. That day, George Kline told us, she had met George Bush, who was in Memphis as part of the Primaries for the Republican Congress. 'How many presidents is that you met, Betty?'

She stood up. 'I met three. I shook 'em by the hand. Richard Nixon, Ronald Reagan and now George Bush.'

George shared with us his view of the President. 'He's an American first. I ain't saying I agree with all his politics. Some of them are dumb, but he got shot down in the war, by the Japanese wa'n't it Richard? And he's an American first. But sorry, Betty, about the Elvis stamp. You was saying?'

'For me it has to be the young Elvis. He was sooo cute when he was startin' out.'

George had a mobile phone, and when he wasn't pretending to broadcast live he made it ring and pretended he had George Bush on the line. Bush was asking for Richie.

'Take his number,' said Richie.

It was a good joke, worth retelling, so he did, frequently. 'He's over in the Wilson World Hotel [a pink palace across the street from Graceland with a giant portrait of Elvis in a white jump suit in the lobby]. Wants you to go see him.'

'Take his number.'

George and Richard were a double act, Richard the straight man and helper. He made sure we all had a number, and in between the Elvis records George played and the monologues drawn from decades spent following the King, he would jump up and spin a numbered wheel hooked to the wall. Everyone won something. The guy before me got a replica of George's TCB necklace. Elvis's motto, George explained to us, was 'Taking care of business in a flash', hence the letters TCB and a flash of lightning. I would have liked that, but when my turn came all I got was an LP, signed by George, that contained a radio show, designed for broadcast by local stations, about a fifties songwriter I had never heard of.

At first I felt strangely privileged to be allowed in here. These people – Elvis's friends, Graceland employees, the organizers of fan clubs and editors of magazines – were the inner circle. They were true believers and yet they welcomed all comers. I certainly didn't share their absolute devotion. My view of Elvis is that he squandered his talent and destroyed his life. I see his story as one of tragic waste. But I do believe he changed the world before he fell apart. Nothing was the same after he hit the scene in the mid-fifties. With him, rock and roll became fully formed. Not only was his music electrifying, he was, too. His sexuality was explosive. And with him, and one or two others like James Dean, the teenager, and teen rebellion, were born.

Before Elvis you went from repressed adolescence to dull, conformist adulthood. He set us all free. Thanks to Elvis, a thirty-five-year-old like me can spend months travelling across America writing a book about his rock heroes. But Elvis's story is a sad one. After a couple of short, wonderful years, his terminal decline set in. He joined the Army. And when he came out he made a series of moronic movies and lousy records. He wore those revolting jump suits, he was persuaded he should become a family entertainer. And he slowly destroyed himself with prescription drugs.

But it was fun for a while to be sitting in a little bar sharing small talk about the King, listening to a bunch of middle-aged men reminiscing about a dead friend. George Kline rambled on between records as if thinking aloud. About the time, 'We was up in Columbus, Ohio and we was at breakfast in the motel when this guy built like Hulk Hogan comes up to Elvis and shows him a billfold.

' "Look at this picture," he says to Elvis. Elvis does and it's a picture of him. "That's my wife's billfold," the Hulk says to him. "Well, what can I do about that?" says Elvis. "I'm gonna teach you a lesson," and this guy goes for Elvis and we grabs him, I've got his legs and the other guys have got him round the neck, by the arms, trying to drag him off Elvis. We did it, but, boy, was he a strong guy.'

There was no particular theme to the reminiscences. George passed them on as they came to mind: 'I asked Elvis one time what it was like in the Army. Elvis said, "Well, you gotta be careful the snow snakes don't getcha." "Snow snakes? What are they, Elvis?" "Well, snow snakes crawl up your ass and freeze you to death!"'

George was the star of his anecdotes because they always placed him alongside the King. Their subtext was: 'Elvis and me, we were *that* close'. He would say: 'Elvis only wrote six or seven letters in his life. I have one of them.'

A lot of his monologues were defensive. '*Entertainment Tonight* say they got three Elvis bodyguards on the show but well shucks, one of 'em, he wa'n't no bodyguard 'cept mebbe a wannabe bodyguard and they didn't think to come down here and ask us.'

George had another complaint: 'Hank Williams Jr, he said his daddy invented rockabilly. Well, I don't like to say this of a dead man but Hank Williams, he wrote some great songs but, hell, no, Hank Williams didn't invent rockabilly. Elvis invented rockabilly and I think Hank Williams Jr, if you listen real close, he ain't that good a singer. I think that's one boy is in his daddy's shadow.'

During the records I looked around at the disciples. At a table packed with a dozen or so Graceland employees was Wayne, a pale twenty-year-old in a baseball cap and shorts. When Elvis records played he was far away, eyes closed and head swaying, hands and knees jumping. The disciples showed encyclopedic knowledge of Elvis's material. Darnell was usually deferred to in the discussions of whether Elvis ever recorded a song by x, whether he ever met y, what song Elvis and z both recorded.

So it went on. In short, it got pretty boring after an hour or so, and I moved into the main bar area to get something to eat.

It was a dark room, the only light coming from little pink lamps on the tables, and in from the headlights on the highway and the neon of the surrounding fast-food outlets. There were old enamelled advertisements for

Sinclair Petroleum, and Elvis's picture above an old British Railways sign.

When the waitress came I asked her about the fan club next door. Didn't they know he was dead?

'They're full of shit,' she said with sudden vehemence. 'They are local, got nothing better to do with their time than come up here on a Thursday night and run me ragged and not tip.'

But did they all know him?

'They say a lot of things. I really don't know.'

There was sudden lightning and a heavy downpour. The rain rebounded two feet up from the car park and drummed on the roof louder than the Elvis records coming from the next room. Thunder and lightning were rolling closer all the time until the boom and crack seemed right overhead. The four lanes of traffic on the highway were crawling past blindly, the green sheen that the huge clover-leaf logo gave the rain made the bar feel subterranean.

In the next room George Kline was asking Richie a question: 'Dean Martin. Would you say Dean Martin was the biggest influence on Elvis as a ballad singer?'

'Well,' said Richie, 'if you mean of any white singer – white singer – then I'd have to say it was Dean.'

I was coming back from the bathroom when a guy who told me his name was Paul called me over. 'You wuz in the Elvis room?' he asked. 'Where ya from?'

I told him.

'You gonna see Graceland while you're here?'

I told him I was, in the morning, and he introduced me to his sister, a mousy girl in glasses.

'I love Elvis too,' she said.

'She ain't never been to Graceland, though,' said Paul. 'Lives in Memphis, ain't never been to the house. You going tomorrow, you say?'

'I'm off tomorrow,' said his sister.

Paul started nodding his forehead, from me to her, and widening his eyes.

Oh no, I thought. I've only just got shot of the hitchhiker, I don't want another hanger-on.

Back at the Memory Lane Inn I sat in bed watching the Elvis channel.

In the movie Elvis was a rich guy who meets up with a poor guy. Elvis is trying to escape from the pressures of being a rich man's son and the other guy thinks money is the solution to everything. So they exchange identities. Then Elvis falls for a girl and although she really likes him she says, 'Look, don't waste your time on me. I'm a gold-digger and I know you are too.' Then a real rich guy comes on to her in a really boorish way but she goes with him because of his wealth. Elvis wants her but he knows he must win her through his charm and innate worth and she must not know he is really rich, otherwise how will Elvis know whether she really loves him? She has to want him poor.

Elvis is a lot cuter. The rich guy has weird hair in two shades of brown, smeared down across his crown like he dumps a lump of shit on his head every day and pats it into place.

So in the end the girl makes the right decision and Elvis gets to beat the grungy guy up.

My room boasted an Elvis portrait from the reverential school, a cheap cardboard affair in a frame of gold-coloured plastic, in which he looked like a Puerto Rican Springsteen.

I sat looking at it when the movie got unbearable, thinking, 'Here I am, across the road from Graceland, watching an Elvis movie, having spent the evening with Elvis's buddies.' It was all pretty weird. When I had set out on my journey around America I had had no idea how close I could get to my subjects, particularly the dead ones. In both Athens and Memphis I had felt very close indeed. It was strange. I had got so used

57

to the idea of idols being distant, now I was finding that it seemed possible just to turn up, make a few phone calls, talk to a couple of people, hang out in the right places and pretty much step straight into their lives, or the lives of those who were closest to them.

Next day I went to Graceland. In my mind there were two Gracelands. One was Graceland as the most notable example of a tasteless millionaire rock star's excesses of bad taste. The other was the one Paul Simon sings about in the title track of his album, *Graceland*: a place of pilgrimage.

Simon sings of coming, with his nine-year-old son, to a place where he is confident he will be received. He sings of wanting to come but of not being able to explain why. Graceland, in his song, is the promised land. The song says nothing of the ugliness, exploitation and commercialism you usually hear about.

Graceland didn't fit either picture, although I did share Paul Simon's feeling that I had had to come, because it is the most visible and personal memorial to Elvis.

The striking thing about Graceland is not how large and opulent it is, but how small. You come in, there is a dining room to your left, a lounge with a fifteen-foot sofa and ten-foot coffee table to your right. (The guides are big on numbers.) You can see from end to end of the house. The stairs are in front of you. Elvis put in mirrors to try and give a sense of space. In the basement are a TV room and a pool room. On the first floor you see the jungle room and some other bits and pieces. You are in and out in twenty minutes, left with just the peripheral stuff out back and the graves to look forward to.

It is nowhere near as vulgar as I was led to expect. Some of it has a rather attractive sixties period feel, particularly the TV room with its black sofas and yellow carpets, walls and cushions. In one corner is a bar with lemon-yellow leather stools. There are three old-fashioned televisions in one wall. Elvis got the idea from Lyndon B. Johnson, who watched three news programmes simultaneously. Elvis substituted football games.

In the jungle room, for which we were told Elvis purchased the furniture in thirty minutes, I felt relieved he hadn't had an hour to spare. The armchairs could have been carved out of whole trees, or shaped from petrified crocodiles. The carpeting on the ceiling was a design innovation of Elvis's, creating ideal acoustics. Two albums were recorded here, the guide told us. I bet they were both crap.

We wouldn't see his bedroom or his bathroom, we were told, out of respect for the King.

Graceland was plain boring. It was quite clear that, as they used to say to shift audiences out of concert halls after performances, Elvis has left the building. Out back were lots of single-storey extensions, the sort of thing you see when an old house has been taken over by an institution. Outside the trophy room, which is full of gold discs, I met Wayne again, the young kid from Malone's, standing in his blue guard's uniform. When a woman strayed on to the brown grass, he called, 'Keep off the grass please, mam.'

I felt someone should have said to him, 'Wayne, that grass, and Elvis, are both dead. Go out and live a life.'

And then there were the graves. Elvis and his mother in a garden of remembrance, their graves bedecked with piles of garishly-coloured flowers, a fountain playing. The fans cannot make their mark here, but the 160-yard wall along the front of the estate on Elvis Presley Boulevard is covered with messages. One or two of them were rather good.

Elvis, come back from Burger King

Elvis, why haven't you called? Larry Elvis Reynolds.

Nice House, Bob

I'd rather live in his shack

Back across the street there were his two aeroplanes, the motor museum with some nice cars in it, and all the Elvis souvenirs you could ever wish to see. None of it interested me at all.

I headed into town, for places that could give me a less sanitized feel of the King. To understand Elvis and Memphis fully I had to go back fifty years before the birth of rock and roll, to the turn of the century.

Memphis is probably *the* most important city in the world as far as music is concerned. The blues, the first American music, was created here in the early years of this century. Fifty years later, rock and roll was invented here too.

The catalyst for both was Beale Street, which runs east from the slow brown Mississippi. I drove there, through the black ghetto of south Memphis, and into an elegant Victorian downtown that has suffered decades of neglect but is now being revived.

Memphis was founded in 1819, a frontier town, river port and huge cotton-trading centre. With the fall of the Confederacy and the triumph of the Union in the Civil War, vast tonnages of cotton – white gold – poured into Memphis from the Mississippi Delta. From Front Street alongside the river the cotton went by ship direct to Liverpool and the English cotton mills.

In the late nineteenth century cholera and yellow fever ravaged the white inhabitants but the newly emancipated black population was left largely unscathed, having brought with it a natural immunity from Africa. Newspapers demanded that Memphis be burned and abandoned, but it was rebuilt as a smart modern business city. Blacks were attracted from throughout the south by the work the cotton and timber industries offered, and blacks from the professional classes came from the north and set up businesses. Beale Street was the focus for their enterprise. A new and lively black community grew up with theatres, bars and bordellos. And, along with the economic and social revolution that was taking place, a new form of music developed too.

The blacks who came to town from Louisiana, Kentucky, Tennessee, Arkansas and the rest brought with them their own versions of folk music, of field chants, refrains and gospel. These different strands of music came together on Beale Street and were melded there into a form that became known as the blues.

In the early years of this century a young bandleader called W.C. (William Christopher) Handy discovered the rich new music on Beale street and decided to put it down on paper. He began to compose music in this style as well. In 1910 he wrote a campaign song for E.H. Crump, who was running for mayor of Memphis. It had a new sound: it used the blue notes Handy had picked up from the blacks, and was published as 'Memphis Blues'. America had its first indigenous music. It is the root from which all other American forms of music have stemmed: jazz, ragtime, rock and roll, the lot. Handy also wrote 'St Louis Blues', one of the most popular blues songs of all time, and became known as the Father of the blues.

I found Handy's house, a little wooden hut very like the Presley home in Tupelo, at 352 Beale Street. You can go round it, but just peering through the glass of the door is enough. You don't need to go inside to see how crowded it must have been with himself, his wife and his six children. On a patch of grass before the house a blues band was playing a lazy number well suited to the hot afternoon.

Musicians came to Memphis from all over America to learn the blues. One who came in the 1940s was

Riley King, who became known as the Beale Street Blues Boy, or B.B. King. King is playing his part in the renovation of Beale Street. His blues club sits on a corner, has live music every night and serves a mean strawberry daiquiri.

In the forties the music was changing, taking on an urban sound which became known as rhythm and blues, and using electronic amplification. But it was not just blacks who were into this kind of music, or who were coming to Memphis to escape from rural poverty.

In the early fifties Sam Phillips was an influential disc jockey and owner of Memphis Recording Services, a studio on Hope Avenue, three blocks north of Beale Street. He also had a blues record label, called Sun, on which he recorded the top black artists of the day. But he had a dream: 'If I could find a white man who had the negro sound and the negro feel, I could make a billion dollars.'

In 1948 the family of Vernon, Gladys and Elvis Presley were among the poor whites who came to Memphis hoping to find a better life. They settled in the white ghetto ten blocks north of Beale. Their first home was a once-elegant house at 572 Poplar Avenue. When they lived there each of its sixteen rooms had been converted into a flat that housed an entire family. Sixty people lived in a bug-infested, collapsing building. After a year the Presleys moved to Apartment 328 Lauderdale Courts, 185 Winchester Street, where they lived until 1953.

Elvis had a Saturday job as an usher at Loews State Theatre, which stood at 152 South Main Street but has since been demolished, and during his meal breaks he would come down to Beale Street. When Elvis left school he drove a truck for the Crown Electric Company, his guitar on the seat beside him. At night he haunted Beale Street.

When Elvis came here it was still a tough part of

town, and his would have been possibly the only white face. He came to hear his first live performances of the blues, and to buy clothes. Today Bernie Lansky's store at 126 Beale Street, in sight of the nine-foot bronze Elvis statue, sells Elvis T-shirts, but in the early fifties Bernie would see Elvis the schoolboy usher peering in the window. He came in eventually and started buying shirts with big flipped-over collars, one-button pink jackets with high collars, and peg pants. These were the sharp clothes loved by young blacks. Elvis liked black clothes, and black music too.

Handy was entranced by Beale Street. He once said of it: 'The seven wonders of the world I have seen, and many are the places I have been. Take my advice folks, and see Beale Street first.' Today you can safely leave it until last. It has been done up as a series of places selling T-shirts and tourist trash. On the forthcoming attractions list outside one club was a band called Five Who Killed Elvis.

Sam Phillips's studio was just a few blocks north of Beale, and one Saturday Elvis went in and spent four dollars recording a couple of songs as a gift for his mother. He sang two Inkspots numbers – 'My Happiness' and 'When Your Heartaches Begin'. The engineer was impressed and kept a tape for Sam to hear. Six months later Elvis was called in to record some country songs. When that didn't work Phillips suggested some blues songs by a Sun recording artist called Arthur Big Boy Crudup. Among them was 'That's Alright Mama', which Presley performed with powerful vocals against a fast country backing. Coming from a white man, the sound was a revelation. Phillips had found his singer, and rock and roll was born.

True, the phrase rock and roll had been common in blues from the forties as a euphemism for the sex act. The man who lifted it from blues parlance and used it to describe a new strand of music was Alan Freed, a Cleveland disc jockey, in 1951. He had noticed white youngsters asking for black, urban rhythm and blues records at record stores, and he began broadcasting such music on a radio show called *Moondog's Rock and Roll Party*.

Elvis was the white with the black sound who opened the floodgates. He also came along at the time the teenager was about to be invented. Post war, for the first time, young people were financially independent, local radio was expanding, 78s were being replaced by less fragile, more easily distributed 45rpm singles.

Sun studio closed soon after its mid-fifties heyday and for thirty years it was a barber's shop, a store room and a repair workshop. Today it is back in business as a recording studio and a tourist attraction. The two-storey brick building has the one-room studio on the ground floor left, with a café to the right. Upstairs, in what was a rooming house for the musicians who recorded here, is now a record shop. You buy your ticket in the café and then shuffle next door to the studio where you stand on one side of the room while the guide stands on the other. You get a twenty-minute potted history interspersed with snippets from some of the songs recorded here. The sawtooth ceiling still has its original acoustic tiles in place, and there are period instruments and photographs on the walls. The contrast between this ordinary little room and the wonderful music made in it is quite remarkable. Here 'Blue Suede Shoes' was recorded by Carl Perkins, 'I Walk The Line' by Johnny Cash, 'Great Balls Of Fire' by Jerry Lee Lewis.

People like Jerry Lee and Roy Orbison would record in the studio, eat in the café and sleep upstairs. These days the studio is for tourists during the day and musicians at night. U2 put it back on the map in 1988 when they recorded three tracks for their album *Rattle*

And Hum: 'The Angel Of Harlem', 'Love Rescue Me', and 'When Love Comes To Town'.

Although Elvis was invented here, it was not until Sam Phillips sold him to a major label, RCA, which could market him worldwide, that rock and roll reached the mass audience. His first song for RCA, released in January 1956, was 'Heartbreak Hotel'. No longer just a cult figure for switched-on teenagers, Elvis was now a revelation for millions.

Two blocks south from Beale, on Mulberry Street, in an area of shut-down hotels and warehouses, is a place called the Lorraine Motel. Its two-storey Victorian front has had a substantial 1950s extension tacked on to it. The stylish fifties neon sign is lit up in contrast to the broken hoardings of the hotels that surround it. It is only when you get right up to the door that you realize this is not a motel but a museum.

It was here that Martin Luther King's trip to the Promised Land of freedom and equality was stopped short, with an assassin's bullet. He was shot on 4 March 1968, on the balcony of room 306. Born in Atlanta, murdered in Memphis. I had started out following the journey Chuck Berry made in a song. On the way I had picked up Elvis's trek from Tupelo, Mississippi to Memphis. I had also mirrored the journey of Martin Luther King. Put this and Elvis together and what have you got? The white man stealing the black man's music and killing his leaders, keeping him down. OK, a simplistic thought, but one that occurs in Memphis, nevertheless.

The bullet was fired from a flophouse sixty yards away, on South Main Street. King was in town to support a strike by city sanitation workers and had stayed, as a mark of solidarity, at the modest Lorraine, rather than the plush Peabody which prominent blacks usually preferred. Walter Bailey, the Lorraine's owner at the time of the assassination, died in 1988 and it closed. There was a plan to run a cable car from the flophouse to the motel and call it the Bullet's Flight, and to rent out 307, where King actually slept, at $300 a night. Fortunately the idea was dropped, and the motel has become the National Civil Rights Museum instead. A leading light behind it is d'Army Bailey, a black judge, who had carefully nurtured some of the exhibits that are now on display in the reconstructed rooms that King last used. In a cardboard box at his home Bailey had kept the plates, cups, cutlery, salt and pepper shakers that were used at King's last meal, and a bloodstained pink bedspread which was wrapped around King after he was shot.

You stand in one of the rooms he rented and look into the bedroom, shielded behind glass. On the balcony outside was a huge red and white wreath, and across the street a group of protesters with banners. 'D'Army is a sell out' read one of them. 'The Museum of National Disgrace — another Graceland' read another. I couldn't agree. This was not about nostalgia, sentiment and cheap entertainment, as Graceland is. The museum's exhibits bore witness to the tale of right being smashed by the forces of oppression, of a gradual black ground swell that became an unstoppable tide, of tough battles and hard-won victories. The story culminated in the pointless evil of Martin Luther King's assassination. The story is one of national disgrace – there is nothing disgraceful about the museum.

On the ground beneath King's rooms was a plaque with a quotation from Genesis:

'They said one to another
Behold here cometh the dreamer
Let us slay him
And we shall see what will become of his dreams.'

A few months after my visit four white LA police officers, who had been videoed beating a black motorist close to death, were found not guilty of assault by a jury of ten whites, one Hispanic and an Asian. Los Angeles erupted into flames and murder. It didn't make me feel white America had learned much. Whether you use a bullet or a verdict, it is still injustice, still oppression.

'So,' said Bill Burk as he tucked into his 'All you can eat for $4.95' breakfast in the Elvis room at Shoney's, just down the street from Graceland, 'what Elvis story are you interested in? The one that he is still alive or that he was making love to his mother?'

I didn't really blame his being defensive. Bill had known Elvis for twenty years, and had written around four hundred stories about him for the Memphis newspaper, the *Press-Scimitar*. And I had to admit that I was interested in that sort of stuff too, because it struck me as strange that the myths that surround dead Elvis don't surround dead John Lennon, or Jim Morrison, or Roy Orbison or Buddy Holly.

Bill saw Elvis right through, from the first years of fame, saw the difference in him after his army service, the traumas he went through after the death of his mother Gladys and divorce from his wife, Priscilla. He watched as Elvis gradually withdrew behind the walls of Graceland, became lonelier, unhappier and increasingly sick. Bill had much first-hand experience of the long decline that Elvis's life was after he left the Army in 1960, and it was that which we talked about as we ploughed through our piles of sausage, bacon, egg, grits, hash browns and waffles. As he ate, beads of sweat formed on Bill's forehead and trickled down from his temples, through his sideburns and down to his chin. It's hard work getting through everything you can eat. I wasn't even hungry but I was ploughing in too, just to keep him company. I felt guilty that I wasn't sweating like Bill. Goddam English, too stuck-up to sweat over their food.

Bill started on the *Press-Scimitar* in 1957. As the cub reporter he had the night shift. A smart editor, realizing that Elvis was big and likely to be around for a while, suggested he went up to Graceland each night with a photographer.

'I was told, anything he does, write about it. My photographer had gone to high school with him for four years. In addition my first wife had dated his first drummer and been in the back seat of the car many times when Elvis was in the front, in '54 before I met her. So I had the perfect entrée.

'Elvis didn't wake up until about five o'clock. We'd come here about five or six and in those days Elvis would still come down to the gates on the highway every afternoon. Nobody grabbed him then. He'd just sit and talk to the people, and sometimes he'd invite some of them up to the house. It was like sitting talking to a neighbour. In fact he was a neighbour to me, I lived right here too. He was very accessible. I got his trust real fast, and I never wrote anything that embarrassed him.

'Then he coped with his fame pretty well, but I saw a change after he got back from the Army in March of '60. People started grabbing off of him and pushing him further back behind the walls.

'One night in May of that year Elvis called me about midnight. He never called before midnight, and he never said, "This is Elvis" he just started talking, and you just had to recognize him. He said, "Can you come down to the house?"

'So I went down and there was just something preying on his mind. He was sitting at the piano, which still stands at the far end of the lounge on the ground floor of Graceland, to your right as you enter the front door. And not playing a tune but just hitting the keys and talking to me all the time. He had a Bible on top of the piano and he just thumbed it every so often. Never opened it, just thumbed the edge of the pages. The one topic that ran through most of what he said was his mother and how much she meant to him and how much he missed her.'

[Gladys had died on 14 August 1958. Their relationship was very close. After her death Elvis said of her: 'Everything I have is gone, I lived my whole life for you.']

'After a couple of hours I got up to leave and as we got to where my car was parked right in front of the door he said, "I wish I could be like you. You can go through that gate tonight and they ain't going to grab you. If I went through there they'd tear my hair and tear my clothes."

'I said the main reason for that is you got yourself locked up behind these walls. You don't go down to the gate like you used to. You are inaccessible, so what little moment they can get with you they are grabbing at. If you go to the gate every afternoon, after a while you will be right back to where you were because you won't be so inaccessible.

'He said, "You really think so?" I said, "I know so. Hop in a car right now, I'm gonna go over and open the gate. We'll go down there, they'll grab you tonight but I'll be back tomorrow night and we'll go back there again and I'll be there tomorrow night and tomorrow night and tomorrow night, and after two weeks they gonna say, 'Hell, here comes Elvis again,' like it was commonplace. Two weeks, you be going down to the supermarket, you be going to the movies, you be doing everything."

'For a while he was teetering but then he pulled back and refused to go through it with me. If there is one moment in my life I wish I could change it is that one. If I had made him do it everything might have turned out different.'

It sounded to me as if Bill Burk had witnessed a

crucial moment in Elvis's life. Having seen how the members of R.E.M. were determined to lead ordinary lives, in contact with ordinary people, not shut away like stars, and how it seemed to be working for them, made me feel that Elvis had made the worst possible decision that night.

Elvis also told Bill that he was not happy with the way his career was going. He did not like the films he was making, he wanted to tackle serious roles rather than the froth of comedy, musicals and romances.

The more Elvis shut himself away the more lonely life got, the more unreal, the more he needed buddies around him to keep him company. What Bill describes as the second big hurdle Elvis could not leap, his divorce from Priscilla in 1973, sent him lurching into an ever steeper decline.

Bill watched life at Graceland get weirder and weirder. 'By '75 it was a wild scene, there was rampant shooting of weapons down there. It was like Graceland was its own city with its own laws and because he was Elvis the police looked the other way. Elvis would go down to the Holiday Inn, a high-rise hotel down on the river, and just take the gun and shoot out lights, shoot up the television and shoot up the walls and just walk out and say, "Send me the bill."'

Bill refused to go to Graceland with all the shooting going on, but he tried to warn Elvis in his column that he was in a very serious condition. 'After seeing him in concert in Las Vegas, when he couldn't remember the words or even read the cue cards when they were held up in front of him, I suggested maybe he should think of walking away from it for a while. I asked of the fans in that column, "Why do they still go? Perhaps they think it will be the last time."'

In May of '77 Elvis called Bill as a result of the column. 'He told me he couldn't take a break, that he owed it to the fans. I told him he owed it to himself to stay alive. I think he paid a supreme price for that feeling of loyalty.'

I was sitting in my car, waiting to see Elvis's psychic. The day was blazing hot but I felt shivery. I began to wonder if I hadn't got sunstroke. How ridiculous. Couldn't work up a sweat over breakfast, couldn't get warm in the Memphis sun. I was early for my appointment with Dolores Cunningham and I killed time reading a copy of *Weekly World News* that I had picked up in a souvenir shop. I had been attracted by its front-page banner headline: 'New Wave of Elvis Sightings!' Beside it was an 'amazing computer-enhanced photo' put together by 'police experts' of what Elvis looks like today, based on these sightings. He still had the sideburns but they were flecked with grey. He hadn't gone bald. He must have had quite a few All you can eat breakfasts.

The sub-heading read, 'Eight people who can PROVE the King is alive.' These eight said things like, 'He gave me a brand new Cadillac.' 'We shook hands in Seattle.' 'He loaned me $5.' 'We shopped together at Wal-mart.' 'He saved my life with CPR.' 'We met at the Grand ole Opry.' 'He used my phone to call a pal.' 'We shared ice cream in Michigan.'

It seemed these were just a few of two thousand sightings, a wealth of evidence that 'proves the King faked his death . . . they indicate that he's preparing to go public and make a comeback'. The paper was old and the deadline for that comeback had passed. Cummon Elvis, we're waiting!

Martha Yoder, who shared the ice cream, reported from Muskegon, Mich: 'At first I couldn't believe my eyes. I looked, then I looked again. It was the most beautiful double take you'll ever see. He was right there . . . standing just a few feet away from me . . . Elvis . . . alive! I know it was Elvis, there's absolutely no way I could be mistaken. No-one else has those steamy, sexy eyes. God! What they do to me.' Another said, 'His T-shirt was so white it seemed to glow.'

The woman whose life he saved was drowning in a pond: 'The next thing I knew . . . I was lying on blessed solid ground, and the handsomest man I'd ever seen was giving me the kiss of life. "Welcome to the land of the living, honey," he said to me, and that voice –that "honey" – hit me like a truck. Then I looked into that fabulous face and I knew it was Elvis.' The man who saw him in Wal-mart said Elvis was buying styling gel for his hair.

I was expecting to get more of this stuff from Dolores. I knew that Elvis had consulted her after his mother's death and that she had been able to tell him how she was faring on the other side. Since Elvis's death she had had regular encounters with him. Should be funny to listen to, I had thought.

But it didn't turn out like that. I was shown into a book-lined lounge in an elegant southern house to find a frail figure in a pink leisure suit lying doll-like on a brown corduroy recliner. She lifted her head a little as I entered, and raised her hand when I held out mine to shake it, but there was no strength in her fingers, and none in her voice when she spoke. Miss Cunningham was dying. She apologized for it. She had been terminally ill for a year. I felt terribly guilty.

I sat across the room on the edge of a chaise longue while her nurse came and helped her to sip from the cardboard Pepsi carton that stood on a table beside her. He lifted her head and brought her lips to the cup, dabbing her chin after each of the two small sips that she took. If I could have left then, I would. I said I hoped this would not be too tiring, but she said no, she was always happy to talk about Elvis.

She told me he had come to her after his mother's death because he believed in an afterlife and wanted to discuss it with a parapsychologist. 'His dream was to join his mother and he truly believed he would see her again,' she said, pausing to swallow carefully. Miss Cunningham spoke quietly and slowly, but her mind was clear. She was not the fool, crank or eccentric I had expected. 'I was someone to talk about it with,' she went on. 'It was reassuring to him. He was very close to his mother, closer than I believe any man I've ever seen. Elvis had a mother complex. It was a problem for him.

'He didn't try and contact her through me, he wanted perhaps to share some of my belief systems. To see if I really felt there was an afterlife and that we did see our loved ones, which I believe we do. I've seen that afterlife and I've seen loved ones that had passed on and they are alive as we are here.'

She looked at me coolly. I somehow felt, dying as she was, that the two of us were already in different states from each other. I had a sudden mental image of her floating on a blue cloth over water. The speed of the flow increased and she slipped from sight over a waterfall and was lost to sight. I could feel the hairs standing up on the back of my neck. I didn't for one minute believe this stuff, but it was affecting me, nevertheless.

Dolores told me how she had discovered her powers, how as a child her parents noticed first that she had a psychic sense of smell. She could smell rain, and tell the difference between an approaching hurricane and a tornado, she said. Then she began to have visions. Pictures would form in her mind of events that would happen the next day. And then there were dreams.

'I've had more out of dreams than anything else,' she said. 'I denied my powers at about age eleven. It was embarrassing. It wasn't mentioned, we didn't talk about it. But later, much later when I was a young woman of twenty-seven, I had a clinical death. I had been bitten by a poisonous insect and died in hospital. There really is such a thing as a death that you go through and then you get, or choose – I'm not sure which – to be revived. You get another chance.

'It was an out-of-body experience. I was up in the corner of the room looking down on my body, and it wasn't an unpleasant experience at all. But I didn't want to go back into my body and I was forced, I was slammed back into my body. I argued with the force, I said, "No I'm not going back," but I was slammed, slammed back. That is a terrible feeling.'

For some reason I got the distinct impression that she was going to talk about me, was going to ask me questions that I would not want to answer. My father had died a year ago and in the times that I had spent alone on this trip I had felt a very strong sense of his presence. The time since his death had been very busy. I had purposely kept it so. I had left myself no time for thought, but now when I was driving, or alone in a hotel room, I could often feel his presence. Each time I asked her a question about Elvis it was as if I were changing the subject, steering the conversation away from me on to some third party whose experiences were safely distant from my own.

So I asked her what she had been able to tell Elvis about his mother, and she said she had been able to reassure him. She was at peace. And so, she added, was Elvis, because on the other side we live the type of life we want to live and at the age we want to be.

'Some will tell you he isn't dead,' she went on, 'but I don't believe that. Eight to ten hours after he died I could feel him thrashing around on the other side, just like he was having epileptic fits. That happened because he could not adjust, but we have helpers, there are angels who help us through that transition. I saw that.

'He made contact with me shortly after his death.

There was a party, some kind of celebration, and Elvis was singing at it. He is an entertainer. We take with us exactly what we have learned and accomplished here. Michelangelo would be a painter. In fact I saw him, on the other side, wanting paints. We are able to do things we have always wanted to do, and live the way we always wanted to live. We gather like-minded people around us. A musician would gather with musicians, an artist with artists.'

I told her about Bill Burk's conversation in which Elvis said he was sick of being Elvis. 'He is free of that now,' she said. 'He looks well, like he did when he was about thirty-two.' And then she gave me the sort of quote others before me had come for and got, and gone away chuckling. She said, 'I've seen Elvis entertaining on the other side. He was singing his own songs. I remember he sang "Teddy Bear".'

But somehow it didn't seem funny. She was dying, I was sitting here shivering, in a cold sweat, feeling sick, and thinking about my dead father. I'd watched a TV show with Jonathan Ross in this room, talking to this woman, and asking her if Elvis wore jump suits in heaven, and finding it quite amusing. It didn't feel like that now. And I felt sure she would ask me about myself soon. I was worried about it because if she did I thought I was going to cry. So I asked her if she had known Elvis was going to die.

'I knew, it was obvious. And it wasn't just me. A bunch of psychics in Memphis all knew. One of them called me and pleaded with me to tell Elvis he was going to die but I refused. I would never tell a man that. I might say be careful, but never that. Another told me he had had a vision of a telegram which said Elvis will be shot today and naming the correct day. I wonder if that shot wasn't the fatal drug shot that killed him. I don't know.'

And then I asked her about numerology, which was

a mistake, because she used the question to turn the conversation around to me. It forms the basis of parapsychology, she explained, because numerology states there is order in the universe and therefore events can be anticipated. Everything is in order and everything has a number. Numbers unlock the secrets. Know a person's date of birth and you can outline their character.

'When is your birthday?' Dolores asked me.

'It's the tenth of July.'

'What year?'

'Nineteen fifty-six.'

There was a pause while she thought, and then she reeled off a concise and completely accurate summary of my character: 'You break from family tradition,' she began. 'You are not like anyone else in your family. And you always will break from tradition because the only way you are going to succeed is to not follow the family line. You make a better leader than a follower. You will never be happy following, so you should always place yourself in a position where you can rise to lead rather than follow.'

'That's all true,' I said.

'Now, I took that from numerology, from the ten. You have another number, fifty-six. Let's see. Your other number makes you very charming and a public type of personality. So you can go public at any time. And people really enjoy you, they really love you. You don't especially like to be alone although you could be, if you have to, but that's not your goal.'

I suspected that this was only half the story, that my number, if numerology worked, would also have me down as selfish, jealous, spiteful, easily enraged, shallow and a range of even less appealing traits. But Dolores didn't go into that. Instead she asked me if I had ever had an out-of-body experience. And I said no, but found myself going on to tell her about my father, about sensing his presence, and of how in the past month the sense had become incredibly strong at times.

As I spoke I avoided looking at her, but could feel her gaze on me. There was a pause. 'A sense of his presence would mean that was his presence,' she said, and I found myself fighting not to cry. 'That is the way he is making contact.'

I was shivering uncontrollably now. I tried to relax to stop my body shaking and managed it to some extent. I can't really remember the conversation from there, but I know I spent a long time telling her about my father, about my anger that he had died at sixty-two, before he got old, only eighteen months after retiring. About my guilt and loss over not having had a closer relationship with him, of having spent too many years using him as a benchmark for everything I did not want to become when I probably should have used him as a role model. But why was I telling her all this, instead of asking what colour jump suit the dead King was wearing today, or whether Dad had met Elvis yet?

'Your father is in a good place,' she said when I finally stopped talking and got up to leave. I had told her I was an atheist and that the concept of a Christian heaven meant nothing to me. 'I'm not thinking about a Christian heaven,' she went on, 'where you just walk around smiling and holding hands. The dead learn things. They study, they are productive. Your father is a teacher there too, he has people around him who want to learn from him.'

By the time I got back to the hotel I was feeling really ill. I made it to the room just in time to throw up. I turned the Elvis channel on low and went to bed, still shivering, and had to get up hourly to puke or shit. I was in this state for twenty-four hours, with the Do Not Disturb sign on the door, in a state somewhere

77

between sleeping and waking, dreaming distorted dreams about my father, and Dolores, and Elvis. I only got up then because I had a plane to catch, for Nashville. I drove to the airport in a daze, my stomach kept in check with the strongest drugs the pharmacist would give me without a prescription, sensing my father in the seat next to me, one hand clutching the door handle, right foot jabbing automatically for the brake he did not control. He never did like my driving, especially not the time I rushed him to hospital after a heart attack, feeling mad as hell and jumping every red light. What a stupid thing to have done.

At the airport there were delays. A plane was out of action because of a faulty radio, hours to wait before they found another. At Nashville it was all I could do to go through the process of hiring a car, finding a cheap enough motel and falling back into bed.

Chapter Four

The Twitty Bird and the titty cup

Nashville is hell. I've never been to such a crass place. It would have made me puke, if I wasn't already puking. Nashville is America at its shallowest, most schmaltzy, money-grubbing and exploitative. It is also the home of country music. Need one say more?

It calls itself Music City, USA. It *is* Country Music City, certainly. The industry is here, this is where the stars come to be discovered, where they live, where the records are made. Country music got its big break here in 1925 with a radio show called the *WSM Barn Dance*, later renamed *The Grand Ole Opry*. Broadcast every Saturday night since then, it has disseminated country music through the whole of the USA east of the Rockies and has been largely responsible for its development as one of the most popular forms of modern music. Today it is broadcast from an auditorium in a theme park called Opryland, which boasts a thousand-bed hotel enclosing a stadium-sized atrium in which a tropical landscape flourishes. The owners, Gaylord Entertainment, also own two cable channels, The Nashville Network (TNN) and Country Music Television, the hillbilly's MTV. Through the Country Music Association, a sort of music freemasonry, the entire city seems geared to promoting and exploiting country music in every way.

But what did it all mean to me? Nothing. The only country music I can bear is by Patsy Cline, plus Elvis Costello's album *Almost Blue* and Bob Dylan's

79

Nashville Skyline. I had tried to come with an open mind, keen to test the stories that country music had come of age and captured popular music's mainstream, but for two days I was too sick to venture far from my hotel room. So I watched TV. TNN churned out a succession of music shows and talent contests, and Country Music Television was like MTV for your parents.

TNN was as maudlin, shallow and sentimental as I had expected. A comedian won the audience round by saying, 'My daughter got elected cheerleader.' They applauded, and when the camera panned to show their reaction, waved and held up signs reading 'Hi Mom!' The shows were sponsored either by laxative manufacturers – Ex-lax, Docolax – or Preparation H for haemorrhoids and Great Looking Gray ('makes your dull gray hair look great'). What did this say about the audience profile?

The talent shows were like tele-evangelism. Nobodies were brought on one by one. Instead of showing us their infirmities they brandished their musical abilities. We were invited to pray that they would be delivered from their anonymity into the golden light of fame. And it was in our power to help them, through our telephone votes. Lordy lordy. Will this little girl from Winnebago be saved?

There were visits from past supplicants. One was telling the host how she had made a record. (Applause, hi Mom.) And this week it had had the most adds to playlists of any record around.

'What does that mean?' the host asked her.

'It means I think we have a hit!' She turned to the audience and asked, 'Do we? Do we?' They cried back 'Yes!' The cameras panned over them, they waved and held up their 'Hi Mom!' boards and 'Howdy y'all in Des Moines' banners. Allelujah! Ah think she can wawk!

* * *

When my temperature and nausea had subsided sufficiently I ventured out into the surreal world of the Opryland Hotel. Wandering after dark in my feverish state, through the massive undercover tropical garden, past streams lit pink and waterfalls green, beneath orange fountains, was a truly bizarre experience.

I escaped to the relative sanity of Bob Martin's Country Store for lemon tea and plain toast. The place was done up like a mock-rustic motorway service station, with souvenirs on sale, bentwood chairs and gingham tie-back curtains. A team of old-age pensioners were doomed to serve. One poor old dear circled endlessly with a basket of bread. This was catering the Samuel Beckett way. And the condiment bottles on the table wore cowboy hats. In the souvenir area more sauce bottles, jars of jelly, relish and peanut butter were also wearing cowboy hats. I really didn't want to sit at a table where the sauce wore a stetson, so I took them off. But on her next circuit the old lady with the bread basket noticed they were out of place and popped them back on, giving me a broad smile as she did so.

Then I ventured downtown. On Broadway I found the Ernest Tubb Record Store. From a back room the *Grand Ole Opry* radio show was broadcast in its early years. Today the deep narrow store is shabby but well stocked with tapes and CDs. I was the only customer and the girl at the cash desk was in the middle of a long phone conversation about how 'No-one wants to do nothing on the weekends'. She kept the conversation running uninterrupted as she sold me the Roy Orbison and Patsy Cline cassettes I had selected. Broadway was seedy, but not especially so. Next to the record store was the Rose Loan Co., which specialized in pawning guns and guitars. Nearby were the Wheel Adult Emporium, General Lee's Flea Market and the Music

City Lounge. I would have liked a drink in what was a cosy-looking bar, but doubted they stretched to lemon tea. The lounge was among the stars' watering holes after shows at Tubbs and later at the Ryman Auditorium, a former church hall to which the Opry moved in 1934. In 1974 Opryland was opened, and the decline of downtown accelerated. Now the place is called the District, and the Victorian warehouses alongside the Cumberland river have been converted into restaurants, galleries and antique stores.

Drive north on Demonbreun and you come to Music Row, where all the record-company offices and recording studios are. First you must navigate a golden mile of trash, a chain of cheap and nasty souvenir stores which bear the names of some of the biggest country stars. There is Loretta Lyn's Western Wear, Barbara Mandrell Country, which boasts a full-size replica of her bedroom, Conway Twitty's Twitty Bird Record Shop, George Jones's Store, Hank Williams Jnr's Store, and Elvis Presley's Gift Shop and Museum.

In Conway Twitty's, while Rickie Lee sang that makin' love don't always make love grow, I toyed with the idea of buying a 3-D Last Supper place mat, a mug with a little penis inside it or a titty cup – you drink through the nipple.

In Hank Williams's I could have bought a hat with the slogan 'If heaven ain't like Dixie [the south] I don't wanna go', or one branded 'Shithead' which had a lurid turd sitting on the brim. A sign asked 'Please don't try on the T-shirts'. Honey, I wouldn't piss on the T-shirts if they were aflame. In Elvis Presley's I bought a bottle of Elvis Presley Love Me Tender Conditioning Shampoo. On the label I read, 'Elvis Presley had a precious gift, a great talent that he shared with the world, capturing the love of young and old. Elvis was respected and admired as an entertainer and a generous caring person. He revolutionized the field of music and became a legend in his own time.' 'Elvis performed "Love Me Tender" in 1956. This beautiful love song remains one of the most popular recordings of all time.' 'Elvis Presley Love Me Tender products are a commemorative to the King, made with the finest ingredients, to be used and enjoyed daily.' 'Love Me Tender conditioning shampoo cleans and conditions your hair with a rich, thick, luxurious lather.' The shampoo was blue and smelled of almonds. An ideal gift for an unloved one.

This place resembled a thrift store. There was a chipped Elvis plate marked 'reduced', and a singing Elvis In Concert doll with a note attached which read: 'Tape plays, it is just a little deep.' This seemed rather like saying, 'Elvis is alive, he is just a little buried in the ground.'

It all made Graceland look positively tasteful.

At the top of the street was the Country Music Hall of Fame and Museum, which I had hoped could persuade me that country music was worth serious consideration, but instead showed me Dolly Parton's stage outfit and Elvis's gold-plated Cadillac. One room was called the Johnny Cash Collection. On a TV screen a video played, with Johnny in his den at home picking up items and talking about them. 'This is my private room,' he said. 'I want to show you around a little.' He picked up books, pointed to photographs, held up Indian artifacts. When the video ended I looked around and found that all these items were not in his private room at all but here, in glass cases. Magical!

There was not much attempt to explain the roots of country music. Basically, while the blues was the music of the poor blacks, country was the province of poor, uneducated southern whites. It was the music the white man didn't have to steal. It has its roots in the folk music brought to America by British settlers, but because of the particular conditions in the south, where reliance on black slavery for white prosperity led to disapproval and insularity, the music was geographically restricted. The south was isolated and the music became inward-looking and defensive. It was not until the *Grand Ole Opry* and other radio shows that country music broke out, but it is still often seen as part of a pride in Dixie and an embodiment of southern separateness.

Just beyond the Country Music Hall of Fame and Museum is Music Row. Here, on three long blocks bounded by Music Square East and Music Square West, are the offices of the record companies. It was on Music Row in 1939 that the second big influence on the spread of country music occurred: the foundation of Broadcast Music Incorporated (BMI). Up until then there had only been one organization in America, the American Society of Composers, Authors and Publishers (ASCAP), which looked after songwriters' interests, monitoring the use of their compositions and collecting royalties. The ASCAP was not interested in country – hillbilly – music. BMI gave country performers national exposure and protection.

In the fifties, when rock and roll was created, country music was one of its elements. Elvis was a hillbilly, after all. The fifties generation of young country performers, including Carl Perkins and Jerry Lee Lewis, blended the white and black influences, but pure country music remained a minority interest. In the sixties it gained popularity, partly as a reaction to the way rock music was going, becoming more complex and experimental. Country music maintained its simple style, and its lyrical concerns were still those of love, infidelity, loss, bravery and suffering. Politically it was often right-wing and reactionary, and appealed to those who disapproved of the permissive society of the sixties. What a betrayal, then, that at the height of hippiedom Dylan should go into the enemy camp and record a country album!

In 1969, the same year that the hippies made the pilgrimage to Dylan's upstate New York home village for the Woodstock Festival, the biggest expression of the counter culture, Dylan came to Nashville. He made *Nashville Skyline*, an album of country love songs which were simple without being crass. It was good! Many rocks stars followed him because he had made country respectable, weaving it in with the mainstream.

The third area with country music connections is Hendersonville, a rich man's suburb twenty miles out of town on the shores of Old Hickory Lake. There seemed to be a lot of churches on the way out, each with a slogan on a billboard. 'Attitudes are contagious. Is yours worth catching?' read one. Another declared: 'Friendship is like vitamins. We supplement each other's minimum daily requirement.'

Out here, just off the Johnny Cash Parkway opposite the House of Cash store and June Carter Cash antiques, is Music Village, a gathering of more tourist attractions. I resisted Willie Nelson and Friends ('New and exciting. Willie's personal items') and Encore Celebrity Pre-owned Clothing, heading for the biggest star-related tourist attraction in Nashville: Conway Twitty's Twitty City. The annotated map at the gate promised total exposure of the star. Conway was a new one on me, but I discovered that he had a number one hit in 1958 with 'It's Only Make Believe', and thirteen more hits in 1962 alone. It listed: 'Observation point for children's homes. All of Conway's children live and work here at Twitty City. Guest home: Home for Conway's and Mickey's mothers when visiting Twitty City. Conway's home here at Twitty City has over 10,000 sq. ft. Conway spends as much time as possible visiting with fans and visitors to Twitty City. Garage:

Conway's buses are parked here (when not on tour) for easy viewing by fans and visitors.'

A photograph revealed Conway to be a grinning, tanned old character with a bouffant hair-do. To make the tour of Twitty City I had first to wait for a Gray Line busload of blue rinses to arrive. We were ushered into a cinema where a film started. It's night. The Twitty house is in darkness. Conway is snoring. The phone rings. It is the Twitty Bird, a yellow cartoon character, calling about the balloon trip the next day over Twitty City. 'I'm frightened, Conway, I can't fly.' 'You don't have to go – but we will,' and off we go, over the house where 500,000 lights shine each Christmas, into the private world of the star.

Conway, it turns out on the tour, was an Elvis wannabe who switched from country to rock and roll in the fifties and back to country in 1965. As his biography unfolds and he gets older I notice that his hair seems to get younger, more bouffant. We hear he has more gold records than Elvis or the Beatles, that he clocked up fifty-five number one records over thirty years. They cover a whole wall.

An old lady is puzzled: 'How old is he?' she asks.

'We are allowed to say over forty.'

'Well, I say over fifty.'

The climax of the tour comes when you enter Conway's house itself. Who knows, he might come tripping down the stairs in his golfing slacks right this minute. Of course, he does not, and as we are shepherded round the ground floor, which is all we get to see, the house has a distinctly unlived-in feel. There are acres of pale blue unwalked-on carpet, hotel-like furniture and – a really phoney touch this – a huge Norman Rockwell volume left casually on the coffee table.

As we look glumly around, the guide confesses the Twittys have just finished building another house – for privacy. I feel cheated. You are enticed into this place with the promise that it is the star's privacy which is being sold to you. Country stars pretend to be real down-home and friendly, the opposite of rock and roll, where the stars trade on untouchability, where mystique is part of the image and appeal. Here the message is: 'Come into my home, see everything, join the family.'

I had met R.E.M. in Athens, no problem, but Conway in Twitty City? No chance. All this star stuff was like virtual reality. You are in their stores, looking at their clothes, their personal effects, in their private dens, invited into their homes, but nothing is quite what it seems. It is all a simulation.

I was pleased to see that Twitty's sensational LP *Merry Twismas* was reduced to $2.99 in his souvenir shop. I didn't buy one, but did pick up a copy of a map that promised to identify over 128 stars' homes, from Bill Anderson to Sheb Wooley. No matter that I had heard of neither of them. No matter that, true to form, while showing where the superstars lived, the map also ran a disclaimer to the effect that if I loitered outside their houses I could be breaking a bye-law. I wanted to find Roy Orbison's former home. It turned out to be right around the corner.

A narrow lane called Caudill Drive led to the lakeside, passing between the substantial detached houses. Orbison's former house ('large white stucco wall, two angels in wall') stands next to Johnny Cash's, with its twenty-four-hour security post at the gate. The best of the houses of the rich lead down to the water where there will be a smart boat moored at a private dock. Just round the headland on which the three-storey stone and wood house stands was an inlet with a public launching point. It was empty today. From where I sat on a concrete dock I saw no-one except the occasional gardener and security man and the Gray Line Country and Western tour buses, turning at the circle just past

87

Cash's house. The breeze was up, the water choppy in the inlet, rocking the boat at Roy's old dock and setting a corrugated iron landing stage creaking.

If there is a true-life story that matches the tragedy of the gloomiest of country songs, it is that of Roy Orbison. Later on my journey I would visit the little town of Wink in the west Texas desert where he was brought up. Hendersonville was where he came when he made it, with songs like 'Only the Lonely' and 'Claudette'. On an 11,000-acre plot, larger than the town he came from, he built a rambling house equipped with a cavernous music room, an entrance hall with a waterfall, a swimming pool in the living room and a lift to the beach.

Claudette was Roy's wife. They loved motorcycling and were coming back on 7 June 1965 from the national drag races 200 miles away at Bristol, he on his Harley Davidson, she on her BMW, when Claudette was killed. A few miles north-east of Old Hickory a truck pulled out of a side turning and Claudette went beneath the wheels.

On 16 September 1968 while he was on tour in England, Orbison heard that his house had burned down. Two of his three sons, Roy and Tony, were killed. They had been playing with petrol stored in the basement. The air conditioning system had helped the fire spread through the house.

Orbison thought he would go mad. For days he hid away in a darkened Nashville hotel room, but was consoled by Barbara Wellnoener-Jacobs, whom he eventually married. Orbison sold the site of the house to Johnny Cash, who planted an orchard there, and built himself a new home a few hundred yards away along the headland. That was the house I could see from the dock.

In December 1988, his career having taken off again

after years in the doldrums, Roy Orbison died of a heart attack. His collaboration in the Travelin' Wilburys with Bob Dylan, George Harrison, Tom Petty and Jeff Lynne had put him back in the charts. A new solo album, the first for years, was about to be released. It was a big hit after his death.

So far I had seen and heard nothing in Nashville to persuade me that there was much of any real merit in country music, but I was still open to persuasion. There are those who believe that country is now the most vital form of popular music. Rock has split into a hundred camps, the argument goes; it is merely the music of tribes, from heavy metal for white longhairs to rap for urban blacks. Country stars and fans tend to be white, and the music has been likened to the aural equivalent of white flight, the phenomenon of whites leaving mixed-race areas for comfort and security of suburbia. The thirty- and fortysomethings, the ones who buy the most records, are turning to the security of country.

Jim Rooney, partner in a Music Row recording and publishing business called Jack's Tracks, is one who sees a great future for country. Together with his partner Allen Reynolds he has played a substantial part in the success of some of the most prominent of the new wave of country stars, including Hal Ketchum, Garth Brooks and Kathy Mattea.

I found Jack's Tracks at the bottom end of Music Row, in a little two-storey wooden house which had been converted into a studio.

'Nashville is the hottest music centre in the United States,' Jim told me. 'It has always been in third place behind New York and Los Angeles, but in the past two or three years country music has come to the point where, in terms of radio plays, it is second only to adult contemporary.

'Pop music just seems to have run out of gas. The

most exciting awards at the Grammies went to Natalie Cole [daughter of Nat King Cole, for an album of his songs to which she had added her voice] and Bonnie Raitt. Both of them are in their forties. There is some alternative rock happening like R.E.M. and Nirvana, but country music right now is selling in very large numbers and attracting a whole new audience of young people.'

Jim drew a parallel between this and the scene in the early sixties, when Bob Dylan spearheaded the emergence of folk as the primary, most creative force in popular music. Those with talent tended to express it through folk rather than any other form. Today, Jim believes, young people will be attracted to the country form rather than any other.

'There have been eight or ten artists in the last three years who have come from absolutely nowhere to multi-platinum status,' he went on. 'Clint Black, Garth Brooks, Alan Jackson, Trisha Yearwood. I guess part of it we'd like to take credit for.

'The major artists who are coming up, all guys in their twenties, grew up on a mix of southern rock music and folk: the Allman Brothers, Lynard Skynard, Crosby, Stills, Nash and Young. James Taylor is one name that keeps coming up again and again. Women very frequently mention Joni Mitchell. They have been influenced by artists with folk roots who also have in common that the lyrics to their songs were quite important. That obviously sank in. Plus they also have listened to the normal country artists like Dolly Parton, Merl Haggard, Johnny Cash and Waylon Jennings. All these are really good songwriters.'

Jim, whose first musical experience was in the folk scene in Boston in the early sixties, came to Nashville in 1973, where he met up with Allen Reynolds and switched from being principally a musician to producing.

'I recorded an album in 1984 with Nancy Griffith called *Once In A Very Blue Moon*, which used a mix of acoustic with steel guitar, electric guitar and drums. The sound worked and, shortly after that, that sound started showing up on other records. Randy Travis was one of the first to use it. When I mixed the second album with Nancy, *Last Of The True Believers*, Allen heard it a lot. He had just started working with Kathy Mattea, and he recorded a track from that album with Kathy called "Love At The Five And Dime" which was her first top ten hit. He also recorded "Going Gone" and that was Kathy's first number one single.

'That sound, a folk and country combination, just started to blossom. We started a publishing company and discovered a young songwriter called Hal Ketchum. We saw him as primarily a songwriter but when we did some demos with him, in a simple guitar, bass and drums setting, we were very impressed with him as a performer. We got him a record deal. We were in the middle of an album and released a song called "Small Town Saturday Night", which became the most played single of 1991. He went on to have two more hits from the first album and now we have just finished his second.'

As I left, Jim asked me if I'd like some tapes. He opened a cupboard and started tossing out a pile of things produced by Allen or himself including Garth Brooks, Hal Ketchum, Don Williams, Kathy Mattea and Emmylou Harris.

I listened to them on the plane to St Louis. I willed them to contain something new and exciting. Don Williams and Emmylou Harris I had to junk after a track or two. Kathy Mattea was passable but too soft for me. Hal Ketchum started well. The first track was 'Small Town Saturday Night', which rocked along like a reasonable Springsteen imitation, with evocative lyrics about the limits of small-town life, but trailed off somewhat from there. Lots of stuff about not needing money because he knew where to find true love. Most of the time I could forget this was country music, which made it bearable, but when it got to a track with the title 'Don't Strike a Match (To the Book of Love)' I felt I was right back to cornsville. Garth Brooks I had the highest hopes for. After all, he outsells Michael Jackson and Guns N' Roses. I had 1991's *Ropin' The Wind*, the first country album to go into the *Billboard* chart at No. 1.

Country's loudest proponents would have you believe pop music's line of progression goes Elvis, the Beatles, Brooks. I listened for the lyrical inventiveness of John Lennon, some hint of the sexual charisma of Elvis. The picture on the sleeve showed a slightly rotund thirtysomething in a black stetson, worn, I hear, to cover his receding hairline. His voice and his sound seemed very mainstream country to me. I found it just too comfortable, too down-home, too corny.

So no, I can't see country as the popular music of the future, though I will confess I am humming 'I Know Where Love Lives', from the Hal Ketchum album, as I write this.

Chapter Five

Johnny B. Goode tonight

Joe Edwards and I were looking at a guitar. A white guitar in a glass case just inside the door of Joe's bar and restaurant in St Louis. 'Chuck Berry wrote and recorded all of his greatest songs on that guitar,' Joe told me. ' "Johnny B. Goode", "Roll Over Beethoven", "Sweet Little Sixteen"; it's the most influential guitar in the history of rock and roll.

'Chuck gave it to me. We were rebuilding the front of the bar and putting a display case here and he said he'd give me a guitar to put in it. I was thrilled but he has twenty or thirty guitars at his place in Wentzville and I never expected it to be this one. I went out with Linda, my wife, and as he pulled out the guitar I could tell what one it was from the case. I couldn't believe it. And it's so nice because everyone gets to see it this way. We put glass both sides so you can see front and back. I like to watch people come up and put their ear near the case and do the duck walk or start dancing or something. It's almost like they can hear him play it right there and then. It's an ES 350 T hollow body Gibson. I've had offers, but I would never sell something that a friend had given me. Besides, it belongs in St Louis.'

Indeed, it was Chuck Berry who had brought me to St Louis. It is his town. He was born here in 1926 and still lives within thirty miles of the place. St Louis is another crumbling city that grew great on river-borne trade, as Memphis and Nashville had. Here it was the fur trade, and St Louis is still America's second busiest inland port. I was back on the Mississippi again. I hadn't seen it since Memphis so I went down to take a look. Although I was three hundred miles upriver from Memphis, the Mississippi seemed just as wide, brown and slow-rolling. Beside the grimy brick façade and four huge rusting chimneys of the Union Light and Power Company were a couple of rows of former warehouses, now well scrubbed and converted into restaurants and gift shops. There were three or four paddle steamers moored, one of them converted into a McDonald's. Looking back to the city I saw a tower block framed by the soaring concrete arc of the Gateway Arch, looking for all the world like the largest ever manifestation of the famous McDonald's M.

St Louis was at the same time the blackest and the most European of the cities I had passed through. Downtown the narrow streets were cool, shaded by the office blocks and echoing with the roar from the elevated Interstate which follows the sweep of the river around the city. I didn't like it much. There was a bullet hole in my hotel window, the impact sculpting an aperture shaped like the base of a wine glass in the centimetre-thick pane. Driving north to the yuppified University City area to meet Joe I passed through a great swathe of poverty. Once-grand houses, now tumbling down, teamed with children. There was a gas station converted into a thrift store and a stall offering the world's best shoe shine.

On Delmar there had been a wreck. A fat old Buick seemed to have tried to pass between two cars turning left, one from the north, the other from the south, and we had a Buick sandwich blocking the road. The junction was littered with bits of rusty cars and red glass. Traffic crawled up on to the sidewalks to ease past, and in the beat-up houses everyone was leaning from the windows, enjoying the incident that had added a little interest to an empty day.

But when I got to Joe's I felt lucky. I had found the best bar in the world, and it was run by one of Chuck Berry's few close friends. Maybe the fact that I felt well enough to have my first drink in over a week influenced me, but entering Joe's bar, which he had named Blueberry Hill after the Fats Domino song, was like stepping into the home you never knew you had. Blueberry Hill was converted in 1972 from a warehouse covering half a Victorian block. It is arranged as a series of dark-blue painted rooms, one full of pinball tables, another housing the 2,000-selection CD jukebox which Joe claims is the best in the world. The selections are changed completely every three months. The walls are filled with framed sheet music, single and album sleeves and other rock and roll memorabilia, and downstairs there is an Elvis room where they have live music. In 1986 Joe launched his own Blueberry Hill record label; he had clocked up twenty-three releases of local bands when I spoke to him. He has his own specially brewed beers, too: a bottled brew called Rock and Roll and a draught called Spirit of St Louis. Oh, and his hamburgers are the best in town. In short, going to Blueberry Hill is like wriggling into a rock and roll cocoon. If a rock star is in town, he comes here.

Chuck Berry likes the place as well. He can often be seen, sitting at the bar facing the huge airbrushed picture of him doing the duck walk. 'He doesn't drink,' said Joe. 'He has his tall orange juice with no ice. He likes the soups here a lot, too. I think he feels comfortable here because people don't bother him. Occasionally a person will come up for an autograph but generally they respect his privacy, and let him alone.'

Of course, I was hoping he would be in that day, but I was out of luck. I had heard he was the most reclusive of people. More private than Dylan, even. Joe said that was probably true. 'He's somewhat a hard guy to get to know. He is cautious. A lot of people come to him with not friendship in mind but some kind of exploitative thing. Once he starts to trust a person he is very open, it just takes a while. I get along with him very well, but I wouldn't say he knows a lot of people in that way.

'I met Chuck after a concert in a small venue many years ago. Then about ten years later we were involved in a business deal and we got to know each other, little by little. We didn't even realize we were becoming friends. So now I'll go out to his house, he'll come to my house. He likes to sit at the piano and play blues.

'He is a very reclusive figure but just a magnificent person. He goes through his times of adverse publicity but the man is a genius, one of the two greatest rock poets. Dylan is the other one. Even though Elvis got to be bigger culturally I think, musically Chuck Berry is more important. He has influenced more musicians than anybody. Every band knows some of his songs, he can go to any city and find musicians who can play with him straight away. A lot of people learned to play guitar with "Johnny B. Goode" and "Roll Over Beethoven".'

I agreed with Joe. One of the most interesting things about Chuck Berry is that while Elvis was a white man who drew from black music to create his own unique blend, Chuck Berry was a black man who drew from white music. Elvis was a hillbilly who sounded black, Chuck was a black who could sound like a hillbilly. In his early days playing the St Louis clubs he consciously tried to play in a style that would appeal to both black and white. In 1955 his first hit, 'Maybellene', put new lyrics to an old country song called 'Ida Red', and he was one of the few black artists who had a white teenage audience. Over the next four years he produced a stream of unsurpassable rock and roll songs including 'Roll Over Beethoven', 'Johnny B. Goode', 'Sweet Little Sixteen' and 'Brown-Eyed Handsome Man'.

Lyrically he was totally in tune with teenagers' obsessions and aspirations. 'Maybellene' is about a race between the singer's V8 Ford and a Cadillac. While the verses tell the story of the race, the choruses are a plea to an errant girlfriend to be faithful. 'No Money Down' is about how car-hungry teenagers are bamboozled by salesmen, 'Little Queenie' about lusting after a beautiful girl standing by a jukebox. 'No Particular Place To Go' is about cruising with your girl at night, the radio playing, and 'Brown-Eyed Handsome Man' captures perfectly the terrible misfortune of being young, good-looking and put upon.

Hot cars, hot women, and rock and roll. Life's essentials. No wonder Chuck Berry has been called the Poet Laureate of American teenagers. Perhaps the strangest tribute is that 'Johnny B. Goode' is the only rock song included in the Sounds Of Earth gold record mounted on the Voyager I and Voyager II spacecraft on its journey from Uranus to Neptune. Chuck is rock and roll's representative to the universe.

One of the highlights of knowing Chuck for Joe Edwards came in 1986. Chuck was sixty that year, and to mark the occasion there was a big concert in the Fox Theater in town, which because of segregation Chuck could not enter as a young man. It was to be filmed and Chuck's band was to include Eric Clapton and Keith Richards. They stayed at Berry Park, Chuck's country estate near the small town of Wentzville, for a week of rehearsals. Joe was there throughout. Snapshots he took during that week are pinned to the walls of Blueberry Hill. He pointed them out to me proudly. Me and Eric. Me and Keith. Me and Keith and Eric. Chuck and Keith and Eric and me.

Was Berry Park easy to find, I asked, fishing for an

invitation to go out there. 'Right off the beaten path,' said Joe. 'And Chuck is very, very private right now.' So what should I do to meet him? Joe went quiet, making it clear I would get no introduction from him. 'But,' he went on, 'if you want to talk to someone else who knows him, you should catch Johnnie Johnson. He's here Saturday.'

I had heard of Johnnie. He had played with Chuck in the very early years. You hear him at his best on 'Roll Over Beethoven'. In fact it was Chuck who joined Johnnie's band. Johnnie wanted a singer and guitarist, but the man he brought in stole the show to such an extent that Johnnie ended up as Chuck's piano player. He toured with Chuck for four years, but then quit, returning to St Louis where he has played the clubs ever since. Joe has released three solo albums by Johnnie on his label, and on Saturday Johnnie Johnson and his Magnificent Four would be at Blueberry Hill. I came back for the show, and in between sets chatted to Johnnie, a big, lumbering, amiable guy in his late sixties.

I thought maybe there would be some lingering resentment in being the bit player in the Chuck Berry story. Johnnie was quiet for a second when I asked him, then said, 'Chuck came to me one day and said, "Johnnie, what do you think about changing the name to the Chuck Berry Trio?" I said, "Hey, OK, because you are a go-getter and I think we will go much further with you out front." Simple as that.

'First thing I knew, he made a tape of "Ida Red", this old country song he used to do in the show, and he was off to Chicago trying to get a record contract. He got turned down a lot of times, but finally Leonard Chess, of Chess Records, said he'd record the song.'

Chess, the home of Berry rhythm and blues heroes such as Muddy Waters, Howlin' Wolf and Bo Diddley, was as pioneering as Sun.

'Then one night I was driving home after a show and I heard "Maybellene" on the radio. I told Chuck, and then other people started hearing it and we had a hit. I was young and I never thought of making music a career. I was working in the steel foundry at the time, I just thought of playing locally. I stuck with it about four years, but I don't like flying so finally I decided to quit and go back home.'

I asked him about the story that 'Johnny B. Goode' was about him. He smiled. 'Chuck says the song is about Chuck Berry, but that he wrote it for me. Work that one out if you can. Chuck was born on Goode Avenue, so that's him not me. Anyway, in that song, the line about some day you will be a millionaire with your name in lights. Well, that sure as hell ain't me.'

I wondered if Johnnie could introduce me to Chuck. 'Chuck and me get together now and then, he comes and sees me when we're playing locally and sits in sometimes. But no, I ain't gonna be able to help you there.'

So I went out west to Wentzville to try and find Chuck Berry for myself. It was a tiny country town, built straddling the railroad line like a baby Birmingham, Alabama. It too was a purely functional place, a place for getting things on and off trains. The country around was rolling grassland, and it reminded me of Ireland. In St Louis the majority of faces were black; here everyone was white.

I had heard stories that Chuck Berry is not entirely approved of in this small town. Some say it has something to do with his criminal record. As a teenager he was sent to reform school after committing two robberies and holding up a motorist with an unusable gun. He was sent to prison in 1961 for violating the Mann Act, which outlaws transporting a woman across the state line for immoral purposes. Chuck's defence was that she was simply a hostess in his club, but the prosecution claimed she was only fourteen and had been a prostitute in El Paso. He got three years and a $10,000 fine. Berry went to jail again in 1979 for evading payment of nearly $110,000 in federal income tax. They tend to take a dim view of such things in small towns.

I had been told Chuck often used the Crossroads Cafeteria, so I went there. The café offered 'Homestyle cooking. Drive in, carry out'. From my window seat I could see anything that moved in Wentzville. It was good to be away from the cities I had frequented during the past weeks and watch a small town go about its afternoon business. In the street I could see all the essentials: a Farmers' Bank, a livestock provisions store, a grocer, a hardware shop. The café was opposite a flower shop called Anne's Bokay Korner, which was the only concession to luxury goods. A string of yellow school buses swung out of a side street. The occasional pick-up and tractor were the only other traffic.

Somehow, flying from city to city as I had over the past three weeks gave me a feeling of not having travelled at all. The driving I had done so far made me thirst for more, but not on Interstates. From now on I would be taking two-lane highways through small towns all the way to L.A.

The waitress was busy gossiping with a couple of farmers when I arrived, but when they had gone she came over to talk and I asked her about Chuck. 'Oh,' she said, 'he comes here quite a lot. He don't say much, though. He did leave a ten-dollar tip once, so I've heard. Matter of fact he was in this morning, and I saw him head home not an hour ago.'

I asked her for directions to Chuck's place.

'You just go south on Route 3, it's about three miles out, a big place, kinda low and white. Once you're out there you can ask.'

100

Chuck built Berry Park as a non-racial country club, inspired by the whites-only places he had occasionally visited as a youth when helping his father, who was a carpenter. There would be fishing and hunting, swimming and dancing. It would be his own mini-Disneyland with rides, a lodge to stay in, and a seventy-six-foot guitar-shaped swimming pool. In 1960 he opened it to the public. But there were problems. Chuck allowed pop festivals to take place here, but a promoter pulled a con trick, announcing bands that had never been booked and consequently did not turn up. A riot ensued and the place was closed. Today it is just Chuck's private country retreat.

I drove to it along a narrow lane through farmland. The few houses that I saw were ranch-like, with horses grazing in paddocks beside the road. I went more than three miles and had seen only one place that fitted the description I had been given, of a gathering of several white concrete buildings. I doubled back to it and stopped outside. There was nobody about to ask if this was Berry Park, and no sign. I walked up to the door and knocked.

No-one came, so I knocked again. Then the inner door opened abruptly and I was looking through the mesh of the screen door. The sun was so bright that, inside, the house seemed pitch black in contrast. I could see no figure at all, nothing but a black hand holding the door open. A man's voice said, 'Yes?'

I asked if this was Chuck Berry's place.

'What do you want with him?'

My eyes were a little more accustomed to the dark inside now and I could make out the figure of a black man, his left arm resting up the edge of the door.

What *did* I want with Chuck Berry? That was a good question. The truth was I didn't know. What should I say? For some reason I blurted out, 'I just wanted to come and shake his hand.'

The figure pushed the screen door towards me with his right hand. I sidestepped. He pressed a bare foot against the base of the screen door to keep it open and extended his right hand towards me. I found myself looking down at it. I shook it. The hand was withdrawn, the screen door snapped shut and the inner door closed after it. I turned and left, with no idea if I had shaken hands with Chuck Berry or not. At my car I stopped and looked back at the house. I could see no-one.

It might have been Chuck Berry's hand, it might not. But it felt like mission accomplished. I could move on.

Chapter Six

Get Your Kicks

Who hasn't sung about Route 66? From the Andrews Sisters to the Rolling Stones, from Nat King Cole to Depeche Mode, plus every two-bit rock and roll band that ever was, all of them have covered a 1946 song by Bobby Troup called '(Get Your Kicks On) Route 66'.

The song is not the only tribute to America's most famous road. In the 1960s it got its own TV series, too. In 116 episodes of *Route 66* two teenagers called Buz and Tod travelled the road in their Corvette.

Named in 1926, and covering 2,448 miles from Chicago to Los Angeles, Route 66 spans eight states, crossing mountains, deserts, plains and canyons. It has earned many names, from Main Street America to The Way West. In his novel *The Grapes of Wrath*, about mid-Western farmers thrown off their land during the Depression, John Steinbeck calls it the Mother Road, their route to the Promised Land of California.

During the Second World War Route 66 was used to move millions of troops, and even more American tourists have come to know and love it over the decades. Even before it was created, out of a string of local roads and farm tracks, the route was responsible for some historic shifts. The movie men came this way from Chicago and founded Hollywood. In the winter of 1907, a film-maker called Francis Boggs was despairing of finishing his twelve-minute movie about the Count of Monte Cristo. The light would be too poor for outdoor filming in Chicago for months, so he went west in search of sun. He found it in Los Angeles, and the following year set up shop there. Others followed.

It was a national institution: a part of the American consciousness, a concrete expression of the American ideal of total freedom of movement. Because of this road you could simply get in your car and go, right across the country if you wanted to, to find better times, escape unhappiness, discover whatever it was you were looking for. A myth and an illusion perhaps, but one on which America is built.

As the song says:

'Well if you ever plan to motor west
Then take my way, it's the highway that's the best
Get your kicks on Route 66.'

When I came to plan my trip around America, Route 66 was one of the first things I decided to include. But when I looked on a map, I could not find it. Route 66 had vanished. It no longer existed. This puzzled me, because I heard it referred to in all sorts of places. Bizarrest of all, I saw it on a poster in Old Street tube station, London, a few days before I set off. The ad was for a Japanese motorbike, a very sleek and modern-looking thing. The commercial for this up-to-the-minute piece of machinery was shot beside a sharp bend on a mountain road in America. Beside the highway was a sign identifying it as Route 66.

The simple truth is that in modern, disposable America, Route 66 outlived its usefulness. During the 1980s it was superseded by a clutch of Interstates, and as these were opened, Route 66 was stripped of its identifying markings and signs. This is sad, because the American love of the open road is rooted in the belief that a succession of towns of the utmost ordinariness add up, if you go through enough of them, to a journey of epic proportions. The interstates, which rush you from A to B without encountering anything in between, rob travel of its savour and its meaning.

The fact that it was not on any map did not matter too much. The lyrics told me where it went. I could sing my way across America if necessary:

'Down to St Louis, Joplin, Missouri,
Oklahoma City is oh so pretty.
You'll see Amarillo, Gallup, New Mexico
Flagstaff, Arizona, don't forget Winona.'

What would make things impossible would be the disappearance of 66 not only from the face of the map, but also from the face of the earth.

That proved not to be the case, as I discovered in St Louis when I met Jim Powell. Jim is president of a preservation society called the Route 66 Association of Missouri, the state organization of the national Route 66 Association. Right across America, I discovered, people like Jim had become determined to save the road, to map its route, to campaign to have the signs put back, and to encourage its use. He gave me a copy of a handbook called *The Route 66 Traveler's Guide* which identified every remaining stretch of the road. I discovered that I could cover a substantial portion of the next section of my trip, the 1,942 miles from St Louis to Los Angeles, on the old road. The fact that the modern Interstates were very often run alongside Route 66 meant that if I got tired of it, I could switch track and zip along swiftly for a while too.

I would make one detour on the way west, going south into Texas on the trail of Buddy Holly, who lived in Lubbock, and Roy Orbison, who spent much of the time, before he became famous and moved to Nashville, in the isolated oil town of Wink, two hundred miles further south.

Jim had driven the whole of Route 66 with his brother Don, but that was before Tom Snyder, founder of the Route 66 Association, wrote the guidebook. I met Jim after hours in his office in downtown St Louis. A little bald-headed guy with a moustache and glasses, he was zipping off to Europe on a business trip the next day, boasting about buying up some computer companies on the cheap, but his anonymous corporate office was festooned with Route 66 memorabilia. On a large easel stood a brown enamelled roadside Route 66 sign, and he dragged out posters, maps, guides and photocopies of articles about the road.

'My brother and I travelled Route 66 as kids on vacation and it held a special place in our hearts,' he explained. 'So when they decertified it in '85 we said, "Before it's gone completely we have to drive it." Don owns a '64 Corvette and while he got the car ready I planned the route. It turned out he had to do almost a full restoration of the Corvette but he still had an easier job than I did. It proved very difficult indeed to identify the route and to establish what sections of it still survived. In the end I flew out to California and got Tom Snyder's help.

'We had a great time, but what really set Route 66 apart were the people. The Interstates are boring. They are designed to get you from one place to another very quickly without really worrying about where you stop or why. An Interstate is a place where you find a Holiday Inn and a McDonald's, you don't find a comfortable old sixteen-room motel with neon out front and somebody who is really glad to see you. And you don't find a place with a big-boned waitress and a greasy hamburger and a wonderful bowl of chilli in a little truck stop or café or diner.

'What's happening in America today is people are really discovering their link with the past. Obviously it's not a very far distant past, but they are rediscovering America and harking back to an earlier time when things were slower and more peaceful. They are rediscovering two-lane highways and taking the time to get in touch with the things they have to offer. They may not make the whole trip on a two-lane road but they will get off in two- or three- or four-hour chunks to drive the really significant pieces. Once they try it, it is amazing how many people get hooked.

'In a sense Route 66 turned out to be its own worst enemy. It was so popular you had to put an Interstate there. Our goal is to get it really busy again. Preserve, promote and develop. We hope that a whole heap of little cities and towns will hook enough people off the Interstates that they generate some serious business for themselves. We are trying to get some stretches of the road into the *Historic Register*, as well as some of the buildings along the way.'

I told Jim of my plans and he gave me a run-down on conditions. 'Missouri is fairly easy to follow,' he said. 'Texas is difficult. Not a lot survives in Texas. In New Mexico there are some big chunks missing, Arizona is pretty easy, California is very easy. But you do have to know where you are going and take the time to stop and look at the map.'

I felt like an archeologist as I drove west from St Louis on the Interstate, looking out for signs to Eureka where I would switch to the old road. I found this talk of discovering the recent past, of the road as a part of popular culture abandoned before it got old, quite inspiring. Route 66 is unregarded, hidden, and yet an ever-powerful myth, why else would it be used in commercials for a state-of-the-art Japanese bike? Japanese technology, American mythology: this is the modern world.

Route 66 dovetailed with the theme of my trip. As America got richer and faster and more efficient it abandoned the old roads that made it. The same, very largely, applies to pop stars. OK, Elvis is an exception, but people like Chuck Berry, Buddy Holly and Roy

Orbison have never been highly regarded in the States after their first flush of fame. They were abandoned too. Hardly anyone thought of looking up their old haunts, the places that shaped them, or thought it worth seeking out the people who knew them in their formative years. Even the rock biographies I had read seemed to do precious little of that.

Some of the stars themselves sought stardom partly as a means of escape: Roy Orbison from the emotional desert of Wink, Bob Dylan from the cold northern wasteland of Minnesota. Even Bruce Springsteen, who has written so much about his homeland of New Jersey, was finally driven to flee the place. Surely it was worth going to see the places they escaped from? It was not inconceivable that the key to what made them tick lay there. These stars, and their music, came from a certain place. With each of them, to contradict Chuck Berry, I had found a particular place to go.

Turning off the Interstate on to Route 66 was like travelling back in time. The businesses along the road were certainly different. Instead of the modern, corporate, Identikit chain restaurants – Taco Bell, Dairy Queen, Pizza Hut and the rest – I found in Eureka a cosy little place with net curtains called Phil's Bar-B-Que. I had stepped into the real America of real places for the first time, more or less, since Athens. I ate a breakfast of ham omelette and fried potatoes that set me up for the day.

The road was rutted and crumbling, snaking through the undulating wooded countryside. I followed the guide book carefully, switching from north of the Interstate to south and back again as the old road plaited its way with the new. It was not until several miles later, at a little place called St Clair, that I saw my first Historic Route 66 marker and I knew it was working. I could make it on the old road. I found everything Jim Powell had promised, the sleepy little towns, the faded 1950s motels and cafés, the roadside grape stalls. I saw a lot of trailer parks too, and barely driveable pick-ups outside two-room shacks. The poor still live on Route 66.

Sometimes the route was confined to a narrow strip between Interstate and railway. I passed a sawmill dwarfed by vast piles of sawdust yellow as sand, heard the whine of the chainsaws and caught the sharp smell of resin that they released into the air. The greatest barrier to progress was not the slowness of the route but the temptation to stop and look at every little place I passed. In Cuba, where the tall water tower so typical of small American towns not only bore the place-name but also a giant witch's hat, I gave in. I found another little town like Wentzville, built straddling the railroad tracks, with Main Avenue North to one side and Main Avenue South to the other. The Cuba Feed and Supply Company had a platform for freight, but it looked as if potential passengers would be unlucky.

This was a one-block town, the centre covering less space than the Standard Oil storage tanks which stood alongside it. There was a welding shop, a huge reconditioned appliance store (this is a great town for buying a second-hand fridge) and the Route 66 café. As I drank my coffee, Cuba's Volunteer Fire Force hit the street, in two battered old pick-ups with fire hoses and pumps bolted on the backs. They were wearing baseball caps and lumberjack shirts and grinning, but they had the sirens on and went powering east on Old 66 as if they meant business.

Mostly I had the road to myself. Sometimes it was hard to work out where the sandy-coloured tar ended and the dead grass on the verges began. If I got someone behind me they'd almost always turn off towards a house or to the Interstate.

At Arlington it got really weird. The narrow country

lane sent me jolting through a series of ruts and ridges, turned sharply through forty-five degrees and dropped me suddenly on a four-lane highway with not a car on it, isolated in the woods. This length used to be thriving, with tourist attractions and diners, but now it serves just a few isolated farms. There were geese strung out across the road outside an abandoned general store, and a sign urging me south, on to a lane completely enclosed by trees. I crossed a river, climbed through the woods and out at Devil's Elbow, where the road scales a cliff above the Big Piney river. I stopped at a summit, pulled over and looked down an almost sheer drop to the valley. Below me the St Louis–San Francisco railroad crossed the river by a blue-painted box-girder bridge. The river fed a lake in the woods. It was a world away from the Interstates.

I was hooked on Route 66. I took my time, slowing the pace from the 65 I had averaged on the Interstates, but still finding I could do 50. The roads were worse, but they were also empty. Driving like this was as relaxing as the freeway, but about a hundred times more interesting. It worked: driving through real places, meeting people with time to talk, was a joy. And as I went on, my journey, which strung together dozens and dozens of insignificant little towns, did begin to feel epic.

On I went, right across Missouri. Just listing the names of the towns I passed through gives a flavour of the variety of the journey: Waynesville, Lebanon, Carthage, Joplin. Then over into Oklahoma, past Quapaw and Miami, Afton and Vinita, leaving 66 when the route got too tortuous or disappeared completely, through Sapulpa, Kellyville, Depew and Stroud. It was too dark to tell whether Oklahoma City was oh so pretty. Later Hydro, Elk City and Sayre rolled by before I reached Texas. You'd know it was

110

Texas without the sign. The country changes almost instantly from rolling wooded hills to the flat endless expanse of the Texas panhandle. This vast, treeless plain continues all the way to New Mexico, but I was to turn south at Amarillo, leaving Route 66 temporarily to head for Lubbock, passing through no-nonsense little towns like Happy, Plainview and New Deal.

It had been a wrench leaving my westward route for this detour. Once on the road I wanted to keep going, waking each morning anxious to press west like some frontiersman, happy to drive all day with Chuck Berry on the tape machine. Bob Dylan was right when he said of Chuck Berry that you had to be out on the highway to appreciate him fully. I wished I still had the white convertible as I bounded along to the sounds of 'No Particular Place To Go'.

But I became very glad that I did turn south for Lubbock, because Peggy Sue was back in town. *The* Peggy Sue. The one in the song 'with a love so rare and true'.

She gave me her business card.

'Rapid Rooter' it said, 'The Drain and Sewer Cleaning Co. Peggy Sue Rackham, Administrator.'

'If you knew, Peggy Sue, then you'd know why I feel blue about Peggy, my Peggy Sue,' sang Buddy Holly. Of course, I didn't know Peggy Sue, and the song furnished few details, apart from the fact that she was 'pretty pretty pretty pretty'. But, in the thirty-five years since Jerry Allison, drummer in Buddy Holly's group the Crickets, wrote that lyric about the girl he would soon marry, her name has come to mean something to me and millions of others.

She is arguably the most famous woman in a song, and here she was, ringing the doorbell, asking to go to the little girl's room, patting her hair before the hall mirror and finally walking across the lounge of a

111

house in suburban Lubbock. She was tall, slim, aged about fifty, but looking younger. Her hair was cut short, and golden blonde. She wore a business-woman's smart tan slacks and white blouse.

Buddy Holly was the most unlikely-looking pop star, a skinny, gangling boy, bespectacled, seemingly uncharismatic. Yet, in the two short years of stardom before he was killed, aged twenty-two, in a plane crash, he recorded some of the very best, most influential, most lasting pop music of all, and had a major influence on the Beatles. His catalogue is small: 'That'll Be The Day', 'Peggy Sue', 'Words Of Love', 'Every Day', 'Not Fade Away', 'Oh Boy', 'Heartbeat', 'Rave On', 'True Love Ways'. The best fit easily on to one tape, and I had junked Chuck Berry's in favour of Buddy's greatest hits as I sailed through the cotton fields on my approach to Lubbock. It struck me forcibly that when you listen to the songs today they seem as vibrant, inventive, exciting and unexpected as ever.

And this genius came out of Lubbock, this lone-some farmers' town on the hot windy high plains of north-west Texas. But Lubbock, it seems, has never been too sure of Buddy Holly. This is the Bible belt, and rock and roll is still the Devil's music. It has been down to one man, Bill Griggs, who runs the Buddy Holly Memorial Society from his home in the town, to fight to put the singer on Lubbock's map. It was Bill who introduced me to Peggy Sue. She enjoys talking about her song, but I felt really nervous meeting her. 'I was very flattered having it written about me,' she said. 'I remember the first time I heard it, at a concert, when I was seventeen and still in high school. It was all just wonderful, unbelievable. I thought it was a great song. I said to Buddy it would become a standard but he laughed and said, "Oh no, come on." But it can also be a little scary at times, thinking that there are millions of

112

people out there that I don't know but who have heard of me and maybe think they know me a little.'

A couple of years later Buddy wrote 'Peggy Sue Got Married', in which he seems to be saying that Peggy Sue is the girl in almost all his songs. But she does not believe she was quite that inspirational.

I had hoped she would let me in on some huge secret, such as that she and Buddy were really lovers. But she didn't. My hints that they might have been more than just friends got a distinctly frosty reception. 'Everyone needs a cheerleader. I hope I was Buddy's cheerleader,' she said.

She brought her story up to date for me. Peggy Sue Got Divorced, after eight years. Then Peggy Sue Got Married Again, to Lynn B. Rackham, and now lives in Sacramento, California, where the family plumbing business is. She has two children, and still likes to listen to her song. 'I have it on CD at home, and on tape in the car. I have a two-hour journey from Sacramento to Reno, where we have a new office, and I listen to music on the road. It still makes me feel good to hear it.'

It seemed to be doing Bill Griggs a lot of good having Peggy Sue in his house. He was dancing around whereas before he had been sitting slumped in front of the weather channel, the drapes drawn, nursing a luke-warm Coke. His wife had left a few months before, he told me, and taken the kids. Their toys were still scattered on the porch. He is a Buddy Holly freak, a collector, one of several rock and roll dealers and archivists I would meet on my travels. Like Joe Edwards in Saint Louis he had a pile of memorabilia. His air conditioning had broken down and the house was stifling, except for the room in which he housed his collection, where a fan the size of an aeroplane propeller had been set up to keep the vast array of Buddy Holly records cool. He showed me an orange soda tin from which Elvis was reputed to have drunk. Nice. Peggy Sue seemed nervous in the room, as if she had entered Buddy's tomb. She shied away from the pinned-up front pages of newspapers announcing his death. 'Ugh,' she said, shivering, 'dead pop stars.'

'What's up?' asked Bill.

Bill was eyeing Peggy Sue like a butterfly collector with a prize specimen. I imagined him sticking a pin through her and adding her to his collection. OK, so she could only be a temporary exhibit, but that was pretty damn good, wasn't it?

It was a mean thought, probably. Bill is a devoted fan of Buddy Holly, and has single-handedly unearthed his haunts in Lubbock; no-one else in the town seems to have been bothered.

I fancied breaking my journey west for a few days here, and decided to do a spot of sightseeing. Bill Griggs had given me a list of the Buddy-related places in town that he had uncovered, and I toured them. Driving around Lubbock, the agricultural and industrial foundations on to which a modern, slick American city is only now being grafted, are clear. Every other vehicle is a pick-up truck. There are rail marshalling yards, iron and steel depots, huge grain silos shaped like pyramids linked by metal tubes. A highrise downtown is only just beginning to emerge. This is still very recognizably the small southern town that shaped Buddy Holly.

The house where Holly lived in 1957 when he was recording much of his best work still stands at 1305 37th street. It was in this house that, in 1958, he married Maria Elena Santiago, a Puerto Rican whom he met in New York. The wedding was semi-secret to avoid upsetting girl fans, but Peggy Sue was there, as Matron of Honour.

'We had been planning a double wedding,' she had told me earlier, 'but Jerry and I jumped the gun. He

114

was Protestant and I am Catholic and there was a family fight over which church it should be in, so in the end it was easier just to run away and do it. We still went on a joint honeymoon, though, to Acapulco.'

Just off Avenue A at 10th street, Bill's list told me, I would find the Fair Park Coliseum, where Buddy Holly and the Crickets were at the bottom of bills headed by Elvis Presley and Bill Haley and the Comets. It is a featureless general-purpose auditorium. Just beyond it was a cattle market and, opposite, a row of wooden shacks like English beach-tea huts, all run by different worthy local organizations. There was the First Foursquare Church Booth ('Dr Pepper. Hot cakes served all day'), the Oakwood Methodist Church ('FRIED PIES') and the Lubbock Optimism Club ('Friend of the boy').

I found the radio station (call sign KRLB), on which Buddy got a spot of his own on Sunday afternoons, at 6602 Quirt Avenue on the southern edge of town. In the fifties, a rock and roll station would never have been tolerated in the centre of town, Bill Griggs had told me. It is a small single-storey metal building surrounded by rough grassland. 'FM99 The Music Station' says the sign they have today.

Sitting outside, watching the trucks appear up the highway through the shimmering heat haze, I tuned in and heard: 'Time to get ready for summer. Got your shades? Check. Got your sunshield? Check. Got your swimwear? No check! Woh, better get down to Mervyn's Swimwear right away.' The temperature was 105F.

There is a tribute to Buddy Holly outside the Civic Center, in the shape of an 8ft 6in bronze of the singer, holding a guitar and standing in the middle of a raised circular flower bed. The huge satellite dish of the La Quinta Inn makes a nice backdrop. 'Buddy Holly,' an inscription reads, 'contributed to the musical heritage of not only West Texas, but the entire world.' They get their priorities right around here. West Texas, then the world.

Around the stone wall enclosing the flower bed were plaques to fourteen other musicians with local links including Roy Orbison and Waylon Jennings, who narrowly missed being on the flight on which Holly and two other rock and roll stars, Ritchie Valens and the Big Bopper, were killed. It happened on a bitterly cold night in February 1959 while Buddy was on a gruelling tour of the Midwest. That night, to escape sleeping once more on a tour bus with a broken heater, he chartered a light plane to take him the 400 miles from Clear Lake, Iowa, to the next gig. There were only three places. Waylon Jennings, a Lubbock DJ who played bass with the Crickets and has gone on to be a very big country star, wanted to come but lost the toss and saved his life. At 1.50 a.m. on 3 February the plane crashed in thick snow, killing all on board. It had hardly gone ten miles. At the time Jerry Allison and Buddy had fallen out, and Jerry was not with the Crickets, yet Peggy Sue remembers a strange premonition.

'About a month before,' she said, sitting in Bill Grigg's chair beneath a rather artless portrait of Buddy and a framed Gold Disc, 'I had had a dream about a plane going into a snowstorm, going straight up and coming straight down. At that point, I thought it was Jerry in the plane, not Buddy. And I had had that dream over and over. When I heard of Buddy's death I was numb, devastated. Jerry and I were driving in from out of state to Jerry's house. We walked in and his mother told us. Buddy was dead. At first I thought they had made a mistake.'

More than 1,500 people came to the funeral, held at Lubbock's Tabernacle Baptist Church. Phil Everly, of the Everly Brothers, was a pallbearer and there was a telegram from Elvis Presley. 'I was still stunned,' said Peggy Sue. 'Before the funeral I was with Buddy's parents, I wanted to be with them. At the church I remember having a hard time finding a place to sit, I ended up in the back, on my own, and I remember thinking how strange it was that Maria Elena wasn't there. Then I heard that she had been so sick, so devastated that she just could not go. I didn't go on to the cemetery, I think it was because of the crowds.' The gravestones of Buddy and his father Lawrence and mother Ella lie flush with the ground. There was the smell of grass baking in the heat, and the hiss of sprinklers, as I walked round the plot later that day. Buddy's stone, a copy of the original, which was stolen, is a rather kitsch affair with a guitar leaning against a Doric column. His surname reverts to the way the family has always spelt it, Holley. Buddy dropped the E after it was accidentally left off an early recording contract. A simple vase held red fabric flowers.

Sometimes there will be fresh flowers on the grave and a note marked 'From Peggy Sue'. In the song 'American Pie' Don Maclean marks the day of Holly's death as that on which the music died. I had asked Peggy Sue if she felt that way. 'For me personally, yes, the music did die that day,' she had said. As I looked down at Buddy's modest grave I noticed a sliver of something sticking up from the hard red soil. I crouched down and extracted a small piece of tortoiseshell plastic. It was a plectrum, placed there in homage by a fan. I put it back where I had found it.

It was two hundred miles south from Lubbock to Wink and Roy Orbison, two hundred miles over increasingly desolate and lonely country. For a long time there was the monotony of passing the one-mile squares of the cotton fields, flashing through the one-block towns dominated by their vast silos. After

Andrews, which survives because it houses an Air Force base, the land got emptier and emptier, turning gradually to desert, where the only crop was oil. The flat, featureless terrain was littered to the horizon with the machines nicknamed nodding donkeys that pump the oil to the surface and the dirty brown tanks in which it is stored. After a town with the joke name of Kermit, I turned off on to a back road signposted for Wink that felt like it was leading nowhere. I expected it to turn a bend and end at a shack beside a sand dune at any moment.

And there was a smell in the air. An inescapable smell as if the earth had bad guts and was seeping a filthy stench from its bowels. It almost turned my stomach. I could taste the stink too, like a heavy licorice residue on my tongue.

It was dusk when I hit Wink, and discovered it offered absolutely nowhere to stay. It barely existed. I carried on down the road to Monahans where I found the Sandhills Motel. In a darkened room off Reception a very old colour TV with a weak picture flickered. A little scrap of a dog came at me yapping and a heavy-set old man rolled himself slowly out of his armchair, surprised to have a visitor. His wife followed him out and gave me the register. My room cost me $16.05, the cheapest place I had stayed on the journey so far. I'd never match it. As I registered the woman said, 'London, England. My, but you're a long way from home.'

As she said it I felt like all the air had been let out of me. I suddenly wanted to talk to people I knew. I asked if there were phones in the rooms.

'No, we don't even have a pay phone since they took away this one out here,' said the old man, gesturing with his head to the road outside.

What the hell, it couldn't get any lonelier. I drove across the courtyard to my little hut, got a beer out of

118

the car and sat on the bonnet drinking it. It was getting dark quickly now, and a cool breeze was beginning to ripple across the land. I looked out over the scrub behind the motel, into an emptiness where nothing was built and no-one would have reason to venture. The sunset was staining the horizon orangey-brown, as if the oil beneath the ground were vaporizing.

It was on hot nights like this, up the road in Wink, that a softly-spoken, introspective, pale-faced boy called Roy Orbison would leave his baking hot shack, the screams of his baby and the complaints of his young wife, and take his guitar out to his wreck of a car. There he would strum away, dreaming idly of how he might make his escape. On one particular summer night in 1959 he began singing to himself a couple of lines that went:

'Only the lonely, know how I feel tonight
Only the lonely, know that this feeling ain't right.'

He had written his ticket to Nashville, fame and fortune. He was delighted to escape. He only came back once to the area he was brought to in 1946 at the age of ten, to play an oil workers' benefit in 1987 at Midland, thirty miles east of Wink on Highway 20. He was another unlikely star. With his pebble-lens glasses and dyed black quiff he could have been Buddy Holly's bulky older brother, but from 1960 to 1966 Orbison wrote a succession of wonderful songs in a distinctive style. He excelled at dolorous, melodramatic ballads like 'It's Over', 'Only The Lonely' and 'Crying'. Occasionally the lyrics were optimistic like 'Oh! Pretty Woman' and 'Running Scared'.

I put my Orbison tape on the car's deck, playing softly, as I sat looking out across the desert. It sounded to me like the antithesis of desert music, which, perhaps, is the whole point. If you wanted to portray the mood here you would go for the kind of spare, searing, howling guitar that Ry Cooder used on the

119

soundtrack to Wim Wenders's film *Paris, Texas*. You would not use words. Sitting in the west Texas desert I could see that the very style of Roy Orbison's music was a means of escape from the land he came from. The songs are full of emotion and often build to a powerful climax, but in this landscape all emotion seems burned away by the heat. The people are monosyllabic and uncommunicative. They carry their burdens silently, they don't howl out, 'It's over' like Orbison did in one of his powerful songs.

My beer finished, I went looking for a phone and a place to eat. I found neither. I was 5,000 miles from home, hungry and alone. My motel was almost the only business still operating in this one-street town. I passed derelict garages, motels, cafés and stores. The payphones had died together with the businesses they stood alongside. I found a Roy Orbison landmark, though. At the far east of town, beside the pink-painted Monahans Motel ('Kitchenettes, weekly rates') was the Fraternal Order of Eagles, once the Archway Club, where Roy Orbison met a girl called Claudette. He was nineteen, she was fourteen. Two years later, in 1957, they married.

Next morning I drove back to Wink. I had noticed a storefront with a cut-out of Orbison beside the door, which proved to be the Roy Orbison Museum. It was locked, but a pink Post-it note on the door said the keys were in City Hall, which turned out to be one room at the other end of the block. Walking from one to the other I passed the boarded-up Rig Theater, the former movie house where Orbison used to sit alone in the darkness watching the latest glamorous fantasy from Hollywood and dreaming of stardom.

'Orbison! Ooby Dooby!' said a redneck in an Exxon cap, quoting the title of Roy's first hit, when I asked for the museum keys. They had to phone round the museum committee members to get one. While they dialled, I looked at the photographs on the wall, which showed Wink in the 1930s, its heyday. The strip photos showed a panorama of wooden buildings and, beyond, a forest of oil rigs. The streets were full of signs for hotels, clubs and saloons and were lined with cars. 'Wink, the largest city ever built in two years . . . in the heart of the world's largest oilfield' said a caption on one.

Not any more it ain't. In its heyday, 30,000 people lived here. Today there are 1,200. Wink's fate is inextricably tied to the rise and fall of oil prices. When Orbie Lee and Nadine Orbison, Roy's parents, came here just after the Second World War Wink was already in decline. Today it has almost been wiped off the map.

The ring round for a museum key had drawn a blank. Everybody was out. Could I come back this afternoon? I could. Meantime, why didn't I take a look around town? Not that there was much to see. I found the street on which Roy once lived, which has now been renamed Roy Orbison Ave. His house is gone, and so have a number of others, leaving empty lots. Between Roy Orbison Avenue North and Roy Orbison Avenue South the road disappears into a patch of grassy sand, as if the encroaching desert were making its final advance, and had split the town in two prior to overrunning it.

About the only place to go was Peggy Sue's Café, on the next, and only other block to City Hall. Not that Peggy Sue. This one turned out to have been a school friend of Orbison. So were most of the guys in the Caterpillar caps and checked shirts with shiny red faces and impenetrable accents. They had trouble understanding me, too. 'I'm just enjoyin' sittin' here listenin' to you enunciate,' said one in the pause after my question. They were shy, inarticulate people, not given to passing on insights to strangers. They didn't look like they had one searing ballad amongst them.

I had time to kill so I killed it by driving, back through Kermit and on to Odessa. In the desert I felt as if I could disappear off the face of the earth. There was no sensation of speed or motion, only the rumbling of the tyres on the road. The dials in front of me were all static except for the slowly turning tumblers of the odometer. You could become invisible out here. I passed a place called Notrees. And, certainly, there were none. After half an hour on the featureless land something happened. The road climbed a gentle gradient for perhaps fifty feet up Concho Bluff and passed a gas flame burning at the top of a silver chimney. 'A point of light' said a sign, as if this had the significance, in the west Texas desert, of the star of Bethlehem.

Odessa proved to be another one-street provisions town. I barely stopped, just going into a 7-Eleven for coffee before turning and driving back to Wink. It was numbing, to drive for so many miles to find a next-to-nothing town. How would I have fared growing up in this place?

This time in Wink they did manage to raise someone with a key to the museum. As we walked from City Hall past the Rig Theater, Jean Hadley told me she had lived in the next street to Roy and her yard backed on to his yard. She would often hear him playing. 'I didn't like it at first, to tell you the truth,' she said, 'but my daughter, she loved it. She loved his playing.

'People that knew Roy and knew him real well will tell you that at first he was a loner. He was no good on the football field, he didn't make friends easy and I guess it's true that he got bullied at school. I'd say he didn't have a happy time as a child and that he probably didn't have good memories of Wink. But as he got older, you know, he really changed. It was

122

music that did it. Once he got to playing and found he could do something well he really became somebody. From the first time we heard him, in the back yard, to when we saw him playing a concert over here in the theatre, you could tell the difference. Each time I heard him he got a little better, there was more expression in his singing and playing and in him too.'

We went into the reception area of the museum. There was a right-angled glass cabinet that looked as if it had come from a shop. Inside were some Wink High School yearbooks which featured Roy and listed his ambitions: to be famous and marry a beautiful girl, both of which he achieved. There were a few singles and albums by him. Nothing rare or valuable, just gifts from the collections of people in Wink who knew Roy. Each bore a little yellow sticker marked with the name of the donor. Jean took out a pair of heavy black-framed spectacles with thick, purple, bi-focal lenses. They were donated by Roy's second wife, Barbara, when she came to the annual Roy Orbison Festival the previous summer.

There were also some T-shirts and postcards, but that was it. I eyed the door leading to the back room, imagining it would open on to the museum proper, with glass cases containing clothes and other personal effects, Nashville style. But as Jean kept chatting away about the things in this front room it gradually dawned on me that they were the sum total of the Roy Orbison Museum.

It was quite a contrast to Nashville. As far as I was concerned, Roy Orbison was more important than any number of Conway Twittys and Willie Nelsons, and yet his memorial was this one, a more or less empty room in a tiny town in the desert. How lonely can you get? I asked Jean about Wink, and what it was like to live way out here.

'Wink has changed,' said Jean, looking out at the

123

silent main street and the empty lots across from the museum. 'We came in 1952 and have lived here most of the time since. Back then it was a rough town. There was a honky tonk across the street here which you would not walk past on a Friday or Saturday night unless you wanted to get into a fight.

'It was busy then. It's most all gone since. There used to be stores and bars and buildings all along here.' She swept her arm, indicating the dry grass, parking lots and stubby trees. 'Then we got this here urban renewal and they pulled it all down. The high school is about the only thing that keeps the town going now. It serves two counties.' I had seen it, an impressive art deco place supported with money accruing from old oil revenues. People here are either teachers or work for the oil companies. Jean used to be a teacher, her husband an oil worker. 'But Wink is a good place,' she added quietly. 'I raised two children here and we like it a lot.'

The biggest day of the year is the Roy Orbison Festival. Jean is on the Roy Orbison Memorial Committee ('Dedicated to preserving the memory of a rock and roll legend'), organizers of the event and the power behind the museum. The football pitch up at the high school is the venue.

'We put a Roy Orbison sign across the street from City Hall to a tree,' Jean said. 'We have a Pretty Woman Contest, and a Candy Man contest for the guys and a Dream Baby contest for the little children. This is the programme from last year. We have a real good Roy Orbison imitator called Kenny Morrill, he really sounds like him and looks like him. This is Kenny standing underneath the Roy Orbison Avenue street sign. Kenny said it felt kind of weird coming into Roy's home town, but everybody made him welcome. Wink's known for that, for people coming in.

'Last year Roy's wife Barbara came along for the day

and she opened this museum. Brought her son along too. Peggy Sue has a motor home and she let them use it while they were here. Barbara was very happy to talk with us about Roy, she spent the day with us. The only thing was she wouldn't go out on the stage. I don't think she could. And she didn't stay to listen to Kenny sing, either. But you can imagine, someone singing his songs and imitating him. It would bring it all back to her. So they left.

'We are trying to raise enough money to have a real nice bronze statue of Roy made and placed right here.' She showed me a square of gravel beside the museum. 'But we need $60,000.'

As I left, Jean asked me to sign the visitors' book, which had been covered in an elaborate arrangement of black and white satin and lace. The first line read 'Barbara Orbison, PO Box 2402, Malibu, California'. On the line beneath, Roy's son had added his name: Roy Kelton Orbison.

There had not been many names added in the year since. Not many people make it to Wink on the trail of Roy Orbison. I signed my name, then got in my car and drove away as fast as I could.

I was in New Mexico, driving into a mirage, the road a dark grey cone pointing up to the sky, pale grey desert on either side. The sky was pouring into the road at its very tip, becoming mercury. The road ahead was awash in silver liquid. I looked in the rear-view mirror and it was the same picture behind.

Driving a long, long, straight road over an empty landscape I found my eyes drawn to the furthest point I could make out, so that I focused constantly on the distant horizon. I was always straining to see further. Is that a car up there? It seldom was. Now I could understand why drivers acknowledge one another in this lonely land. It is reassuring to see someone else moving through such a hallucinatory scene. I found I was getting high as I drove, feeling light-headed and shaky when I stopped and got out. I was exhausted and dehydrated, so that when I fuelled up on coffee I set my veins buzzing.

I was sailing across New Mexico, using the Interstate as far as Albuquerque to make up some time. I had the car on cruise. I touched no controls for hour after hour, with the air conditioning streaming into my face. Roy Orbison had taken me out of one time zone in my journey and into another, moving me from the fifties to the sixties. In California I would pursue the decade through the Beach Boys' surf music of the early years to the late sixties psychedelia of Jim Morrison and the Doors.

I picked up my first flavour of Jim Morrison outside Albuquerque. It was on the highway here that Jim experienced what he would later come to see as the most important moment of his life. His father was a Navy man and the family moved home a lot, but during Jim's adolescence he was stationed at the Kirtland Air Base. One day the family was driving on Route 66 when they came across an overturned truck. Beside it were injured Pueblo Indians who had been thrown on to the tarmac in the collision. Jim became hysterical, crying and screaming and shouting that he wanted to help. As they drove away, an Indian died and his soul passed into Jim's body, or so he believed.

You can believe such things in New Mexico. It is the strangest of places. I was soon passing over the painted desert, between the curious flat-topped hills called mesas which give you the sense that you are travelling on the bed of a vast quarry. Between 200 and 300 feet has been shaved off almost the whole of the landscape, with just the odd outcrops of the mesas showing where ground level used to be, like the scattered clues to a massive conspiracy. I could see for thirty miles or more all around me, over the pale green sagebrush desert, and ahead to the blue hills of Arizona. And all this lay beneath a vast sky of a translucent cobalt blue. New Mexico feels like an ancient land, and so it is. There are Indian peublos all around, and every two-bit town along the route offers Indian artifacts. But I did not want sand paintings or silver and turquoise jewellery. I sought out the remains of a much more recent civilization.

I took as many loops off Interstate 40 on to Route 66 as I could. I drove through Laguna and Cubero where Ernest Hemingway, having come to the desert to sharpen his recollection of the ocean, wrote *The Old Man and The Sea*. I went through Grants and Bluewater. In Grants I stopped to take some photographs of the boarded-up main street and the splendid 1950s neon signs outside the wrecked motels. Within the sound of the freeway's roar was a world of relics. 'Hey, you gonna take my picture too?' called a middle-aged honey blonde in shades and tight white slacks. I got her popping gum outside the boarded-up Lux theatre, which was next to the former Grant's State Bank and the Cibola Hospital Auxiliary Thrift. What a woman! Pure Route 66. What a shame she wasn't hitchhiking.

I felt I had been alone for a long time now. It struck me how rarely during my life I had been on my own like this with time to think. I realized that the last time had been fifteen years ago when I was twenty-one. I had just left university and spent a month in an onion-pickling factory – the place I was in when Elvis died – suffering the enforced isolation of work on a production line where, because of the pounding of the machinery, you were obliged to wear ear plugs. Sitting alone in a sou'wester ten yards from the nearest person closely resembled solitary confinement, and gave all the time in the world for thought. I reviewed my whole

127

life in that month: relationships, accomplishments, failures. By the end of it I had nothing left to think about. This time round there was much more past to occupy me.

Just past Thoreau I reached the Continental Divide, America's watershed. To the west of this point all water flows west, to the east it flows east. I was moving from one side of the country to the other. Soon I was in Arizona, the high country, and started seeing signs for Flagstaff, one of the towns that gets a name check in '(Get Your Kicks On) Route 66'. From Flagstaff I would drop through a series of plateaus to California.

But before that, we are told 'Don't forget Winona'. So I didn't. I left the Interstate at nightfall for a look through that town and travelled into Flagstaff by the back road. Winona proved to be a tiny place, very easy to forget, with just a couple of neon-lit motels to encounter before I was looping through a forest, with the ghostly white and grey outlines of San Francisco Peak and Agassiz Peak, both well over 12,000 ft, far ahead of me.

I left the Interstate again at Seligman for a 100-mile sweep of the old road to Kingman. It was a hot, moonlit night, the road was empty and ran straight as a die for twenty miles at a time. I have never felt so alone, but it was a good feeling. I had been thinking the past couple of days about what I had done. This trip was becoming as much about myself as the music I was searching for. Of course, one of the reasons I had wanted to trace the roots of American music was that it meant so much to me. It is, after all, the soundtrack against which I have lived my life. In tracing its origins I was tracing my own roots too, roots I knew next to nothing about, discovering more about the things, the people and the places that had influenced me.

Before I left on this journey I had come to feel that listening to music and having it mean so much without

128

knowing anything about where it came from was, in a curious way, like being an orphan who does not know his parents. The orphan becomes desperate to find them. I had become obsessed about getting as close as I possibly could to finding Elvis, Buddy Holly, Roy Orbison, Jim Morrison, Bob Dylan, Springsteen and the rest of the people in this book. A lot of these stars were dead, but no matter. If you can't find your father you look for someone who can tell you what he was like. I knew that access to the people I sought would not always be easy. No problem. I would get to them somehow, through old friends, people who themselves got close to them for one reason or another.

I had never felt so composed, and confident. I had a job and a family back home, commitments and pressures which never let me stand alone and see how I fared. I wanted those things, very much, but stepping away from them to complete this journey gave me perspective. I felt self-sufficient. I would never be nearly as worried about losing a job as I had in the past.

I had my windows open in the hot night. There was no sense of motion at all. A car's headlights would appear as a white smudge and stay hovering on the horizon for what seemed like an age before suddenly speeding up and flashing past me. Then the red smudge of the tail lights would end up hovering in the far distance for another age before winking off. There were very few cars to disturb my isolation. I felt so calm and relaxed it was like being sedated or hypnotized. I turned my headlights off and travelled on by moonlight. I could drive with just two fingers on the wheel, the car on automatic pilot, and I got that soothing sensation once more that I might just disappear. Then I caught a glimpse in the pale white light of a sign saying 'London Bridge: Next right'. Weird, or what?

*   *   *

I slept at Kingman, in a white boxroom like a prison cell with the TV bolted to a shelf and at least three warning signs about ensuring my own safety. Kingman brought to mind another line from the song 'Route 66', the one that goes 'Kingman, Barstow, San Bernardino', a line which represents half a day's drive and includes the searing Mojave desert. Next day I dropped quickly down to Needles and the gunmetal Colorado river. Crossing it put me in California, and the desert. In the days of the dustbowl there were roadblocks out here, police and vigilantes seeking to turn the refugee farmers back. Now they just ask you if you are bringing any fruit in and wish you a nice day. 'Missing you already,' as my love tractor, Joyce, would say.

I had a hundred miles of open desert to cover from Needles to Barstow, and a wonderful loop of Route 66 in the central section. I planned to have breakfast at the Bagdad Café, in the tiny desert settlement of Bagdad, which was the setting for the film. In the thirties the migrants scurried over at night, terrified that during the day the merciless desert would disable their vehicles and kill them. I kept eyeing the gauges, but I had plenty of fuel and the rest were all at normal. A modern car removes the terrors of the desert. With air conditioning, it couldn't even make me hot.

There were a few people still serving the infrequent travellers on the old road. Roadside signs said café, towing, gas, but most businesses were closed, grave-yards for old cars abandoned in the desert. The Roadrunner restaurant's roof had fallen in on it, the gas stations had lost their pumps. At Amboy there was Roy's Motel and Café but I passed it, knowing Bagdad was only a few miles on. It was hard to keep a sense of the number of miles travelled out here. Like time for children, distances could be covered painfully slowly or in the blink of an eye, depending on how I was feeling. Bagdad seemed to be taking an age to reach, and I began to wonder if I had missed it. But I had felt like this a dozen times before on the remote stretches of my drive, and then found the ten miles I thought had passed were only two. But it did seem a long way. Then I hit Ludlow, and knew I really had missed Bagdad, the place I had looked forward to visiting – because of the movie – since the trip began. I stopped and got out at a coffee shop. A surge of heat hit me as if I had opened an oven door. A line of rail trucks were marooned out in the scrub and a sign offered 'Six acres of desert for sale'.

After Barstow things got much greener and busier. I was back on the Interstate and joining the heavy traffic headed for Los Angeles. The last eighty miles were across the nightmare sprawl of L.A., but I had the vision of the Pacific Ocean to spur me on. Route 66 used to run right to the sea but today it is easier to take Interstate 10 to Santa Monica, turn north on Lincoln Boulevard, west on Santa Monica Boulevard and crawl the few blocks to Ocean Avenue, where the old road ends, on the cliffs above the blue, blue Pacific. And there I parked and found a patch of shade and sat looking out to sea.

As the song says:

'If you get hip to my kind of tip
You might take that California trip.
Get your kicks on Route 66.'

Chapter Seven

The boys on the beach

It was raining in Disneyland. Not real rain, movie rain. The kind that comes down as if a giant power shower has been turned on. The kind of rain you only see in films, which drenches you to the skin in seconds as effectively as a bucket of water over the head. It came down in a vast silver blur, turning a parking lot as big as Wink into one huge car wash. It was headlights at noon, wipers flicking back and forth, throwing off a mugful of water at each swipe. The asphalt was under four inches of rain, the car park a giant network of flash-flood rivers flowing this way and that, bubbling over the inundated drains, swamping my shoes. I don't know, maybe it always rains like this in Los Angeles – in Los Angeles and nowhere else. Perhaps movie rain is copied exactly from L.A. rain. The movie men don't know that L.A. rain is unique, that only they are convinced by it.

I didn't even want to be at Disneyland, but I was under instructions to bring back a Minnie Mouse doll for my four-year-old daughter. She had a Mickey, but Mickey couldn't sleep at night. His sister Minnie was lost in the woods. When I was in America I had to find her and bring her home. I had hoped to be able just to hop out of the car, grab a doll from the souvenir store, and leave. But I had to go into the car park, which cost $5. When I got to the entrance they insisted I had to buy a one-day passport, even if I just wanted to go in for five minutes to get a doll. And that cost $27. This

Minnie was getting expensive. The guy at the ticket booth handed me a slip of paper which burbled on about how into each life a little rain must fall, and we sure were getting our share today.

Inside the theme park everyone was wearing yellow raincoats with a huge Mickey on the back and sheltering in the phoney antique souvenir shops. I had to fight my way into the shop, struggle to the display, squeeze to the till, then sprint back to the car, $50 poorer and with my shoes turned to two shapeless blobs and my feet, I discovered later, dyed black. That's enough Magic Kingdom.

I had to put the heater on full blast to dry myself out, then spend thirty minutes in a jam of fleeing motor cars before I could get back on to the freeway. And the freeway, of course, was packed solid. The radio jabbered a tale of fender benders and rubberneckers, and played a nonstop stream of the sort of air-conditioned rock that has given the West Coast such a bad name. It took me four hours to creep west on 91 past the black ghetto of Compton where the music, from bands like Niggas With Attitude, is just an extension of street-gang chants and beatings and lootings and rapes and cop slayings. What a choice: rap or adult-orientated rock. This is not what made L.A. great.

I was headed for the beach, where I could pick up the story of American music through ten glorious years from 1961. In the sixties the West Coast became a focus for pop music. The surfing groups, of whom the Beach Boys were the most talented, started it, with songs that sprang from this perfect climate and portrayed the teenager's ideal lifestyle of sun, surf, hot rods and two girls for every boy. It was all Fun Fun Fun. Did this teen heaven really exist? It did. This was the true California postwar lifestyle. The baby boomers were in their teens and developing their own peculiarly Californian popular culture.

There had been surfing in Hawaii since at least the eighteenth century, when Captain Cook witnessed it, and the first public performance of surfing in the USA had been given by the Hawaiian surfing champion Duke Hahanamoku in Atlantic City in the 1920s, but it did not catch on in California until the fifties. There were 30,000 surfers here in 1961, when Brian Wilson wrote 'Surfin'', the Beach Boys' first hit. By 1968 there were a million. The whole of America was drawn in. Another Beach Boys song, 'Surfing USA', started with the smart conceit of just supposing that everybody across the USA had an ocean, then they would all be surfing. It struck a chord. Somehow it made teenagers across the country feel that they were not excluded from this exceedingly hip new craze, that even if they lived a thousand miles from the coast they could still be a part of all this. I spoke to someone in San Francisco who remembered being in landlocked Amarillo, Texas, and seeing people with surfboards on top of their cars because it fitted the image. 'Say,' the girls would ask, 'do you surf?' 'Sure,' would come the reply.

By 1965 this simple, hedonistic lifestyle and the music that went with it had been overtaken with concern for weightier matters, and by the protest songs of Bob Dylan. The Byrds kept the focus on L.A. to some extent with their electronic cover version of Dylan's 'Mr Tambourine Man', and helped create a club scene on Sunset Strip, West Hollywood, where seminal late sixties bands like Love and the Doors could learn their craft, but by 1967 the emphasis had moved 450 miles north to San Francisco. The city became known as Liverpool USA, and its youth now had a set of new concerns. Peace had replaced partying, you got your highs from hallucinogenic drugs rather than on a surfboard, and you didn't cruise, you protested against the war in Vietnam.

The big bands were Jefferson Airplane, the Grateful Dead, and Big Brother and the Holding Company. Scott MacKenzie recorded the ultimate San Francisco anthem: 'San Francisco (Be Sure To Wear Some Flowers In Your Hair)'. Now the movement across the country was not of young people headed for the Californian beaches, but toward San Francisco's Haight Ashbury district, world headquarters of hippie-dom. But the Doors, for one, ensured that L.A. was still a potent place up to the end of the decade and into 1971, when Jim Morrison died.

But first things first. I was crawling through the rain to the coast, where the beach culture inspired Brian Wilson, the motive force behind the Beach Boys, to write 'Surfin'' in 1961. His brother Dennis may have suggested the idea, being the only competent surfer in a family which also included Carl. The three brothers plus their cousin Mike Love and friend Al Jardine formed the group, and played their hit song for the first time live in the concrete auditorium at Long Beach. Today it was empty in the rain, the grey breakers dirtying the wet sand, the place deserted and forlorn. I turned back from the shore and picked up the Pacific Coast Highway, the stirringly-named route that would later take me to San Francisco. It wove north through the pastel-painted beach colonies to the three beaches of the Beach Boys' home suburb of Hawthorne: Redondo, Hermosa and Manhattan.

Brian, Dennis and Carl were cruising around Hawthorne in Brian's 1957 Ford one day when the disc jockey announced that three songs would be played. Listeners could phone in and vote for the one they thought the best, and that song would be added to the playlist. 'Surfin'' was among the three, and it won. It was Brian's finest moment. They drove to a place called Fosters Old-Fashioned Freeze, on Hawthorne

Boulevard, to celebrate. Carl drank so many milk shakes he threw up.

Tiring of looking at beaches in the rain I turned inland for the couple of miles to Hawthorne, into a long, slow grid of lower middle-class suburbs and shopping malls. Opposite the blank pink cement-block curtain wall of the big new Hawthorne Plaza I found a store called The Boys, a used-car lot and a little arcade of shops. Next door to Thi Thi's Nails and Hair I found Fosters Old-Fashioned Freeze. 'Burgers and Tacos' read the sign over a little blue-roofed takeaway.

If you ever doubted that the Beach Boys' California existed, you should come here to put your finger on one of the concrete landmarks. Remember the song 'Fun Fun Fun'? The one in which the girl takes her daddy's Thunderbird, telling him she is going to the library to study, when in fact she goes down to the hamburger stand? Well, Fosters is that stand. What a slice of history. I ate a cheeseburger to the memory.

Brian Wilson and Mike Love wrote that song in a car, cruising Hawthorne, while discussing Dennis's predilection for young girls. Dennis had boasted to Mike about a girlfriend who had told her father she was going to the library but had come instead to Dennis's apartment. They used the story as inspiration for a wonderfully well-observed vignette, a perfect sketch of teen life.

In such songs the Beach Boys not only reflected and recorded the ideal early sixties teenage lifestyle, they went a long way to inventing modern California. Brian wrote 'Surf City' for Jan and Dean which has the line about two girls for every boy. There is 'I Get Around', about the virtues of going steady because it wouldn't be fair to leave the best girls languishing at home on a Saturday night, and Hawthorne High School, which Brian attended, inspired 'Be True To Your School'. Simple songs for simple times.

Brian Wilson was a genius, no doubt about it. He created a whole new genre – surf music – with very few influences, combining close four-part harmonies with twangy guitar and his own falsetto soaring above it all. These were the golden years for the Beach Boys, but they didn't last long. Both Brian and Dennis experienced profound problems. Brian had a break-down late in 1964 which led to him ceasing touring with the group and spending ten years in bed. When the Beatles hit America in 1965, Brian was eclipsed creatively and felt it deeply. And when hippy culture took hold, the group were left in a time warp. They sounded hopelessly outdated and naive, although they did still come up with occasional masterworks like 'Good Vibrations'. Now, with the perspective of two decades, the music has a wonderful period feel, but is also timeless. It is about being young.

The story of the Beach Boys was all here on this forty-mile stretch of beach. If I went further north I would find Marina del Ray, scene of the group's unhappiest chapter. It was in this rich man's yacht park in 1983 that Dennis, with a history of drug and alcohol abuse and a broken marriage behind him, drowned. His yacht had been repossessed, but Dennis found himself on a vessel owned by friends in the very next berth. Although the water temperature was only 58F he started diving deeply to try and salvage mementos from his marriage to Karen Lamm, things he had thrown overboard in a rage. He found bits of boat, and a framed wedding photo of himself and Karen. He dived again but did not resurface. Forty-five minutes later his body was found in the mud of the harbour bottom.

Still further north on the outskirts of L.A. I would find Malibu, where Brian Wilson lives now. He has suffered from years of mental illness, but today he seems well, slim, handsome. He's better than he ever was, say those who watch him on his daily jogs along the Malibu shoreline. He was on American television while I was visiting, promoting his new autobiography. So, incidentally were his daughters, Carnie and Wendy. Along with Chynna Phillips, daughter of John and Michelle Phillips of another classic sixties L.A. band, The Mamas and Papas, they have formed a group called Wilson Phillips. Carnie was on the same show saying what a lousy childhood Brian treated them to. At the age of five her mother told her her father had problems, he was a drug addict, a genius, and not like normal people. She had felt abandoned by him for years, she said, and even now he says he will phone but never does.

But I would get to Malibu later. My drive north had brought me to the next beach after Marina Del Ray: Venice. And here I could pick up on the story of the man who was the other reason I was in Los Angeles: Jim Morrison. The rain had stopped, the sun was out and the sand was steaming as I parked and walked down to the beach at Venice to find what I had learned to describe, since arriving in America, as a whole bunch of people hanging out and just having a great time. In other words they were doing nothing. Just sitting around, standing around, lazing around, watching other people walking past, calling out 'Yo' or 'Hey' when they saw someone they knew. I suppose it sounds better, when someone asks you what you are doing, to say, 'I'm just having a great time' than simply 'Nothing'. Or maybe you could compromise: 'Nothing, but I'm just having a great time.' Maybe it's being in California, and the terrible fear of negativity that this engenders. Perhaps if you asked Brian Wilson, during his bleakest periods in the late sixties and the seventies, how he was doing he would say, 'Well, I've been alone in my room for ten years developing schizophrenia, ballooning to 300 lbs and just having a great time.'

Between the pier and the pavilion is a strip of beach which houses hamburger stands and T-shirt shops. The fast-drying walkway was full of people cycling, blade running and playing ball. There was a building with a huge, three-storey mural of Jim Morrison on its end wall. Others were decorated with waves and surf, but no-one was actually surfing that day. The pavilion was the most comprehensively graffitied piece of concrete I have ever seen. Kids on skateboards were trying to ride up its sheer walls. A clown with a red nose attempted to incorporate me in his act until I got Minnie Mouse to give him a kiss on his big red nose. A blond guy on roller skates was zooming along playing electric guitar with two speakers strung around his neck. Clearly, from his totally zonked-out expression, he was just having a greater time than all the rest of us put together.

In 1964, when Jim Morrison became a film student at the University of California at Los Angeles, Venice was the bohemian hang-out it had been since the Beat Generation of the fifties made it their own. In the sixties it was still alternative, with students living in the big Victorian houses and plenty of drugs on the streets. Today it is twee and touristy, suffering from the financial overspill from Marina del Ray. Morrison spent the summer of 1965 living on the roof of an empty warehouse, dropping a lot of acid and dreaming of starting a rock and roll band. He had a name, the Doors. Meaning what, people would ask? There is the known and the unknown, he would say in explanation. Between them is the Door. I want to be that Door. He wrote a lot of rock lyrics that summer too, but it might have come to nothing if it hadn't been for a chance meeting on the beach here in August with Ray Manzarek, whom Jim knew vaguely as a fellow student at UCLA.

139

Ray asked Jim what he was doing and, presumably after going through the ritual about hanging out and just having a great time, Morrison told him he had been writing song lyrics. Ray asked to hear them, and Jim sang a verse of a song that was to become 'Moonlight Drive' on the 1967 album *Strange Days.* Ray listened and was amazed. 'Let's start a rock and roll band and make a million dollars,' he said. So they did.

During that summer, Jim had written songs which were to be the mainstay of the Doors' output. Among them were 'Hello I Love You' about a beautiful black girl he saw walking on the beach one day, which surfaced in 1968 on *Waiting For The Sun*; 'Soul Kitchen' about Olivia's, his favourite beach restaurant, which was on the debut album, *The Doors*, in 1967; 'End Of The Night', also on the first album; 'My Eyes Have Seen You', 'People Are Strange' and 'When The Music's Over', which all appeared on *Strange Days*; and 'Cars Hiss By My Window', which did not appear until *L.A. Woman* in 1971.

Jim made a promotional film for an anti-war song called 'The Unknown Soldier' on Venice beach, in which he is tied to a stake and shot, blood gushing from his mouth. To make it as a rock and roller he moved to a new stamping ground ten miles inland, to the stretch of Sunset Boulevard, known as Sunset Strip in West Hollywood where the rock music clubs were.

I followed him, turning inland on Sunset where it meets the ocean just past Pacific Palisades, winding with it through the canyons and into Beverly Hills, where the movie stars, the rock stars and the (generally) anonymously rich all live. In Beverly Hills I could feel my skin getting younger just breathing that rich, moist air. I passed the avenues with their grand parades of towering palm trees, and the lawns on which the grass is so perfect it looks like a thick woollen carpet. There was a smell in the air which might have been the leftover freshness of the rain, but could also have been the scent of a thousand sparklingly clean swimming pools. There was an army of Mexican gardeners and pool men getting down to work, their battered pick-ups almost outnumbering the Rolls and Mercedes and Lexuses of the residents. They toiled away, giving the lawns their daily shave, catching falling leaves before they could land untidily, clipping back the lush foliage so it would not obscure the yellow and blue badges warning of an Armed Response if any sinner tried to get into these little parcels of heaven on earth. Yellow and blue seemed to be the State colours. It is the same on the licence plates of the cars: yellow for the beach, blue for the ocean. On the street corners other Mexicans sat in folding chairs, a pile of *Maps of the Movie Stars' Homes* on their laps, waggling them lazily at the traffic when it stopped at the lights.

As I passed through I put this niceness against the general nastiness of L.A., typified in the sordid crime stories the *Live at Five* type of eyewitness news programme scoop on to the screen with such relish. The running story that week was about the Syringe Bandit, a man who held up stores while wielding a hypodermic filled with blood which he claimed was AIDS-contaminated. I watched blurred black and white footage from surveillance cameras of terrified clerks leaping over counters to get away from the Syringe Bandit, as he came round to grab the money out of the till. The Los Angeles Police Department spokesman said, 'This man is preying on the fear of AIDS. He is using this syringe like a gun. I think people are right to be afraid – a gun is a quick death, this could be a real slow one.' Three extra patrol cars had been deployed to look for him.

This was all minor unpleasantness compared with what was to come a matter of days after I left. Los Angeles would erupt into riots following the acquittal of police officers videoed beating a black motorist called Rodney King.

The change from Beverly Hills opulence to West Hollywood sleaze is very sudden. This was Jim Morrison's stamping ground, his rock and roll square mile. Bordered by Hollywood Boulevard to the north and Santa Monica Boulevard to the south, it is the area between Vine Street to the east and Beverly Hills to the west, with Sunset Strip wandering through the middle like Jim himself after one of his monumental drinking binges. Within this square you can trace the remainder of the Jim Morrison story. Here is the Whisky, the club where the Doors got famous, alongside other clubs like the Roxy and Gazzarri's. Here is the Duke's Coffee Shop, once a club called the London Fog, where the Doors got their first regular gigs.

I walked a block down La Ciegna Boulevard to the unprepossessing two-storey Alta Ciegna Motel on the corner with Santa Monica. It was in the $10-a-night room 32 on the first floor that Jim lived for several years. Just around the corner on Santa Monica is the Doors' former office, a two-storey wooden affair, now also converted into a coffee shop. In the ground-floor rehearsal room here they recorded *L.A. Woman*, perhaps their best LP, accompanied by a lunatic known as Cigar Pain who burned his vocal cords so he would sound uncannily like Morrison, crooning along through an air-conditioning vent.

Just along Santa Monica is Barney's Beanery, a three-room dive where Jim and Janis Joplin got into a fight in which she hit him over the head with a bottle of Southern Comfort. Janis was boozing here on the night she died, aged twenty-seven, of a heroin overdose.

Heading north from Sunset is Laurel Canyon Boulevard, which snakes through the hills between precariously overhanging houses and signs reading

'Mudslide Stoppers 24 Hours'. After a mile or two I came across the Laurel Canyon Country Store and behind it a narrow lane called Rothdell Trail. In an apartment here Jim lived with Pamela Courson, the woman he always came back to after his repeated booze binges and one-night stands, and whom he eventually married. He used to sit, nursing a beer, on their veranda fifty yards up the hill and watch people coming and going from the store below him. He wrote about it, in the song 'Love Street', as the place where the creatures meet. What do they do in there, he wondered. Well, Jim, when I was there they were taking advantage of the special low price on six packs of Diet Coke. The song is also about Jim and Pamela's relationship, which Morrison seemed to think was OK so far.

Jim wrote other songs inspired by Pamela, who thought he wasted his talents being in a rock and roll band and ought to become a poet, pure and simple. She bought him a leather bag to carry his poems in. There are three songs for her on the *Morrison Hotel* album from 1970: 'Roadhouse Blues', 'Blue Sunday', and 'Queen Of The Highway' in which Pamela is a princess and Morrison a monster in black leather. Then there is 'Riders On The Storm' on *L.A. Woman*, in which he tells her she has got to love her man.

Morrison made quite an impact in 1967, when the Doors' debut album was the first ever to get one of the huge hoardings on Sunset normally reserved for the big new movies. In his tight leather outfits he was described variously as 'like David come to Hollywood, a fist in a glove of black kid'* and a 'surf-born Dionysus . . . a hippy Adonis'.† Clearly this was one

---

*Jerry Hopkins and Danny Sugerman, *No One Here Gets Out Alive*, Plexus Publishing Ltd 1980
†Albert Grossman, *ibid*

generation forward from the grinning, good-time Beach Boys.

On the wall beneath the Rothdell Trail house I noticed someone had scrawled 'Mr Mojo Risin'' which, apart from being a line in a Doors song, is an anagram of Jim Morrison. It is also taken as prophetic by some Doors fans, as an indication that Morrison, who died of a heart attack in his bath in Paris in 1971, may not be dead after all. He used to tell people that he might fake his own death to escape the pressures of stardom, disappear to Africa and use that name when he got in touch. There are those who think Mr Mojo is alive and well.

After my tour I was in the Duke's Coffee Shop on Sunset Strip, eating an omelette of Monterey cheese, hot peppers and spinach, when a guy called Art Fein started talking to me. Art turned out to be a rock and roll junkie who moved to the city twenty years ago from Chicago because, he said, it was Rock City USA. He told me he loved Sunset Strip. 'I don't use the rest of the city,' he said, 'my island is the little bit from here to here,' and he moved his forefinger from the Sweet 'n' Low to the maple syrup.

Art had bumped along all these years on the edges of the rock industry, working for record companies, managing the psychobilly band the Cramps for eighteen months, writing a sort of train-spotter's guide to all the rock and roll landmarks in Los Angeles, making films, compiling rockabilly albums and hosting a cable TV show called *Art Fein's Poker Party*. 'Sure I get rock stars on my show,' he assured me. 'Usually I get them twenty years after they have had a hit. I had Brian Wilson on, then about a month later I met him and he didn't remember a thing about it. I'm thinking there ought to be a band a little like the Travelin' Wilburys but called the Droolin' Wilburys, with Brian

144

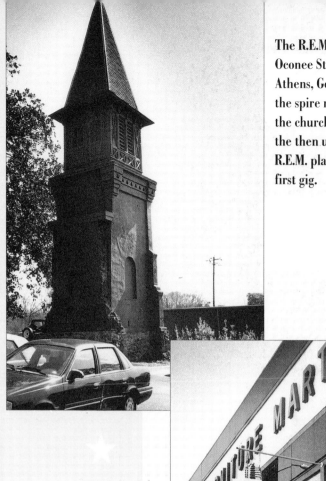

The R.E.M. church, Oconee Street, Athens, Georgia. Only the spire remains of the church in which the then unnamed R.E.M. played their first gig.

The 40 Watt Club, Athens, Georgia, is run by Barrie Berry, wife of Bill, R.E.M.'s drummer.

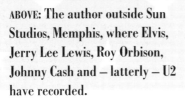

ABOVE: The author outside Sun
Studios, Memphis, where Elvis,
Jerry Lee Lewis, Roy Orbison,
Johnny Cash and – latterly – U2
have recorded.

ABOVE RIGHT: Peggy Sue in
Lubbock, Texas. THE Peggy
Sue, the woman who inspired
the Buddy Holly song.

RIGHT: Buddy Holly statue in
Lubbock, Texas. 'Buddy Holly,'
reads the inscription,
'contributed to the musical
heritage of not only West Texas,
but the entire world.'

ABOVE: The Roy Orbison Museum in Wink, Texas. His high school yearbook, exhibited here, lists his ambitions: to be famous and marry a beautiful girl. He achieved both.

RIGHT: After years during which the highway authorities sought to expunge evidence of the old road and keep the traveller on the sanitized freeways, Historic Route 66 signs are now appearing.

RIGHT: Grants, New Mexico, on Route 66.

BELOW: An abandoned motel on Route 66.

RIGHT: A mural of Jim Morrison on a seafront building at Venice Beach, Los Angeles. On the sands, The Doors were born and their finest songs composed.

LEFT: Bob Dylan's family home on East Seventh Street, Hibbing, Minnesota, the town he escaped from down Highway 61.

BELOW: Hitsville USA in Detroit, home of Motown Records.

LEFT: A visitor to Hitsville USA sits at the piano in the tiny studio used to record the Supremes' 'Stop In the Name of Love' and numerous other hits.

ABOVE: The 59th Street Bridge, subject of Paul Simon's '59th Street Bridge Song (Feelin' Groovy)' seen from Carl Schurz Park, where I met his old friend Monica.

LEFT: David Peel, veteran Manhattan street musician, who befriended John Lennon on his arrival in New York City and whom Lennon immortalized on his album 'Some Time In New York City'.

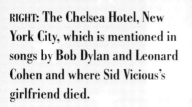

RIGHT: The Chelsea Hotel, New York City, which is mentioned in songs by Bob Dylan and Leonard Cohen and where Sid Vicious's girlfriend died.

LEFT: The cabin in the woods at Woodstock, upstate New York, where Bob Dylan stayed on his first visit to the village which gave its name to a pop festival and a generation.

RIGHT: The café in Woodstock where Bob Dylan had a secret room and wrote two albums.

RIGHT: The Eglise de Notre Dame de Bonsecourse in Montreal, which appears as 'Our Lady Of The Harbour' in Leonard Cohen's song 'Suzanne'.

BELOW: Leonard Cohen's house on Vallieres, Montreal. He lives in Los Angeles now, but when he revisits the city he calls 'the Jerusalem of the north', this is where he stays.

and who's that guy from the Pink Floyd? Yeah, Syd Barrett, mebbe Arthur Lee from Love. Guys who didn't quite make it through the sixties intact.'

'I met Pamela Morrison once,' he told me when I had explained to him that Morrison had brought me to town. 'It was in '73. I knew a girl, a publicist, who was going out with Chuck Berry. We went over to Chuck's house to use the swimming pool — Chuck was out of town. I remember vividly because they were doing coke on the diving board and I didn't know what was happening. Pamela Morrison came over, she was friends with this girl. Pamela was real dipsy, like wow, everything was prefaced with "Jim used to say". She just seemed like she was in outer space. Not long after that she was dead. Heroin.

'I came to L.A. because it is a rock and roll mecca. I'm not a musician but if you aren't what do you do? Hang around musicians. Lately I've been seeing the shortcomings in that. OK, there is this great music and I'm right next to it, but what is that? With the Cramps I had an identity crisis. They get the applause, but what about me? I came here and worked with record companies but it is just a business. If you like sex you don't necessarily go into prostitution. It gets boring.'

He asked who else was I interested in? I ran through some names and when I got to John Lennon he stopped me. 'I met him when I was doing promotion for Capitol. I was promoting one of Yoko's solo albums. I think it was *Fly* or the one after. I'd put Yoko on the phone with a college station in Buffalo or someplace, and me and John would sit around and talk about rock and roll. He'd take out his guitar, I'd bring records in, so for two weeks we just had a party over at the Beverly Hills Hotel.

'Then one night about two years later at the Whisky, Bobby Bland was playing. John is sitting in the corner with Phil Spector. I go "Hi" and John comes flying over saying, "Hey Phil, this is Art Fein, he knows everything about rock and roll." He was on his lost weekend, the year or so he spent away from Yoko getting drunk and whatever. One night in '73 at the Troubadour he and Elton John got on stage with Dr John. I took a lot of photos of the three Johns. It was really cool, he would always fly across the room to greet me. It was like me and my buddy Lennon, so it was pretty good.'

I had arranged to meet someone whose life became entwined with Jim Morrison's when he was only twelve, and who has stayed close to his memory and the work he left behind. For some reason I had formed a mental picture of Danny Sugerman as a David Gower lookalike, but in fact he looked more like John Lennon, circa 1968. He was smaller and slighter, perhaps, but he had the little gold-rimmed glasses, a beaky nose and lank black hair curling to his shoulders. He wore a faded old T-shirt and a brown trilby, but he was driving a white Porsche Carrera soft-top when he came to meet me outside Tower Records on Sunset Strip.

Danny was taken to a Doors concert by a teacher who knew the band, and was given the job of getting Morrison, Manzarek, Bobby Krieger and John Densmore out of their darkened dressing room and on to the stage. Danny's story reads like the dream come true of every rock and roll star-struck kid. Jim understood his inability to fit in with his family or at school, let him hang around the band's office, answer fan mail and write press releases. Jim educated and nurtured him.

Danny has many stories to tell, like the time he had expressed an interest in trying drugs and Jim took him to the Chateau Marmont, the rock and roll hotel on Sunset, to show him the pathetic sight of the singer-songwriter Tim Hardin, so wrecked on heroin he had lost control of his bowels and was begging for a few dollars for a fix.

Danny was with Jim at the Palms Bar, after the deaths of Jimi Hendrix and Janis Joplin, when Jim said to him, 'First Jimi, then Janis, you're drinking with number three.' Just before Jim made his trip to Paris, the one from which he would never return, he said to Danny, 'See you at the big rock concert in the sky.' Danny was eighteen when Jim died. At twenty-one he almost died himself, of heroin addiction. His girl-friend, pregnant with his child, did die.

After Jim's death, Danny went on to manage the three remaining members of the band and to cast a protective eye over the Doors' legacy, which culmi-nated in his involvement with the Oliver Stone film *The Doors.*

I asked him whether it still seemed incredible to him that a boy of twelve should have been taken under the wing of a man like Morrison. 'It seems so unlikely,' he said. 'It's weird. It *is* incredible that I met him, that I worked for the Doors, that I did not just go to college and end up as a lawyer, like my father wanted. Jim's appearance in my life began the most profound relationship I have ever had. He was a phenomenal person and I feel very, very privileged to have known him. As the time passes I find I talk about him more and more often, and about how he lives in my memories. I'll be thirty-eight this year, and it's strange spending a great portion of your life working on something that happened twenty years ago.'

I got the feeling, talking to Danny, that Morrison was more a father to him than his natural father was. He alone seems to have empathized with Danny's alienation from school and family, and to have under-stood the journey that a questing, misfit teenager like Danny had to go through.

'I don't know what is wrong with teenagers,' he said.

'But nobody better expresses the angst and sense of dislocation that teenagers feel than Morrison. He had a four- or five-year dark night of the soul, that is what his lyrics came out of. Everyone must go through it eventually, a lot of people do as teenagers.'

I wondered if Danny's rebellion, and his drug-taking and addiction, were his way of pushing things to the limit. I remembered that I was hungry, as a teenager, to go to the limits. This, in a Home Counties town, meant that I could get the odd bit of cannabis resin. Very occasionally I could get LSD. That was the scope of the drug-related rebellion open to me. The limits for someone like Danny, coming from a rich family and living in Hollywood, were far beyond mine, hence the danger he was in had been far greater. But he didn't see it like that. 'Being a drug addict is not a rejection of society,' he said. 'It is not rebellion, it is more humble. It is actually a desperate attempt to fit in anywhere, because you don't feel you can in any other way. Drugs make you feel you have a place in this world.'

Drugs took Danny on his dark night of the soul, a journey he survived. He hit bottom and came back up. Jim Morrison did not. I wondered what he would be doing now if he had lived.

'I think he'd have an electric blues band,' said Danny, 'or he'd be writing. When I heard *American Prayer*, which is the album the surviving Doors put together in 1978, putting music to recordings of Jim reading his poetry, I thought, this is the album Jim would have done if he had lived. It really seemed like the next step. But so much of who he was is wrapped up in the pursuit of grabbing life whole and swallowing it, that it's hard to picture him as a forty-eight-year-old man, trying perpetually to burn down the night.

'Jack London has a great line about intensity and longevity being ancient enemies, and I think that is really applicable to Morrison. And then Dylan Thomas's mother had another one: "He didn't burn long but he sure burned bright." I think Jim traded longevity for intensity. I wish he hadn't. I wish he was still around. He was the most important person I ever met. He was fun too. He knew how to have a good time because he seized the moment. Making life intense for himself he made it intense for everybody around him.'

So what about Danny now? After he kicked heroin he had decided the things to do were to clean up and get the movie made. 'Now,' he said, 'I want a family. Which is what my father, who has been dead seven years now, always rammed down my throat. The importance of family and how, out of hand, I had rejected it. "Are these guys going to take care of you when you are sick?" he used to say. I've been living with the same girl for two years, we are getting engaged, and I have come to the conclusion that my father was right. That the money isn't important, that the business acclaim isn't important. What's important is being with people who love you unconditionally and who you love unconditionally.'

He didn't say it, but I got the feeling that up until now he had not found anyone since Jim Morrison with whom he had a relationship of unconditional love.

'Are you familiar with the work of Alice Miller?' he asked. I said I was not. 'She wrote a book called *The Drama of the Gifted Child*. She has a line in there about parents assuming that kids know that they are loved. And kids don't assume that they are loved. If a parent punishes them and says they are a bad boy they don't feel loved. I didn't. I felt . . .' he let the sentence trail and picked up the thought with, 'So my father wasn't real good at unconditional love. But it seems that that's the only thing I want now in my life. I'll be real content having a family and writing and taking care of the Doors. 'My girlfriend comes from Washington and is into politics and her mother works in the White House.'

'What's her name?' I asked. There was a pause.

'Aaam. Faun Hall,' he said. One of those names you know but can't immediately put into context. 'The one that worked with Oliver North.'

Now I remembered.

'She's been through quite a lot,' I said.

'Yeah, the media did a real number on her. She was lumped with girls who basically fucked their bosses. Faun never fucked anybody, she was just doing her job as a secretary. The media thrust on her the sudden perception of her as Miss America. On the surface it seems like a real mismatch, me and her. On the other hand, when you get to know her it is not that crazy. She had a pretty wild youth, and Oliver North was her Jim Morrison. He was the one that gave her direction, made her feel that her life had purpose. He galvanized her the same way Jim galvanized me.'

While I listened to Danny I compared myself with him. His real father and his surrogate in Jim Morrison were both dead. My father was dead. I never had a surrogate, but the people I was following on this journey had had more influence on me, given me more support as a troubled teenager, than anyone. Bob Dylan especially. Jim Morrison, too.

I never had the rows with my father that Danny had with his. I was not nearly so rebellious. I wanted to challenge authority, to take it to the limit but not beyond, did not want my rebellion to result in rejection, getting thrown out of home or school. I just wanted to be acknowledged as someone who thought for myself, as a bit of a wild kid, but I wanted to succeed too.

Danny wanted a family now. Well, I had one and wanted it very much and needed it. But there was still this rock and roll trip. If, at the age of eighteen, I could have put aside my ambition for a year and done it then, perhaps I would have got it out of my system. But at that age I was desperate to get through university and make my mark in a career, become a journalist, get my name in the paper as Chuck Berry got his name in lights. In any case, I wouldn't have known what to do then, I would not have realized that this trip and finding out about my idols could complete something unfinished in my life. But now, as I travelled, I found that that was exactly what was happening.

That afternoon, as I drove out through a concrete tunnel into the white sunlight beside the blue, perfect Pacific and headed north for San Francisco, something had changed. The feeling of foreboding at being alone, the misery that sensing my father's presence had been causing me, had gone. I felt at peace for the first time in a year. I had come to terms with my father's loss; I could handle the grief. I didn't have to deny it any more to get by. It had all come into focus when I talked to Danny Sugerman.

The journey had echoes of the Beach Boys. On the 1973 album, *Holland* (named after the country in which it was recorded), is a three-song cycle about this coastline called 'The California Saga'. It includes a hymn to the Big Sur hills south of Carmel, and a celebration of the wonderful, seventy-mile stretch of coastline between Morro Bay and Monterey. Monterey marked one of the band's low points. They were to headline the Monterey Festival in '67, but Brian Wilson had a nervous breakdown and the group had to withdraw. Some say they were scared to appear, fearful of the reception they would get from the hip young audience. Jimi Hendrix played, the concert that made his name in America, and told the audience

151

dismissively of the Beach Boys' pull-out, 'You've heard the last of that surf music.'

Once off the freeway that took me the first fifty miles or so, I was the only car again. Highway 1, to give the road its other title, took me through passes into valleys full of vines, through dinky little towns like Pismo Beach (what a great name), and into a sunset, I swear, that was the most wonderful I have ever seen. Morro Bay was cupped in hills and the sun was setting beyond the dunes. The waves were breaking into a pool of orange, each breaker drawing a silver line down over the sun's reflection.

Then, as darkness fell, I travelled on in the tunnel of white light my headlights cut in the warm, deep blue night. The road got worse, hugging the rocky coastline. I was doing 20, then 15. There were temporary traffic lights and, beyond them, an innocuous little sign which read 'Pavement ends'. This meant the road stopped and I was bouncing over tyre-shredding rocks. I put on the Patsy Cline tape I had bought in Nashville, very low, and let the tape turn and turn for hours. It sounded as if the music were coming from some ancient radio in a back room. It was old-fashioned, and yet . . . that voice! And those songs about wayward men being like the restless wind, wonderful stories about a perfect man who is good in every way. He does this and this and this. So why can't he be you?

I drove through the cypress forest of Big Sur, where all the rustic lodges were full, the restaurants too, through Carmel and down into the lights of Monterey where the only room I could get had rotted rafters in the shower ceiling, but they knocked twenty dollars off its price. They were English, the man a bald-headed Northerner standing in Reception in his vest. He moaned about England when he heard my accent. It was finished. What a great bloke Robert Maxwell had been. It was the Pakkies had done for England. 'OK,' he said, 'here we have the Mexicans but they mix, the Pakkis don't. And they will marry a brother's children. For us that's illegal.' There was more, but I stopped listening. In all my time in America, his was the only dirty room I stayed in.

In June of 1967 the Monterey Pop festival was staged here, one of the main events in the summer of love. The new masters from San Francisco, the Grateful Dead, Jefferson Airplane, and Janis Joplin with Big Brother and the Holding Company, performed here. So did Simon and Garfunkel. I was to hear a story months later in New York about the impact the event had on Paul Simon. This was a seminal event. The world had changed and so had the music. The Beatles had just released *Sergeant Pepper*. Hendrix, Joplin and the Who were unknowns when they played here. Simon and Garfunkel had only just become stars. Country Joe and the Fish would go on to wow everyone at the Woodstock festival two years later with the song that wittily expounded anti-Vietnam feeling – 'Feel Like I'm Fixing To Die Rag'. And a man who was not a musician but who had as much influence on the new consciousness as any of the bands was also here. His name was Augustus Stanley Owsley III and he was the principal manufacturer of LSD, the drug deemed essential to achieving insights into yourself, the universe and everything. He had his pockets full of a special batch of acid he had made for the festival, called Monterey Purple.

Monterey today is just a tourist trap. At its heart is Cannery Row, a shoreline area of former sardine-processing factories after which John Steinbeck named his novel. It is hotel row now, the old canning factories turned into accommodation, souvenir-shop complexes and restaurants. I searched for a shop selling a copy of

Cannery Row, which I had not read. Copies were very rare, considering the number of places trading off Steinbeck's name.

There was a big Sunday-morning queue for the aquarium, and the harbour was full of people struggling into and out of diving gear. They were mocked by hundreds of honking seals, lying on the spur of rock beyond the harbour arm, brown and wet like a forest of seaweed come writhing to life. Absolutely no-one was on acid. Not even me.

Chapter Eight

Never trust a hippy

The tracks were clicking but I couldn't see a tram in any direction. I looked around. Nothing. But I could feel the hum and buzz of one under my feet. Maybe the sound travelled for hundreds of yards through these rails, perhaps it was a mile away. And then it flung itself over the brow beside me, like a whale surfacing, bell clanging madly, people hanging on the outside waving me aside with their free arms. I jumped, right into Mark Gordon. I apologized. He apologized. He had forgotten to warn this foreigner about one of the hazards of San Franciscan street life.

My close encounter with the tram had distracted me from our conversation about 1967. Mark had to repeat his instruction: 'Look into my eye,' he said.

I did.

'Which eye, you are supposed to say. That was the sort of conversation they had in San Francisco in 1967. That was heavy-duty consciousness.'

I'd asked Mark what it was like in San Francisco in the year that was dubbed the Summer of Love, when this small city became, if you were young, the most important place in the world.

'I came to learn to dance,' he said, explaining that he could best answer my question by giving me his reasons for coming, and telling me what he found. 'I was dating an ex-Broadway dancer who said I had a real talent. I came in by Greyhound bus and found a place to live at Anton Leveque's Satanic church on

155

Page Street in the Haight Ashbury district. It was the craziest place I have ever come across. I'd come straight in from deepest rural Vermont, where I was living in a 12 by 12 cabin I had built myself. I had no running water, I'd lived there right through the winter, and I came out here with the ridiculous dream of trying to dance.

'Let me tell you about the people I found myself living with when I got here. In the front room was a revolutionary couple. Every four or five days they'd run through my room, which led to the back yard, with the police chasing them. It was like something out of the Keystone Kops. They and their dog would jump out my window and away over the fence. That first day I had a woman who lived there – who was formerly a man and had only just had the sex-change operation – try to pick me up. Needless to say, having done a lot of chanting, a lot of meditating in Vermont, where my nearest neighbour was a mile away, this was a bit of a culture shock.

'She kept on coming on to me. I had to be very polite. There were no road maps. Then there was another couple in the house, a very, very beautiful young lady and a teacher who seemed pretty normal but was a ranting, raving lunatic. The woman starts being attracted to me and I'm just totally attracted to her and we have some of the most incredible sexual experiences I have ever had to this day . . . and we weren't really using drugs! We had reincarnation flashbacks, both together, of being in the same place at the same time. Of being on the Russian Steppes, in a Chinese garden mandarin type of setting. Maybe it was the time, maybe it was the circumstances. Talk about it now and they'd tell you you were crazy.'

Crazy? Why shouldn't crazy things happen in this crazy city? Crazy in construction apart from anything else. It is built on a promontory seven and a half miles wide, seven and a half miles long and, I'd swear after a morning trying to walk it, seven and a half miles high. It's a pyramid. And don't pyramids focus energy and make all sorts of weird things happen? The roads going north and south are cut into deep grooves in the sides of the hill. Those going east to west must climb to the summit and then plunge down the other side in a series of giant's steps. The roads alternate from flat to precipitous, so suddenly that you feel the car will bottom out at each change in gradient, or take off if you are going downhill. It was the unique topography of San Francisco that had brought me to my close encounter with the tram.

The city has two centres of energy, to use the sort of terminology you can all too easily slip into here. One is in the north-east, between the high-rise of the financial district and the wharfs of the old docks. This area is called North Shore: its ethnic mix is Italian, Japanese and Chinese, the latter spilling over into the former two as Hong Kong Chinese pile in ahead of the handover of Hong Kong to Communist China. North-west of this, towards the point from which the Golden Gate Bridge lopes across to Marin County, is Presidio, a smart neighbourhood and a US Army base. South of Presidio is the Golden Gate Park, on the map a green letter box running from the central spine of the city west to the Pacific. It is planted with eucalyptus trees, their dark leaves drooping around their smooth, mottled trunks as if enervated in the heat. At the park's eastern end you come to Haight Street and, crossing it a few blocks down, Ashbury Street. Together these streets gave their name to an area, a sub-culture and a worldwide youth movement. This is the second centre of energy.

San Francisco is a city, but a manageable one, on a human, European scale. It's a city where people walk, and that makes sense without a car. But it was tough,

157

under the hot sun, climbing those 1 in 3 hills, and it seemed to take so long to get anywhere. To each mile on the map, add another mile for the gradients, and another four for the effort in climbing. Despite his brown suit and brown trilby, Mark Gordon powered along. He is an historian, guide and travel writer these days, contributing to Berlitz's guide to the city and taking walking tours through historic areas. He didn't make it as a dancer. When I asked him for highlights of the golden age of San Francisco, he picked on the Grateful Dead.

'I don't think I've ever experienced anything like my first Dead concert,' he said. 'Everyone will tell you the same. It is seeing the power of what a tribe is all about. We were into alternative realities, we knew the Western ways were fucked. Excuse my French. There was something very empty about them, we tried all the variations. One of the most powerful experiences was at a Dead concert, where you saw three or four or five thousand people getting high together, acting as one. If the Dead know how to do anything, it is how to work with energy. They are energy masters. They would take the energy from the group and bring it back and forth to the audience, getting people higher all the time. And they'd know when things were getting a little rough and they would calm it down. They were so incredibly intuitive. I've never seen anything that comes close. They were the masters of the universe.'

The Grateful Dead were, along with Jefferson Airplane, the twin peaks of the San Francisco music scene in 1967. There were other good bands, Janis Joplin and Big Brother and the Holding Company, Country Joe and the Fish, the Steve Miller Band. But the Summer of Love was only twenty-five per cent about music, and the principal bands were more than just musicians. They were part of a broad cultural and political movement. The movement was anti-war, particularly the war in Vietnam – it was about sexual and personal liberation. The use of hallucinogenic drugs was central to the lifestyle. The music was created under its influence and was therefore a great soundtrack to an LSD trip.

This movement did not spring fully formed into place on the first day of summer 1967. Purists will tell you that the real summers of love were in 1964, '65 and '66. But even if you look to 1967, things started early. On Wednesday 14 January the seeds of the Summer of Love were planted with an event in Golden Gate Park called the Human Be-In. Twenty thousand hippies came together in a mass affirmation of a lifestyle. It was a baptism. They chanted mantras, wore the psychedelic hippy fashions, flashed peace signs, took drugs, ate the free food and listened to the Grateful Dead and the Airplane. Allen Ginsberg, a guiding light, read his poetry. Timothy Leary gave a speech which was to become a clarion call, in which he urged the young to 'Tune in. Turn on. Drop out'. Augustus Owlsey supplied the drugs and wired the PA. Hell's Angels guarded the generator. The Doors were there, a week after the release of their first album, and felt a part of this new movement. Janis Joplin was around too, but got so drunk on Southern Comfort that she was unable to sing.

Time magazine ran a cover story which called Haight Ashbury 'the vibrant epicentre of America's hippy movement'. By the spring, 75,000 young people had hitchhiked here to be a part of it. Gray Line Tours started running buses through the Haight, advertising them as 'Hippy Hop: The only foreign tour within the continental limits of the United States'. The hippies ran alongside the buses holding up mirrors to the tourists, so that what they saw were their own reflections.

Like, wow. More heavy-duty consciousness.

In the summer there was Monterey, a few miles

down the coast, perhaps the musical highlight of the year. But by the autumn, the originators of all this were sick of the whole commercial thing. The Dead and the Airplane were tiring of the mansion communes they lorded it over in the Haight, and were thinking about moving. On 6 October there was another parade marking the death of hippy and the birth of free man. An empty coffin was paraded through the streets into which people threw beads, flowers and other hippy accessories. It was carried to the park, where it was buried. The end of an era, on to the next thing.

And what would that be?

Daah? Like wow, man.

So what did it all amount to? I asked Boz Scaggs, who came to San Francisco in the autumn of 1967 to join the Steve Miller Band, which was one of the discoveries of Monterey. Boz lives now in a rather grand house in Presidio. He was a friend of a friend back home, and proved to be a really nice guy, inviting me along for supper with the family. He cooked the meal himself, after a day spent writing songs for his new album.

'I had heard and read a lot about it,' he said, moving rather anxiously between his stove and his cookery book, kept clean in a dandy little Perspex holder. 'But coming to San Francisco was a great disappointment. A real blow. They were just American kids jumping around in costume, liberated by permissiveness and by drugs and a very liberal city that was absorbing it all and letting it all go on.

'Do you eat shrimp?' he asked, as he shovelled the little pink blighters into the pasta sauce he had bubbling away. 'Monterey Pop was the high point of the whole experience among the musicians. All the bands that had come to prominence in San Francisco, the Dead, Quicksilver Messenger Service, Janis Joplin and Steve Miller – they all played Monterey. They were with Jimi Hendrix and the Who and it became a world-class event. They suddenly saw themselves in the light of musical history alongside the Rolling Stones, the Beatles, Cream. From then on those bands and those musicians set their sights higher and they entered the popular mainstream at that point. It was an exciting time.'

Tourists still come to the Haight Ashbury in the summer looking for hippies, and they find some. The rags of hippiedom still flutter here. There are head shops selling the full range of drug paraphernalia, macrobiotic cafés, second-hand record stores, a church on Divisadero where you can worship to the music of John Coltrane, drugs offered on every corner and a free clinic outside which someone had scrawled 'This is the dawning of the Aids of Aquarius'.

Wow. Heavy-duty consciousness.

In the morning you see the hippies emerging from beneath the bushes in Golden Gate Park, stashing their bedrolls and congregating at the park end of Haight around supermarket trolleys loaded with cans and bottles, in order to reclaim the deposits. On the Haight each store front had a beggar. One old man in a battered hat had a refreshing approach: 'Hi, do you have $100? I'm going into robbery.' A college kid with a bedroll and a camera had two hippies in a door-way chalking a design of a multi-layered heart on the pavement. He got them to flash peace signs for the camera, gave them a dollar each and walked off with his souvenir.

I walked around with Greg Pabst, who today is mar-keting manager for a company that owns two record stations in San Francisco, one a sixties nostalgia channel, the other specializing in vintage big band sounds. Greg came to the city in 1967 with his room mate from Phoenix, Arizona because they could not face another summer there. They landed in San Francisco by chance, because they knew someone they could stay with. They arrived the weekend of Monterey. 'We drove right by, not knowing the concert was happening. My wife, who I didn't know at the time, was there. When we got to town the people we were coming to stay with were not in. They were at Monterey too. We ran out of money so we stayed. We would walk every afternoon up and down Haight just to see who was there and what was happening. You would get rumours like "George Harrison is here" and everyone would be flying around trying to spot him. *Sergeant Pepper* had just come out, it was completely unexpected, something I had never heard before. I can remember everything about the moment I first heard that record. What the apartment smelled like, the angle of light coming through the window. We knew something big was happening, and that in San Francisco we were at the centre of it. It was so exciting to be here, it was the focus for the whole world.'

Greg showed me the two centres of activity in the Haight in 1967, the rambling wooden Victorian houses lived in by the Dead, half a block uphill from Haight at 710 Ashbury Street, and the Airplane's at 2400 Fulton Street. They were communes, inhabited by large, shifting families, with the bands as the focus. Music and lifestyle were inseparable.

'You hear what a wonderful open society it was,' said Greg as we strolled along, 'but in my experience it wasn't. The Dead and the Airplane communes were very cliquey. I didn't feel a part of that, but I felt a part of the political movement, definitely, especially the anti-war movement. I got drafted for Vietnam but managed to find a sympathetic doctor who found a bone chip in one of my knees and got me out of it. I got a job in St Mary's Hospital, right across from Haight, as a psychiatric tech. We had to deal a lot with the unintended victims of the Haight, the kids who had overdosed or were on bad acid trips. So I saw the downside to all the experimentation.

'It turned nasty very quickly after '67. The bodies of those who had OD-ed started to be found in the park on a regular basis; 1968 was the summer of speed. Amphetamines were everywhere. These poor kids were taking them for days at a time and when you take enough it makes you crazy and when you're crazy you don't stop. So it got into a really nasty business. The police would bring them to us, take the cuffs off and shove them through the door. The number of times they had not been properly searched and would come out with razor blades or little knives! I felt more like a cop than a member of one of the helping professions. The drug scene on the Haight was extremely exploitative. The drug dealers would shoot each other for territory, they had no interest at all in peace and love. Within a year it was all gone.'

So did anything that was lasting and valuable come out of San Francisco in 1967? Greg felt that it did, that the hippy movement born here was a force for good. 'The whole idea you could live together in different ways,' he said, 'the whole human potential movement of the seventies grew out of the Haight in the sixties. In a lot of ways people took the movement to heart, whether they were there or not. A lot of movements go back to that time – the ecology movement, vegetarianism, gay liberation. That year it was politically correct to accept anything new. Anything.'

I have a problem with the hippies. I was too young to be one in 1967, when I was eleven, but I had ambitions. I wanted to be a drop-out when I grew up, but then, as I got a couple of years older, I found that the only hippies I ever met were phonies. Their concept of openness and sharing meant that you gave them whatever of yours they wanted. As Malcolm Maclaren, manager of the Sex Pistols, said: 'Never trust a hippy.' Later on, in Woodstock, upstate New York, I would meet people who were more persuasive in their advocacy of the hippy lifestyle, but I have yet to be convinced. I have no real feeling for the music of the Dead and the Airplane either. The Dead plod along in a laid-back sort of way that does nothing for me. The Airplane I actively dislike. Their two big establishing hit singles in 1967 were 'Somebody To Love' and 'White Rabbit'. The first is bearable, I suppose, but the second – oh dear. Some old tosh ripped off from Lewis Caroll, Grace Slick wailing on about a mushroom. One bit makes you big, the other makes you small.

Yeah, yeah.

I thought for a minute I was going to meet Grace Slick. In L.A., Danny Sugerman had got her number out of his Filofax and called her on his car phone for me. But she said no, she was into her animal project right now. Breeding white rabbits, perhaps.

The remnants of the sixties musical movement are still to be found in San Francisco. Many of the musicians have stayed. Some, like the Dead, are still big box-office draws. Others, like Barry Melton, ex Country Joe and the Fish, have followed conventional middle-class careers and only play now as a sideline. Melton is a lawyer across the Bay in Berkeley, but has a regular gig in a bar called the Saloon in the North Shore district. He plays with Peter Albin and Dave Getz from Big Brother and the Holding Company and I enjoyed his blend of blues, folk and rock and roll. It's a nice bar, too, dating from 1880 and in an area I found much more enjoyable than the Haight.

I came back to the Saloon on my last day in San Francisco. It was quiet. Just me, the barman, a drunk and a woman sitting on a stool beside the open door. I had a beer and then wandered down the street. North Shore is an eclectic mix, Italian bakeries, Chinese supermarkets and Japanese restaurants mixed in with a string of dark, welcoming bars and the occasional sex shop. A couple of doors down from the bar was a place with the invitation: 'Talk to a live nude girl', which sounded one up on talking to a dead nude girl. There was an old-fashioned hardware store run by a man in a grey denim coat who said he had come to San Francisco from Italy in 1924. The City Lights Bookshop, owned by the poet Lawrence Ferlinghetti and the focus of a previous San Franciscan subculture – the Beat poets of the fifties – was just across the street from another bookshop, the sort where the wares are sealed in plastic bags. Inside, the old guy with a stained moustache who ran the place was trying to explain the workings of some sort of clitoral stimulator to a customer. 'You put it over the penis,' he was saying. 'You see? Then, when you slide it in this little bit here comes up against her clit and she goes bananas.'

'So, you stick this in the woman?'

'No, no. You put it over the penis.'

He explained again.

The man still didn't understand and was getting impatient.

'Look,' he said, 'do you stick this in the woman?'

'No, no. Look, the clit is on the outside,' and he grabbed one of his magazines to illustrate a quick anatomy lesson.

'OK, OK. I get the fucking picture.'

'Hey shush, shush.'

'What, you don't swear in here?'

'No swearing, no.'

'You can't say fuck? Cu'mahn, everything else in here is fucked.'

The storekeeper turned to me and, when he heard my accent, told me how much he loved England. He often travelled to Europe with his horticultural society, he said. He loved Scotland too, it was so beautiful. Culture. Oh boy, Westminster Abbey, Stratford. 'England has it for culture, the winner every time,' he said as he tidied up his display, straightening magazines called *Back Door Black* and *Miss Chelsea's Bondage Selection*.

Driving to the airport, where I was to catch a plane on the first leg of my journey back east, to Minneapolis, I saw an illuminated sign outside the Lutheran Church. 'Only two choices,' I read. 'God or Self. Heaven or Hell. Now and forever.'

OK, this is San Francisco, I'll take Self and Heaven and I want them now.

Chapter Nine

Highway 61 Revisited

They have something to be proud of in Hibbing. Yes
sir, they sure do. And something to celebrate, too.

Just outside town they have the biggest hole in the
ground in all of America. That's what they're proud of.
And in 1993, Hibbing folk would have been living
here, digging that hole, for one hundred years. This is
what they were planning to celebrate when I came to
town.

In Howard street, one of the two shopping streets in
town, a disused store had become the Hibbing Centennial Committee's headquarters, its plate-glass window
decorated with copies of a booklet called *Hibbing,
Minnesota. On The Move Since 1893.* Inside, sitting in
a threadbare swivel chair, behind a second-hand office
desk was Bob Kitchen. At another desk was a middle-
aged woman, typing very slowly on a beat-up old
manual. Every so often she would click her tongue and
reach inside the Underwood to prise apart keys which
had hit the paper in unison and become jammed.

Bob Kitchen reached me a copy of the booklet from
the window and, wiping dust from it with his sleeve,
handed it over. It had a colour picture of the hole in the
ground, filled with water. The water was blue and
the soil of the steep banks of the hole was a rich, iron-
ore red. Inside was a paragraph headed: About The
Cover. I read: 'In 1979, hematite natural iron-ore
mining ceased in Hibbing's Hull-Rust-Mahoning
Mines which are part of the 30 individual mines that

created this vast manmade pit. The total gross tonnage of ore shipped to date exceeds 680 million tons, and more than 1.4 billion tons of material have been removed. The pit is 3.5 miles long, 1.5 miles wide, 535 feet deep and covers 1,535 acres . . . When mining stopped so did pumping . . . the water was 400ft deep in 1990 . . . 20 billion gallons of water . . . if you put all that water into trucks, they would stretch all round the earth.'

The ore needed to win two world wars, a quarter of America's total output, was mined here, the book told me. It didn't tell me that as the ore reserves became depleted the town had more or less died, but I had guessed that for myself, just walking around the forsaken little place.

But in America, it seems, the less people have the prouder they are of it. Bob Kitchen was certainly proud. 'Our centennial is going to be like no other centennial,' he said. 'We will have events going all year long, even in the winter, not just for a week or two like most folks. We are zeroing in on the history of Hibbing as the home of the world's largest iron-ore pit. We are trying to get a US postage stamp honouring it. Because of the iron ore Hibbing became one of the most beautiful cities in the world. In fact Hibbing High School still draws a lot of ahs. You should see that. The iron ore is mostly depleted now, but we are heavily into tachonite mining, which is extracting iron-ore content from rock by magnetic separation. We have got huge tachonite plants in the area, got one just north called Hibbing Tachonite. You might want to stop there.'

He pointed to the cover of my booklet. 'This line "on the move" is kind of a big joke around here. 'Cos we did move the town, see, lock stock and barrel, to get at the ore underneath. Took us nigh on forty years, starting in 1921, and the Oliver Mining Company built a new town which is the Hibbing you see today. They built the high school, which has been described as a castle in the woods, the Androy hotel and City Hall.'

Bob also gave me a list headed 'Proposed Centennial Projects'. There were nearly 120 of them. They included 'Ice-sculpting contest. Bed races. Wood-carving contest. Ice cream and pie socials. Centennial spaghetti feed. Historical homes tour. Ethnic flag dedication. Centennial quilt project. Tachonite plant tours. Meet your neighbour. Refurbish Hibbing Memorial Building kitchen. Centennial write-on memo pads.'

Returning to my booklet and leafing through it while he talked, I came upon a list headed: 'Famous Hibbing natives'. It read:

'Rudy Perpich, four-term governor of Minnesota
Kevin McHale, NBA basketball star
Jeno Paulucci, businessman/entrepreneur and
    founder of Jeno's Pizza
Bob Dylan, folk musician, songwriter
Roger Maris, baseball player
Vincent Bugliosi, Charles Manson trial prosecutor'

Wait a minute. Wasn't there a giant hidden amongst those minnows? I put my finger on Dylan's name. 'He's sort of what you might call a big star, isn't he?'

'Well. Yeah. He is. Matter of fact,' Bob went on a little reluctantly, sliding a couple of sheets of blue notepaper from beneath a blotter, 'I got a letter right here from a girl from Wisconsin who wants to set up a Bob Dylan display. She needs a space 60ft long and she swears it will be a nice display, spotlighted and everything else.' He sounded unconvinced. 'Will he come home? I don't know. We've asked him before and he hasn't responded. Maybe this time he will.'

There was no picture of Bob Dylan in the book, but there was one of Bob Kitchen's father, Joe. He may not have been one of the most profound influences on a generation, like Dylan, but he had run a peanut and popcorn wagon at the corner of Howard Street and Fourth Avenue for over thirty-five years.

So did the town make any recognition of Bob Dylan? 'Well, no,' said Bob, 'I guess you could say not.' Indeed not. So while Hibbing has the US Hockey Hall of Fame, Iron World USA, the Iron Range Interpretive Centre and the Greyhound Bus Museum (founded here with its first route a fifteen-cent ride from Alice to Hibbing), it does not have a Bob Dylan Museum.

'His house is still here,' said Bob, 'down by the high school. It's sold now. His dad had a store, Zimmerman Electric I believe it was called, just down here on Fourth Avenue. I think he has an uncle in the area.' But Bob urged me to look elsewhere than to Dylan for my enjoyment. 'We got a lot of lakes,' he said, 'fishing, sandy beaches, beautiful woods. Now in summertime it is probably the most beautiful place in the United States.'

It was quite clear that Hibbing, where a skinny little kid called Robert Zimmerman grew up to be Bob Dylan, had turned its back on him. But Dylan, it is fair to say, turned his back very firmly on this place too. In his only novel, *Tarantula*, he talks of being prepared to make a Faustian pact with the Devil in return for escape. He rejected his family, too, claiming in early interviews to be an orphan and to have continually run away from home from a very early age, repeatedly trying to flee until, finally, they were unable to catch him. It was all untrue. His home was comfortable, his parents deeply hurt by the stories, invented partly to satisfy a demand from writers and audiences for folk singers to be homeless, penniless hobos with a colourful past. Changing his name seemed like not just a rejection of them but of his Jewish heritage, too.

It was easy to see why he should reject Hibbing, though. Although I was at the other end of America from Wink, Texas, the towns had a lot in common. In

Wink the decline of oil left it a hard-up, no-hope ghost town. The demise of iron ore had had the same effect on Hibbing. Wink is remote, in a barren landscape two hundred miles from the nearest big town. Hibbing is in the barren north, seventy miles from Duluth which, at the foot of Lake Superior, is the nearest thing to a city. To the north there is nothing, just the empty hinterlands before you hit Canada. In Wink the desert grit and the stink of crude oil are omnipresent. In Hibbing the red dirt of the iron ore is everywhere, on your face, in your mouth. As you breathe you suck in a faint tinge of iron and your teeth carry the tang of it like blood from a busted lip. In both places you feel you are on the edge of nothing. From Hibbing you could walk north to Hudson's Bay. To a teenager with ambitions, Hibbing could very easily become a place of entrapment, as it did for Dylan, and as Wink did for Orbison.

I did the full tour of town, which used up about half an hour. It isn't even a crossroads, just a right angle. Howard Street runs east-west. At its western extremity you hit First Street, which runs south. Go either north or west from this point and you end up in the red mud of the iron works, and the dirt roads run out among mountains of excavated earth optimistically planted with birch trees.

Robert Zimmerman lived here from the age of six until he was eighteen, in 1959. This was the extent of his adolescent world: First Street had the Lybba cinema, where he went to watch his rebellious heroes, James Dean and Marlon Brando. He identified deeply with the alienated figure of Dean, but modelled himself on Brando in *The Wild One*, wearing a leather jacket and burning around town on the Harley Davidson his indulgent parents bought for him.

The Lybba is now a deli. You buy food in the old auditorium and can eat it, if you like, in the former foyer. Go north a block or so past the Stardust bar, which will try and entice you inside with the promise of charitable gambling, and you come to Howard. From here you can see past the city limits in all directions. Just along on Howard is the record store. In Dylan's day it was called Cher Crippa's. Now it is Manseau's Range Music and Video. It sold no rock and roll in Dylan's day, and today it has very little music at all, and only a couple of Dylan cassettes, mostly stocking videos and T-shirts.

A couple of blocks further east on Howard is the Moose Lodge, where Dylan's high school band the Golden Chords played gigs, and right by it the L and B café, where the rock and rollers hung out, Dylan among them. Across the street the Androy Hotel, with a painted sign reading 'Hibbing's finest supper club' and once a proud symbol of prosperity, is now boarded up. Just north of Howard at 4th and 19th was another of Dylan's haunts, Ven Feldt's Snack Bar, where the Golden Chords held Sunday lunchtime jam sessions. Now it is the Overhead Door Company of Hibbing.

Near here too was Dylan's father's store, the Zimmerman Furniture and Appliance Company. Slogan: 'A kitchen range for the Iron Range'.

Turn south off Howard on to Seventh and you pass Hibbing High School, a sprawling, turreted, mock castle which cost the mining company $4 million in 1920 as part of its bribe to the town to move. A few blocks past it at 2425 East Seventh Street is a three-storey grey corner house. This is Dylan's family home, where he plastered the walls of his basement den with James Dean pictures and where the first TV in Hibbing was switched on, in 1952. Dylan would get his brother David to take his picture on his Harley, in leather jacket and with his guitar slung over his shoulder. At night he would strain to hear the faint tones of rock and roll on his radio, tuned to the weak signals of southern stations coming up the Mississippi and Highway 61, the music of Little Richard, Elvis, Buddy Holly and others. In his 1959 high school yearbook he gave his ambition as being to join Little Richard's band.

Bob Dylan has come back only a handful of times since his great escape down Highway 61 in 1959. He came in 1966 to the funeral of his father, Abe, wearing the black hat he sports on the cover of *John Wesley Harding*. He came again three years later for a high school reunion, ten years after he first escaped. Some people in town will tell you he has a cabin out by one of the many lakes in the pine forests. Maybe.

Dylan has spoken and written about Hibbing only rarely, and has claimed it is a place that has nothing to do with him and what he is. This has to be rubbish. If he hated Hibbing so much that he had to escape from it, the town must have been some kind of trigger. Somewhere more bearable might not have made him the way Hibbing made him, and he might not have become Bob Dylan.

The clearest song reference to the place is in 'North Country Blues' on the 1964 album *The Times They Are A-Changin'*, a song about a town that was rich from iron ore but became poor when the ore ran out. In the song the mines are closing because the ore is of poor quality and labour comes cheaper in South America. A man thrown out of work leaves home, a woman is left with three children, knowing they will leave too as soon as they are able.

On the liner notes to that album, Dylan describes Hibbing as the place that has left him his 'legacy visions'. It is neither rich nor poor, but simply dying. He evokes the ghostly feeling in the few remaining ruins of the former town. But now the new town is going the same way, abandoned not for riches but

173

because of poverty. And as he was young enough to flee he fled, and he has been running ever since. He has been a mental and physical refugee, he says; some dreams have faded, some attitudes have been abandoned and fears exorcized. He feels he will go back to the north some day, able to accept his homeland for what it is, and not condemn it for what it could not provide.

That line about having run away and running still was the one that stuck with me as I continued my journey east, to Greenwich Village and Woodstock, where Dylan lived in his periods of greatest fame. His problem there was maintaining his privacy. When he found a secure hiding place with his family it would be discovered, disturbed, destroyed for him and he would have to leave it. He needed fame to escape the crushing monotony of Hibbing. Fame freed him from the nightmare of being ordinary, but fame stole his privacy. To get out of Hibbing he had to become Bob Dylan. But being Bob Dylan was condemning himself to a life on the run.

I drove out into the country, through places with nothing names like Twig, Tower and Embarrass. I went south towards Silica on 73, where Dylan's girlfriend of the late fifties, Echo Helstrom, lived with her mother Martha in a tarpaper shack. There has been speculation that she was Dylan's 'Girl From The North Country', but it seems more likely that the song is based, if on any one woman, on Bonny Beecher, whom he met later at university in Minneapolis.

The roads through the pine woods are flat and straight. The only excitement occurs when you get a sign saying Bump Ahead and then, sure enough, a hundred yards later, a bump. The radio was the dullest of anywhere in America. No rock and roll today, but half-hourly bulletins from Midtown Motors (next to Walmart in Grand Rapids). 'What's the latest, Ralph?'

174

'Well, Jim, we gotta '91 Thunderbird, 14,000 miles ex-rental, we gotta Skylark, got ever'thing on it, it's loaded, man, air, cruise . . .' I drove north through the forest and found Sturgeon, a town hall, a bait shop, a garage and a food store, but no houses. I went east to Buhl, which boasted on its tower that it had 'The finest water in America'. I pressed on to Virginia, the only other real town in the area, and it was just like Hibbing, as if it ran out of money in 1955 and had remained unchanged ever since.

I asked after Dylan in the bars and stores. Most people were only vaguely aware of him, but in a two-bit place out in the woods I found a woman who had known him well. She was happy to talk about him, but insisted that I must not name her. Not that she was still in touch with him, or believed she would ever meet him again, but somehow Dylan's desire for secrecy has filtered through to all sorts of people who knew him. They are protective of him. They don't want his shell punctured, as I would find later in Greenwich Village and Woodstock.

She remembered him at high school, remembered his family, the crowd he hung out with, and said, 'I believe if you want to understand Bob you have come to the most important place. A lot of what he is is down to Hibbing, and his parents.

'Bob is a little bit mad. He gets it from his mother, she was very strange, just could not stop talking. Talking, talking all the time. She never stopped. And his father was a very tough, strict, narrow sort of small-town-businessman kind of a guy. And when you see this kind of family against a place like Hibbing it all fits, you see exactly why Bob is like he is, and why he had to get out of this place and publicly disowned his folks in the early years. The father was harsh and the mother was kind of cuckoo. And the future was nothing.

'I used to think that way too, I left but I came back. I guess you just kind of mellow, or maybe it's that however much you hate the place you were born in, it's got a hold on you that just seems to get stronger as you get older. Pulls you back to base. It's done that to me.

'But Bob is a strange guy. He's not a very nice guy, to be honest. And one of his problems is he is totally ambivalent about everything under the sun. He is just like his mother in that respect. He will start a sentence saying yes and end the sentence saying no, start a sentence saying I don't know and end up talking for two hours. That sort of ambivalence. Maybe that's a strength in his writing, maybe it makes him able to see other points of view, take on personas, but it's a problem in everyday life and in relationships, I'd say.

'I love him, but he can be contradictory, difficult, moody. He cannot hold a friendship for any length of time. Ultimately, he clashes with everybody he gets close to. Nobody can get on with that guy, you can't work with him, you can't be a friend. And yet people still feel protective about him even if disenchanted. I sure as hell know I do.'

Hibbing was a hard place to be in for any length of time without getting bored. One day I drove to one of the many lakes, found a wooden landing stage and lay out on it in the sun, thinking about Dylan and where he fitted in to the great musical scheme of things. In my survey of popular music I had been finding out about the blues, country and rock and roll; Dylan added another ingredient: folk. He took his influences from the folk singers of the 1930s, principal among them Woody Guthrie, and the radical politics he espoused. Woody was from Oklahoma, where many of the migrants taking Route 66 to California originated, and he first became famous for the Dust Bowl Ballads he wrote about those people and their experiences.

Dylan identified with these homeless travellers, with the first union movements. The sixties was a time of calls for Civil Rights for blacks, women and others, and folk music was the ready-made music of protest. It naturally appealed to an idealistic generation of young people, not just because of its subject matter but also because it had developed apart from the mainstream of popular music, and was considered non-commercial. Folk music left a free spirit like Dylan with more freedom to experiment, to sing serious songs outside the constraints that pop worked within in the late fifties and early sixties. This suited Dylan's personality, his beliefs and his ambitions. When folk became limiting, he moved into rock.

Also, by the late fifties rock and roll had gone through its first great five-year burst of creativity. Elvis was in the Army, to be replaced at the top of the charts by pale imitations like Fabian and Frankie Avalon. Folk burst upon the scene as strongly as punk did in London in 1977 or New York in 1978.

Among the many great contributions Dylan made was that he was one of the first singer songwriters. He made songwriting and popular music the natural outlet for the poet. Woody Guthrie had written about contemporary events, and Dylan did the same. He could see parallels with Guthrie's experience in his own life. Guthrie was among people thrown off their land and left homeless, travelling to find a new life. Although Dylan himself was from a reasonably comfortable middle-class background, he was in a godforsaken place that was dying and so forcing working people to move to seek jobs elsewhere. And while Oklahoma was turned into an unproductive dust bowl by foolish farming practices, Hibbing's environment was being destroyed by that vast hole in the ground. Dylan took a huge amount from Woody Guthrie, from his singing style to his lyrical concerns, right down to the harmonica on a stand around his neck. Guthrie sang for the people who had lost what little they had. Dylan's lost souls were not just the dirt poor but a generation of alienated teenagers, rich or poor, from north, south, east or west.

Perhaps the one supreme thing Dylan did for popular music is summed up in something Bruce Springsteen once said: 'Dylan was a revolutionary. Bob freed your mind the way Elvis freed your body.'

While Dylan was growing up few of his musical heroes came to town, but on 31 January 1959 Buddy Holly arrived in Duluth. He and the Crickets were on the Winter Dance Party, a low-rent tour of the frozen Midwest, where in January the temperature can be 40F below and travel is hazardous. That night Buddy played to 2,000 teenagers at the National Guard Armoury in Duluth. The local paper called it 'one of the biggest dances in the history of the city'. Supporting him on the bill were a Texas DJ called the Big Bopper who was enjoying a sizeable hit with a novelty rock and roll song called 'Chantilly Lace'; Ritchie Valens, who had written a song about his girlfriend, Donna, and was also in the charts, and Dion and the Belmonts. Holly had just released 'It Doesn't Matter Any More'. He was only on the tour because he needed the money. He had just split with his manager Norman Petty and had a cash-flow problem.

Dylan sat in the front row, a slight, nervous, dark-haired kid, who could have been Buddy's younger brother. Three days later Holly was dead, killed during a blizzard in a light plane crash (see p. 116). The death seems to have had a profound influence on Dylan. Another idol, James Dean, was already dead, now Buddy was gone too. Suddenly Dylan was in an even greater hurry than before. He seemed to take it as a sign that if he wanted to get anywhere he had to do it fast, and young. Buddy was only twenty-two when he died, at that time Dylan was seventeen, approaching eighteen. Maybe he had only four years left.

I drove down to Duluth on my way to Minneapolis and the airport, which would take me to my next stop east, Detroit, the home of Motown. Duluth is three streets of cobbles running parallel with grey, choppy Lake Superior. The lake is cut off by a chain of multi-storey car parks and the Interstate. Duluth is a dull little place where, if you wanted a taste of sophisti-cation, you might order a Cherry Seven-Up. 'Down-town Duluth welcomes . . . Canadians' read a sign on a hotel. 'Canada dollar at par' said another. That settled it. If this is where Canadians go to live a little, forget it. I left town fast.

As I travelled south on Interstate 35 I was shadowed by another old road, contemporary of Route 66 and Highway One, called Highway 61. In 1965 Bob Dylan sang a song about it – 'Highway 61 Revisited' – and named an album after it. As with the other old roads I had followed, I could trace it, with perseverance. When Dylan wrote about it the road was still one of the great north-south arteries, running over a thousand miles from Canada to the Gulf of Mexico. It linked him – at least in his imagination – with the great southern states and the great centres of popular music: places I had already visited like St Louis and Memphis, and others that I had had to miss out like New Orleans.

I played *Highway 61 Revisited* on my drive. What's it all about, I wondered, listening carefully to the lyrics. God asked Abraham to kill him a son out on Highway 61. Dylan's father was called Abe, so maybe the son was Dylan getting the chop out on the highway, at the place where a thousand telephones that did not ring would be dumped and where World War Three would be promoted. It sounded to me like a celebration, a surreal, wonderfully obscure in-joke, the euphoric song of a man who thought he was doomed but who escaped.

This road had enormous significance for Dylan. It linked him with his musical influences, with the blues and rock and roll that came up from the south, with Woody Guthrie and the barren Midwest. And it really was his route of first escape, to the university at Minneapolis where he stayed for a year before moving on to New York.

I was escaping from Hibbing down Old Highway 61, too. Fleeing to Minneapolis as Dylan had before me, heading for the airport, and Detroit.

Out of the frying pan, into the fire.

Chapter Ten

Panic in Detroit

It was Saturday night in Detroit, the city the rest of America shakes its head over, the place where the American Dream has festered, a town seething with racial hatred and fear, dragged down by crime and drugs. 'The city where' to quote a T-shirt that sells rather well here among the suburbanites who dare themselves to go downtown for an evening's fearful fun, 'the weak are killed and eaten'.

But Detroit is also the city of Motown Records, where a black car-plant worker called Berry Gordy turned a series of local, talented unknowns including Diana Ross and the Supremes, Stevie Wonder, Martha Reeves and the Vandellas, Smokey Robinson, Michael Jackson, Mary Wells, Gladys Knight, the Temptations, the Four Tops, Stevie Wonder and Marvin Gaye into international stars and built up the largest black-owned corporation in America. Motown Records created exuberant, magical music in a now-desperate city.

It was 1 a.m. when I hit Clubland, *the* downtown nightclub; a smart, cool place in the most trashed, derelict and deserted area. I wouldn't have ventured here alone, but I had met up with a couple of guys who knew how to keep out of trouble and were happy to show me around. Greg Suter was white: big, black-haired and bear-like in a pale grey suit and black open-necked shirt. He looked like he could handle himself. Odell Waller was black, small, and pretty gloomy.

Greg was an ex-line worker in a car factory who is now a writer and researcher for Elmore Leonard, the Detroit crime writer. Leonard's hard-boiled, wryly witty tales of the good guy versus the scumbags are based in this city. Odell works in a bookshop.

Clubland is a former theatre, with an elegant, round auditorium, the stalls converted into a bar area with little high tables and stools stepping down to the dance floor, which is on the old stage. Greg had recommended we came here at the end of the evening, so I could see Detroit at its most boisterous. So we sat with our beers and watched the people.

There was a guy with a Mexican moustache and shoulder-length black corkscrew hair sticking out from beneath his black leather trilby. He was wearing shorts with an overall bib, thick long socks pushed down round his ankles and hiking boots. He danced at the very edge of the raised dance floor, always facing out to the cocktail crowd seated at the tables, in a style that was all his own, a combination of aerobics, karate and silly walks. His girl took the minimalist approach to getting noticed, keeping her back to us and barely moving. In her sheath-like, backless black dress you could see her buttocks flexing to the music and occasionally she swished her waist-length black hair over her bare shoulders.

Then there was the little black girl in a strapless green velvet mini dress. She danced hunched in a way that suggested that if she straightened up either her breasts or her crotch would spring into view, which was probably the case. She wore a bolero jacket which had slipped down to the crook of her elbows, but halfway through Marvin Gaye's 'Let's Get It On' she threw it off and danced with the heel of her hand pressed against her groin, fingers fluttering.

There were pretty white girls from the suburbs dancing with a kind of passionless abandon, their

182

boyfriends stuggling to keep up; a very skinny, very tall black man dancing as if with an invisible double bass, and two fat girls in matching flowing smocks like peach duvets.

When Greg had suggested coming to Clubland, Odell had rolled his eyes behind his big glasses and said, 'When Jesus comes back the first place he will destroy will be Clubland.'

'Odell is a little nervous,' Greg explained to me, out of his friend's earshot, on the way. When we were there he proceeded to wind him up about his fears.

'Where are the hoods, Odell?' he asked him.

'Oh, they're here, don't worry about that.'

'It seems pretty OK,' I said.

'Oh, year, it's OK, but it used to be really hot. Then someone got shot and some other stuff happened here and now it's just OK.'

I sensed no menace at all, and as for glamour, it was just about on a par with a hen night in Swindon. I'd felt a lot more threatened in clubs in London. There had been no weapons search on the door, and we were drinking from glass, not the usual plastic flowerpots designed to be useless in a fight.

'What do you make of this?' Greg asked, showing me a picture of a stripped and burned-out car at the side of a main street. 'I was coming down here on 194 last week when I saw this, it's a late model Chevy Camero, on the Expressway mind you, totally stripped like vultures had descended on it. No engine, no wheels. This is the first nightmare of the suburbanites. That's what they think will happen to them if they come downtown. And it can, oh boy it can.'

As he was talking I watched a little old black guy, very dapper in black suit, bowler hat and cane, carrying a basket of roses as he came pirouetting down the steps towards the dance floor. He sold a few here and there, and then a slow smoochy number was played. He went up on to the stage and asked one of the peach duvets to dance, and she did, cheek to cheek straight away, the flower-seller with one arm round her and the other extended to keep his flower basket away from the folds of her dress.

Odell told me about the latest crime craze in Detroit: carjacking. 'They come up to you if you are stopped at the lights,' he said, 'or if you are going along they might force you off the road and say gimme the car, holding a gun on you, and if you don't hand the car over you get shot. This is running at dozens a week. I have a friend was killed. She was in a Suzuki jeep. She was with a boy but he ran off. He said he was going to get help but I know he was chicken and he was running. She got shot dead.'

The smooch number ended and 'My Girl' by the Temptations came on. It was the third Motown track in half an hour.

Earlier in the evening Greg had shown me a bird's-eye view of the city. We had risen in glass elevators to the observation lounge of the Renaissance Center, a vast, black-glass grain silo of a place buttressed with matching twin obelisks housing offices. The Ren Cen, as Detroiters call it, towers above the Detroit river, which marks the border with Canada. We stood up there planning our Saturday night out, but looking down I noticed half of Detroit heading elsewhere for its pleasure. The streets around the Ren Cen were jammed with cars queuing to pass through the tunnel under the river for a night out in the Canadian town of Windsor, where the beer is stronger, the streets are safe, and the girls in the go-go bars look like *Penthouse* models rather than crack whores.

High above it all, Detroit's problems and contradictions were even clearer than at ground level, but the statistics about the city's dangers and decline alone were chilling enough. Detroiters have an annual one in 1,718 chance of being murdered. In the past forty years the city has lost half its population – nearly a million people. In a place where seventy-five per cent are black, white flight into the suburbs means that a virtual apartheid exists. Ninety per cent of whites live in the suburbs, eighty per cent of black people in the city. If there was one thing that set the city on its path of inexorable decline, it was the Detroit riots of 1967. In five days of burning and looting forty-three people, mostly blacks, were killed. The area in which the trouble started, to the west around Martin Luther King Boulevard, was distinguishable even from this distance by the vast empty spaces, like windblown hayfields, where rows of modest homes once stood. When the riots erupted, Martha Reeves was on stage in Detroit singing 'Dancing In The Street'. Somehow, that song became heard by some as a call to blacks to take to the streets, not to dance but to burn. As Martha Reeves said at the time, 'Lord, that is a party song.'

As I gazed down, the city appeared as the most amazing amalgam of dereliction and riches, as if a sliver of Manhattan had been planted in Beirut. Looking north over the downtown area it was as if the place had been razed almost to the ground, yet dotted on this alien territory were a number of safe havens. These brave clusters of buildings rise, like the Ren Cen itself, from the general desolation like fortresses in enemy territory. Most date from the optimistic attempts at urban renewal of the seventies and eighties, but others, beautiful but careworn art deco giants, were built in the earlier part of the century.

Five or six miles away, in midtown, I could see the largest haven after the Ren Cen. The General Motors World Headquarters, the St Regis hotel (where I was staying), the Fisher Building topped with a gold radio mast, a couple of shopping malls and an entertainment complex were linked by secure pedestrian skyways and tunnels. It meant that one could work, shop, see a show, eat and sleep, all without venturing outside. People move between these islands of safety only in a car, doors locked. The nightmare is a breakdown on one of the dangerous streets in between, in which the only pedestrians are the poor, the derelict, prostitutes, muggers and drug dealers.

It was just possible to see that there had once been a grand plan for Detroit. A number of radiating avenues had been laid out. There was Gratiot running, straight as a die, north-east to the rich suburbs of Grosse Pointe and St Clair Shores, where the car company bosses live in mock-Tudor splendour, and Grand River running north-west. Between them was the grey ribbon of Woodward, following the line of an old Indian route to the river, now more like a tarmac sewer through the worst of downtown, moving out through the once-smart suburb of Highland Park and on to safety.

Detroit was born in Highland Park, and so was the affordable motor car. It was there that Henry Ford invented the automobile production line. He went on to build a massive plant here, General Motors and Chrysler did the same, and Detroit became the city that put the wheels under the American Dream. On a map of the city, car plants are shaded pink like the British Empire on a prewar globe, and cover just as large a proportion of the land. The relatively high wages of the industry sucked poor blacks from the southern states. With them they brought their music, their gospel and their blues. This, when combined with the rhythms of the car plants which pounded through the workers' bodies every day, would create a mix that eventually would result in the soul music of the sixties.

As we walked around the 360-degree observation lounge, I was trying to make out the landscape of Motown. I knew that just to the west of the Fisher

Building was Hitsville USA, the little two-storey clapboard house in which, from 1961 to 1972, Motown churned out a hundred *Billboard* Top 100 hits. I could see the cluster of eighteen ochre tower blocks of the Brewster Projects, where the Supremes were just one of the many groups formed on street corners by kids gathering to sing and dance the hot summer nights away.

If there is one song, one sound that for me typifies the joy of Motown music, it is the 'OOOOOOH-HOOOOOO' that Diana Ross lets out at the start of 'Baby Love'. But, looking down on Detroit thirty years after the song was recorded, it was hard to imagine such music, such fun and excitement coming out of this place. Instead what the city brought to mind was a song by David Bowie: 'Panic In Detroit'.

In an impressionistic, disjointed way, the lyric expresses some of the fear and loathing that exists here. It flashes images of a weirdo who could easily fit into the pages of a novel by Elmore Leonard, a van driver who looks like Che Guevara, the last remaining member of some crackpot revolutionary/criminal gang who keeps a gun handy and will some day erupt into crazy, random shooting.

There was an obvious place to start my search for the Detroit of Motown: at Hitsville USA, at 2648 West Grand Boulevard. Next day, after a night of dreams filled with carjackers and gunshots, I went to pick up my car from the valet parking attendant – always leave your car attended, I had been warned – to find that Detroit's car-safety system was not foolproof. The valet avoided my eye.

'Oh,' he said, 'I'll try to drive it. It's been in a crash.'

'It's been in a what?'

'Yeah, some guy was parking his truck and he went into it.'

In fact it was just a scrape, so I was on my way, out of my hermetically sealed midtown safe haven, alone on the streets. But Detroit by daylight seemed more sad than frightening. In my short drive I passed the huge rich Henry Ford Hospital. Outside it on the central reservation squatted a sick and dirty-looking young black. He looked like he should be inside the hospital. His left arm was in a grubby, improvised sling and he held up a cardboard sign to the cars that passed. It said: 'Will work for food.'

Hitsville USA couldn't be less impressive, yet from this little place came a succession of wonderful songs sung by brilliant performers. It was like finding that the Queen really lives in a council house. It had a shop window containing pictures of the stars and, in large blue script right across the front, Hitsville USA. The door was locked, and bore a No Soliciting sign, but there was a buzzer.

In the lobby, a tatty room dominated by a life-size cut-out of Diana Ross in evening dress, trailing a white mink coat, there was a till and the smell of dust and old carpet. A sign read, 'Welcome to the birthplace of the MOTOWN SOUND, where it all began.'

I was ushered down the hall and into a room on the right, where twenty plastic chairs faced a TV on which a video was playing. There were three black couples already watching. The tape was badly edited and jumped abruptly between the bits of old newsreel, stills of stars and other odds and ends from which it had been thrown together. It did give a potted history of Motown, but I was glad it was a story I already knew.

The basics were there: Berry Gordy, a former boxer, began writing songs while working on the production line at Cadillac. 'Money (That's What I Want)', one of his compositions, was later covered by the Beatles and others. He met a young guy called Smokey Robinson who persuaded him that the only way to make money out of music was to form his own record company. Berry took that advice, bought this house with the idea of living upstairs and recording downstairs. Through a brilliant feel for compelling pop music, he built up a string of his own record labels – of which Motown is the most famous – and music-publishing and artist-management companies. He amassed an amazing roster of stars, drawing mostly on the talent in Detroit.

When Gordy was asked the secret of the Motown sound he would answer, 'Rats, roaches, love and guts'. Those of a more analytic mind have talked of a joyful sound built on an urban industrial rhythm, and overlaid with vocals that told a story with a universal application.

You can try and define it further, listing the ingredients: drumsticks pounding the skins on every beat, the bass bounding along, a clutter of guitar, piano and organ, blustery horns and weirdly arranged strings. Or you could just say 'OOOOOOH-HOOOOOO!' Either way, when Gordy dubbed Motown 'The sound of young America' nobody argued. In 1964, when the Beatles swamped the American charts, only Motown and the Beach Boys could compete. In that year alone the Supremes, Motown's flagship act, the biggest female group ever, had three number one hits. Bob Dylan called Smokey Robinson, one of Motown's most successful artists and songwriters, 'America's greatest living poet'.

But then, in 1971, Gordy moved the company to Los Angeles to pursue expansion into the movie industry. By 1988, when he sold out to MCA, Motown had been dead, as a musical force, for years.

As the video crackled to an end a young black guy came in to tell us he was Carl and would be our guide. He took us to the end of the short corridor, where five open steps led down into the recording studio. It was just a little room, twenty feet by fifteen. There was a concert grand piano to the left, and in the corner beyond it a red and blue drum booth. At the far end were two rows of microphones and music stands. Before them, in the centre of the room, was the microphone where the lead singer, the star, would stand. It took a minute or two to realize that this place they called the Snakepit was really where it had all happened. I stood on the spot where Diana Ross recorded 'Baby Love', where Martha Reeves sang 'Dancing In The Street', Smokey Robinson stood for 'Tears Of A Clown', Stevie Wonder sang 'My Cherie Amour', Marvin Gaye and Kim Weston performed 'It Takes Two', and Edwin Starr had grunted out the opening of his most famous song: 'War? Huh!'

Starr had told me what it felt like to be crammed in here for that session: 'It was just great. By chance that basement had perfect acoustics, everything you could want from a recording studio, but it was really tiny. Recording live, with the whole string section in there, and the band and everything, it was pretty damn crowded. I loved that song right from the start, it is one of the most powerful songs of all time.'

Starr has lived in England for some while, and it was years since he had been back to Detroit, but he told me he had heard that the sheet music on the stands was for 'War', and asked me to look and see. I did, but a medley of Supremes hits had taken his place.

'Now that actual piano,' Carl was saying, 'has been on "Stop In The Name of Love", it's been on all kinds of stuff.' I touched it tentatively, expecting to be told I couldn't, but Carl didn't say a thing, not even when a guy in a *Playboy* T-shirt sat down and said, 'OK, any requests?' and began to pick out, at my suggestion, the opening notes to 'My Cherie Amour'.

We went back up the steps and into the cramped control room, where the original equipment still stood.

The lino tiles were worn through from the tapping feet of countless producers working on innumerable hits. This little studio never stopped. Records were made around the clock. Many of the lesser-known artists were still working at the car plants, and would come in at night when their shifts were over. Complaints about the noise from neighbours were such that Gordy had to buy up all the surrounding houses.

Carl was launching into an explanation of the recording equipment, how they had started with two-track in 1959, then moved up in stages to eight, when he broke off. The young black guy in our little group was giving a more succinct explanation to his girlfriend.

'Hey,' said Carl, 'you know all about this stuff. You in a band, you a rapper or som'png?'

'Right.'

'Do you have a band? What are you called?'

'We call ourselves United Poets in Society, UPS.'

'UPS? I bet they call you U-Piss! Are you recording?'

'Well, we're tryin' to get together a demo tape an' Chrysalis are interested in us.'

'Well all right,' said Carl, with murmurs of approval from the rest of us. We moved upstairs. The house smelled like an old person's home, unaired, undusted. We came to rooms containing old black and white and faded colour photographs, album covers and gold discs. It looked like a church hall set out for a jumble sale. I wandered around, scanning the pictures. There was a copy of Berry Gordy's first hit, 'Come To Me' by Mary Johnson, and snapshots of stars drawn to Hitsville. The Clash were there, the B52s, Elvis Costello. There was a framed Testimonial and Resolution by Detroit City Council headed 'In memoriam John Lennon' which intoned, 'Whereas John Lennon, as a member of the Beatles, visited Detroit in 1964 to express appreciation for the influence of Motown in the development of the Beatles Sound . . .'

There were lots of pictures, but nothing very interesting. Nothing to explain what a beacon of hope Motown was to Detroit blacks faced with a life on the line at a car plant. What Gordy offered to a few lucky, talented individuals was success and wealth, but for every black in Detroit, and throughout America, Motown stood for assimilation, integration and aspiration. Motown stars were symbols of black success. Gordy set up a charm school in one of the houses he bought near Hitsville, in which the stars were taught how to behave with presidents and royalty – and they certainly met them. When groups like the Supremes went on stage they were immaculately dressed, made up and coiffured, each performer a role model for blacks, a sign that it was possible to make it in white society. Who is to deny that Gordy helped to fuel the optimism of the sixties?

The highlight of Hitsville is supposed to be the Michael Jackson room. 'He donated $125,000 to the museum,' said Carl, 'so he gets his own room.' Clearly, none of the money had been frittered away in here. There was a glass case holding Jackson's trademark single sequined glove and a black hat. On the wall hung one of his costumes from the days of the Jackson Five, in which a pre-teen Michael was the squeaky-voiced lead singer. It was a hideous little green and orange Bri-nylon number with the name 'Michael' in ballpoint on the label. There were big fabric flowers stitched on to it and the trousers were generously flared.

I wandered into another room, but behind me I could hear Carl giving the rapper some Motown advice.

'When you're sampling,' he was saying, 'don't just steal, don't just sample everybody else's recordings and rap over it. Be creative. And don't do a gangster rap, it's so old. Are you going to do a video?'

'I hope.'

'Well, please, don't be ghetto in your video, it's such a cliché. Three things not to do,' he counted them off on his fingers, 'don't be in an alley, don't show no burned-up houses, and don't go out on Belle Isle.'

I'd been out on Belle Isle, a park in the middle of the Detroit river, the day before. It was there that Motown staff, who in the early days behaved like one big happy family that worked, ate and played together, went for picnics, fun and games. There was even a blob of yellow on my map marked Detroit Beach. I had been the only person there, as if Detroiters were allergic to grass and fresh air.

The tour was over, but as I walked back through the lobby the cut-out of Diana Ross caught my eye. On this spot in 1962 they sat here after school: the girls who would be made into the Supremes within a year or two, wide-eyed at the succession of stars coming and going. None of the Supremes lives in Detroit today. In '71 when Gordy moved the operation to L.A., they were among the big stars he took with him. He left behind dozens more who could not afford to make the move, and I would be meeting some of them tomorrow, but for that afternoon I decided to take myself on a Supremes tour of Detroit.

I drove downtown on Woodward and out to the Brewster-Douglas Project, the tower blocks I had spotted from the top of the Ren Cen. This huddle of eighteen tower blocks and surrounding low-rise homes was high-quality public housing built for Detroit's post-World War Two black population. Diana Ross, one of six children born to Ernestine and Fred Ross, lived here, as did Mary Wilson and Florence Ballard. Diana's father was an assembly-line worker, her mother a cleaner for rich whites in Crosse Pointe.

There were street gangs here in the late fifties and

early sixties, just as there were now as I drove through the scruffy streets. But back then there was another, more peaceful way for kids to compete: music. There were groups singing a cappella on every street corner in those days, each seeing who could best imitate the current hits. Today they lounged on the scrappy grass doing nothing. A few streets away I passed the works of the Wonderloaf bakery. When the Supremes hit the big time many accolades were bestowed upon them: NASA mission control played 'Where Did Our Love Go' for the *Gemini V* astronauts as they orbited the earth, the girls showed their dry armpits in a 'Stop In The Name Of Love' pose for an Arrid Extra Dry commercial, and Supremes white sliced bread went on sale, complete with the girls' pictures wrapped round the loaves.

In 1965, when they were big stars, each bought a house for herself on Buena Vista Drive in Highland Park, which I reached by heading back up Woodward. Diana's mother came to live with her here, Flo bought a place across the street and was joined by several members of her family, while Mary bought a duplex for herself and a separate house for her mother a block and a half away.

It was a rich neighbourhood then. Today, Highland Park is almost totally trashed. The shops on Woodward have had their windows replaced with ash blocks and metal grilles. I passed a place that still had Highland Park State Bank carved into its imposing frontage but was now a two-screen porno cinema offering gay sex on one, straight on the other. It was just along from the 'Club D'Elegance – surveillance parking in rear'. There was hardly anybody about, apart from people talking on the pay phones grouped at regular intervals. These, I had been told, were crack phones, used for doing drug deals. Above one block of four busy phones by a gas station were two giant hoardings. 'Want some crack? Then crack your Bible!' read one, while the other, with what was meant to look like blood running down it, said: 'You need a gun like a hole in the head.'

In Buena Vista itself, the gardens were overgrown and piled with rubbish and wrecked cars. Some of the houses were derelict and gutted, others had half the windows boarded up. Black faces watched suspiciously as I cruised slowly down the street. There was a whole family sitting on two old sofas on the front porch of what I had been told was Diana Ross's former house. When I stopped and called out to them they watched me without speaking for what seemed like a long time before a kid shouted, 'Get outta here!'

When I persisted someone else called out, 'Diana Ross, you say? She done left. Couldn't afford the rent no more, poor chile.'

A couple of streets away was Boston Boulevard, where Berry Gordy bought Boston House, a $3 million mansion, in 1967. Things were not so grim here. The street was split into two narrow carriageways with a wide, tree-planted verge between them. The substantial houses had retained a look of affluence: they are the homes of Detroit's successful blacks. Boston House stands out still as a real mansion, a three-storey stone affair with a Mediterranean look, fountains in the garden and a separate pool house.

This place must have been the most tangible symbol that Berry Gordy and Motown had really made it. Detroiters who visited it during Motown's heyday still talk of the opulence of its furnishings: the marble floors, gold trim on the walls and a bizarre painting of Berry dressed as Napoleon which hung in the drawing room.

That night I drove out to Novi, a white suburb half an hour away, for dinner with an English couple,

Christine and John Lister, who were friends of friends back home. They had come out to work in the car industry but had now set up their own marketing and publicity company. They operated this from the basement of their substantial modern detached house. John was a classic expat, reading a week-old copy of the *Sunday Times* and drinking imported Bass beer. He pumped me for news of home and told me how he could pick up *Prime Minister's Question Time* on cable TV.

Kindly, they had invited some people round that night, and introduced me to a Detroit photographer called Kurt Taylor who remembered a photo session at Boston House with Diana Ross. Over the dips and beers Kurt told me: 'The session was in the pool house, which you reached through an underground tunnel from the main residence. There were dozens of photographers there, and a lot of guests in evening dress, all sitting at tables around the pool. It looked pretty strange, the pool empty of swimmers and everyone really smart sitting around it. Diana was about an hour and a half late and I was wondering whether she would show when there she was, in a beautiful floor-length fur coat. She stood at the side of the pool and tossed the coat off. She had a magnificent gold gown underneath it. Everyone applauded, she blew kisses, it was very showbiz. Then suddenly she just dived, fully-clothed, straight into the pool, came to the surface and started swimming. The place went wild, everyone applauding and whooping and flashlights popping like crazy. She just swam along, sweeping her hair out of her face. Then she got out, took a bow and was gone.'

Up to now my search for Motown had been all in the past, but next day I discovered just how many of Motown's second and third division stars, the ones who could not afford to move to L.A. with Berry

Gordy, still live in Detroit. I had been invited to 1611 Webb, home of one-time Motown songwriter Sylvia Moy. In her basement she has a recording studio where many of the old Motown acts are still turning out records. While the rest of the street was rundown and roamed by gangs of kids, there was a new Mercedes in the drive beside this house, a faint echo of the way the Cadillacs used to be lined up outside Hitsville.

Sylvia is convinced that she is now carrying the Motown torch. 'It is just as exciting here as the original Hitsville,' she said as she gave me a tour of the two studios and other facilities which fill the basement. 'I was motivated to a great extent by Berry Gordy, and I've held on to it. He proved it was possible to record in Detroit and get your music all around the world and I'd like to think I can do the same.'

Sylvia had invited over some other Motown veterans for me to meet, and we sat drinking coffee and chatting in the spacious lounge. The room has a couple of inches of insulation beneath the white carpets to muffle the sounds from the studio. There was Kim Weston, most famous for her duets with Marvin Gaye on 'It Takes Two', Ivy Hunter who co-wrote 'Dancing In The Street', the Elgins who sang 'Heaven Must Have Sent You' and Pat Lewis who, as a member of the Andantes, sang backing vocals on countless Motown hits. They were keen I should see that the Motown family was still together, and as we sat around the stories started to flow, everyone chipping in with their pieces of the Motown story.

First Sylvia told me about how she saved the career of Stevie Wonder.

'Stevie went through a hard time when he was thirteen or fourteen and his voice broke,' she said. 'His sales were falling and nobody seemed to know how to deal with the new Stevie. Every Monday they had production meetings and the producers would all be assigned an artist to work with. This particular Monday when the A and R manager got down the list and they came to W for Wonder, it was mentioned that his voice had changed and we were asked if there were any volunteers to work with him. There weren't. There was some discussion and people were saying that maybe he had had his day, that he had made some money as a child star and that maybe this was it. I was just an assistant to the producers then so I didn't feel I could volunteer, but after the meeting I went up to the A and R manager and said, "Give me a chance at it. I don't think it is over for Stevie."

'They gave me a chance but I was told, "If you can come up with a hit on Stevie Wonder we will keep him. If you can't we are going to have to let him go." I didn't tell Stevie that but I think he knew things were pretty serious for him. We went into a rehearsal room and he sat at the piano and I said, "I want to hear every ditty you got." We went through everything and I was convinced at the end of it that there wasn't anything there that could be a hit. I said, "Stevie, are you sure you don't have anything else?" and he said, "No, that's it," but then he started playing a little ditty that went "Baby, everything is all right, uptight" and that's as much as he had but I said, "Stevie, that's it, that's the one." And from there we began to work up the rest of it and I did a vocal melody and lyrics to it and we had the song "Uptight".

'It was top five, Stevie had turned the corner. I kept with him very closely from then on. We wrote "Shoobie Do", "I Was Made To Love Her", "My Cherie Amour", "Sylvia", quite a few.

'"My Cherie Amour" has been good to me, it is a standard, it will live longer than me and I'm proud of it. When Stevie first played me the melody, it was called "Oh Marsha". He called most of his songs after

198

girls he knew. If he met a new one, a new girl's name came into the songs. I said, "No Stevie, we've had so many girls' names here I'm going to change it," and I came up with "My Cherie Amour".'

Ivy Hunter joined us and I began chatting to him about 'Dancing In The Street'. He looked like Richard Pryor playing a grandfather. He had come straight from a three-hour tennis game and was hobbling around like an old man. He wore a black baseball cap and satin bomber jacket and had a lot of gold jewellery: pendants, bracelets, watch and rings. He told me about the accidental writing of what is one of my favourite Motown songs. 'I was sitting in Mickey Stevenson's [a notable Motown songwriter] attic,' he said. 'Marvin Gaye was there too, and I had cut this very strong track and I was trying to write a set of lyrics to it. The lyrics were kind of melancholy, but Marvin made the comment, "Man, that's not a sad song, that song is more like dancing in the street," and I said, "Dancing in the street? OK, sounds good to me," so I wrote lyrics to that theme. But when I heard the finished product I said no, I don't like this, because I had had something else in mind. Ever since then I have learned not to pass judgement on my own work, because that one song has been looking after me for thirty years.'

Kim Weston was listening to the story. When the song was written, she told me, she had been married to Mickey Stevenson. 'I can remember hearing it take shape up in our rehearsal room,' she said, 'and I went up there and put in my little two cents' worth. I told Mickey I would love to record the song but what happened at the time was that if an artist was hot and they were coming off a hot record they naturally tried to find something to keep the momentum going. And at that time Martha Reeves fitted the bill and she got it. That wasn't as disappointing as not getting "My Baby

Loves Me", which Mickey wrote about me. Martha got that one too. Come to think of it, most of the things Mickey wrote were for me – "Stubborn Kind Of Fellow", for example, which he wrote with Marvin Gaye and which Marvin sang.'

I asked her about singing with Marvin.

'We had a great rapport,' she said. 'Like sister and brother. He was like a big brother who was teaching me the ropes, very protective, a very gentle guy.'

Gaye's death was an appalling tragedy. In 1984 he was shot by his father during a family row. Kim said she could see how such a thing could happen in a strongly religious family – Marvin Gaye Snr was a minister – if a child challenged his father as Gaye seems to have done, siding with his mother in an argument she was having with his father and striking him.

'I know of many parents who have said, if a child ever raised their hand at me I'd kill them, and of course you hear these words and think it is just something that is said, but it's my understanding that Marvin pushed his father. He didn't really hurt him, and I'm sure that was the first time he put his hands on his dad, but at that particular time it was just the wrong thing to do.'

We got to talking about the Motown sound, and where it had come from. I mentioned the opening sequence of the film *Blue Collar*, which is about the car factories of Detroit, in which the pounding of the machines is blended on the soundtrack with a Howlin' Wolf blues to show that the inspiration for the music came directly from the rhythms of industrial life. Sylvia Moy said she thought that applied to Motown. 'Motown borrowed a great deal from the factories,' she said, 'from the assembly lines. You can hear it in the music, in the drumbeat and the emphasis on the back beat, the two and the four, that's the sound of the assembly line sure enough.'

It was intriguing to imagine Berry Gordy in 1955, fixing chrome strip and nailing upholstery trim in Lincoln-Mercurys, being inspired by the rhythms of the machines around him as he took to humming melodies and making up lyrics.

Ivy Hunter had a good explanation of the enduring appeal of Motown. 'The sound,' he said, 'is like an old lover. You may be married and have children but if somebody mentions that name, Motown . . . oh boy. The feeling is not going to go away. Motown is a special place in time that will never come again, but will never be forgotten.'

Clearly it would never die for those who were a part of it. 'It was a neighbourhood thing,' said Kim Weston. 'The kid next door signs a contract with Motown and you look around and there they are on television. And still, when you say Diana Ross or Martha Reeves, people will say, "Hey, I went to school with those people." We worked together, we slept together, we played together and we looked out for each other. We competed with each other because whoever was hot had the spot. To look back and say, out of that little house history was made, is like looking at Abraham Lincoln's cabin, something like that. Because I was there I can believe it, but it is still incredible, phenomenal.'

As I got up to go, Sylvia Moy's little white dog came yapping at my heels.

'Come here, Cherie,' she called.

'Cherie?'

'Yes, I named this dog My Cherie Amour.'

Definitely, it was time to leave.

Chapter Eleven

Greetings from Asbury Park

The Stone Pony was in darkness. I rattled the door but it was locked and bolted. On the next block the Club Seduction Go Go bar promised it was 'rockin' every nite in October', but at the place where Bruce Springsteen learnt his trade, and later kicked off the biggest tour in rock history, there was no sign of life at all.

The latest band list included Stray Cats and the Blue Oyster Cult and others that I had not heard of. In the cement sidewalk someone had written 'Arn the wild one' and 'Glen the cute one'. A sign on the door said: 'SPC is closed until further notice. Call this number for further information.' So I wrote it down, to ring later, standing in the rain outside a breeze-block shack in a decrepit little seaside town and feeling my Saturday night getting washed down the drain.

The Stone Pony is on Ocean Boulevard, home of the Ocean Cruise, once a Saturday night institution in which the kids cruised up and down the shore, beginning in the little town of Long Branch and passing through Asbury Park to Belmar. But no-one was racing tonight.

Only Bruce Springsteen could bring me to New Jersey in the fag end of autumn when the weather had turned unseasonably grotty. Only the way he has drawn such a detailed map of such a tiny place in so many wonderful songs could make Asbury Park worth a trip down Highway 9.

This was Springsteen's stamping ground, the place that made him and that he made famous. Right from his first album, *Greetings From Asbury Park NJ*, in 1973, he has chronicled the town with a close and loving attention to detail. Visit it today and it feels like nowhere, a yesterday place with all its former attractions gone broke and shut down.

The Stone Pony was supposed to be the last remaining attraction: the little club where Springsteen had performed countless times, stepping in unannounced during the sets of Jimmy Cliff, Nils Lofgren or local unknowns like the Brown Bears. Other times, such as when his *Born In The USA* tour was about to take him around the world for two and a half years, he and the E Street Band would take to the stage in the early hours and play the night away. On that occasion he introduced the song 'My Hometown' with the comment 'This song is a way of reminding me where I come from.'

So here I was: where Bruce came from. An Asbury Park pilgrim, all dressed up with no place to go. What should I do? I knew what Springsteen's advice would be. I had the key to the promised land in my pocket. It fitted my hire car. So I left town, deciding to try the brand of Springsteenian freedom that the open road brings.

After all, that's what it's all about, isn't it? This place may be nowhere, but the road at least goes somewhere. That's the theory, at any rate, the logic behind so many of Bruce's songs. So I took the advice and headed out on to Highway 9, the road that had already brought me south from Newark airport, where I had flown in from Detroit. But I had to admit that I was not feeling the spirit of the thing. In the song 'Born to Run', Springsteen sings about people who spend their days in sweated toil, their nights driving. You are meant to find an overwhelming sense of freedom out on roads like Highway 9. I just felt trapped in my metal box.

OK, my Ford Tempo wasn't exactly one of the suicide machines of 'Born to Run'. It certainly wasn't the souped-up 69 Chevy of another song, called 'Racing In The Street', in which driving takes you out of the workaday world into a better place. But even if it had been, on this dark, wet night Highway 9 could have worked no magic on me. For some reason, unlike Route 66 and Highway 61, it did not feel like any means of escape from small-town America, just another four lanes of tarmac packed with cars, smeared white and red from their lights, the traffic flow interrupted every couple of miles by a stop light. Highway 9 was merely a ribbon between the usual modern American detritus of malls, car lots and fast-food outlets. But it had some pleasingly mad hoardings, such as the one reading:

'Ruptured?

Dial 1–800 Hernia.

Same day surgery!'

and another saying:

'God Makes House Call

The family that prays together stays together.'

Maybe it was the nasty taste that Detroit had left in my mouth, the smell of fear it left on my clothes. Perhaps it was the months spent travelling, the thousands of miles already driven, the plane flights and the many places visited so far on my mammoth loop around musical America. Perhaps I had had enough. But I doubted that. In fact, what I really needed after the anonymity of big-city Detroit was the cosiness of a faded American small town, where people show interest in a stranger, get talking to you, ask you where you are from. Unfortunately Asbury Park was too dead to give me what I needed.

I gave up, and found myself a warm, comfortable and expensive motel with a restaurant. I spent my

Saturday night listening to a classical guitarist grudgingly accede to requests for Andrew Lloyd Webber and watching a bored waitress pulling the pink petals out of the carnations she was supposed to be arranging into table decorations. Things would look better in the morning, I hoped.

After dinner I had nothing better to do so I phoned the number I had taken down at the Stone Pony. Perhaps it would be open again soon? I found myself talking to a rock and roll accountant, a receiver of bankrupt businesses. He was called Roger D. Timpson, he told me, and he worked for a Manhattan firm of accountants, R. G. Quintero and Co. 'The Stone Pony,' he said, 'has gone broke.'

This was all the information I needed, really, but on a wet night when you know no-one even an accountant is worth talking to. He dealt with bankrupt businesses all the time, he told me, but it was the rock-and-roll-related cases that he really enjoyed. 'You meet the oddest collection of people. Rock and roll is a business of will of the wisps,' he said, with relish. 'Dealing with the Stone Pony has been A-mazing.'

I wasn't the first to call this number, he added. 'Every manner of crackpot has approached us – always they drop big names. Six people at least have mentioned Bruce Springsteen, the Hard Rock Café has called, so has Crazy George who used to have a show on cable TV where he stopped women on the street and persuaded them to strip in public on camera. I put him in the Smoke But No Fire category.'

He offered to fax me the details sent out to prospective purchasers, and I agreed, thankful for something to read. I got five sheets, telling me everything I could possibly want to know about the Stone Pony, from the price asked for beer to the fees paid to performers. It was nothing for unknown groups, up to $10,000 for stars. And, most amazingly, the turnover, which had been 'As high as $1,000,000 in recent years'. I felt like putting in a bid myself.

Next day the rain still poured down and the wind off the ocean buffeted the car, but at least I could see where I was going. I drove the Ocean strip, starting in the north at Long Branch where the wrecked pier had an optimistic sign 'For sale or lease with attendant rights' and the Café Bar the equally hopeful 'Will rock the boards all winter long'.

On the outskirts of Asbury Park there were cars in the parking lots of the big wooden churches, the grass verges were clipped and the hedges trimmed, and there were mansions quietly mouldering along the seafront. How wild can you get?

It hardly looked a place for racing in the street, and it wasn't. A chicane made me slow to 20mph and then, as I hit the long straight road through Asbury Park, I saw what finally put paid to the races when they were introduced in the seventies: a string of traffic lights spaced at 200-yard intervals, guarding crossroads through which no-one else wanted to drive on a road serving empty lots. They were timed to perfection. I had to stop for what seemed like two minutes at every one, watching the dumb things swinging in the wind, showing their green lights to all the empty roads that crossed my path. It was quicker to get out and walk to the seafront.

At the north end of town a towering brick building called the Convention Hall straddles the boardwalk. With its square tower on top and its plain elevations broken with panels of purple glazed brick and decorated with garlands of green and gold, it looked like a cross between an Italian *duomo* and a market hall. Its marquee welcomed the Aquarium Fish Association. The boardwalk runs south for half a mile from here, many of the planks soft underfoot from rot, the benches so decrepit that lumps from the seats lie on the ground like dropped turds. I stood looking down past the runs of boarded-up arcades and a rusty old Howard Johnson restaurant beside a sign on a lamp post reading: 'The Jersey Shoreline. Keep It Perfect.'

Actually, the sea looked pretty perfect. Great foaming breakers were smashing on to a blonde beach that was showing its grey roots. Out to sea the rain met the waves in a glowering black haze. And all of a sudden as I walked on down the boardwalk, the magic of the place really did hit me. Here was Asbury Park, deserted and unregarded on a bitter day, and yet carefully, lovingly evoked on a whole string of albums. Springsteen more than anyone has taken the minutiae of his early, everyday surroundings and used them as the settings for his songs. I had never been here before, but I recognized almost every building from the albums. The only difference was that the songs evoked places like the Casino and the Fun House when they were still full of life, and now they were closed down and boarded up. I could see the Empress motel just up the street, which I recognized from the cover of the 'Hungry Heart' single. But it had lost the final S in its red neon sign and looked decidedly dowdy.

The accountant had told me that there were strong rumours of a very big developer with ambitious plans for Asbury Park. That would inevitably mean tearing down what was left of the place and starting again. At least, I thought, Asbury Park, classic seaside America, is preserved in the songs of Bruce Springsteen.

The boardwalk crops up on several tracks. Springsteen has often introduced 'The E Street Shuffle' with a tale of a dark and windy night here, not unlike the one I had experienced. He will talk of leaving a bar at 4 a.m. with Miami Steve, from his band, who carries his guitar. As they huddle against the wind and rain there appears a figure all in white, walking as if there were no storm blowing, and carrying his saxophone.

The man is Clarence Clemons, and it seems to be a true tale. Clemons joined the band; he became Springsteen's foil on stage and his sax central to the E Street Band's sound.

Then there is 'Sandy (Asbury Park Fourth of July)' which portrays the boardwalk as a place of lost youth and innocence, and broken romance. The singer's girlfriend, a boardwalk waitress, has left him and he is looking for a new girl. And one of the landmarks mentioned is the fortune-teller's booth, Madame Marie's.

Sure enough, at the far end of the boardwalk, just before the wrecked casino, its concrete roof pitted and holed as if from shellfire, was the little palm-reading booth. But it seemed to be under new management now, the sign reading 'M. Sylvia Reader and Advisor'. It was closed and for a consultation I would have to ring a long distance number. The casino is in the song too, as the place from which the open-shirted boys spill out to dance on the shore.

The beach itself appears in the song 'Walk Like A Man' from the *Tunnel Of Love* album, in which Springsteen sings of being a child, walking behind an adult, perhaps his father, and trying to widen his stride sufficiently to step on his footprints.

Just past the casino was the Palace Fun House which once, the faded signs painted on its walls told me, housed the Tunnel of Love among other attractions, the same Tunnel of Love after which Springsteen named his 1987 album and where he filmed the video that accompanied the single. Above a side door was an indication that someone, some time, had tried to cash in on the Springsteen connection. A sign read 'The Asbury Park Rock and Roll Museum', but the building was empty, a padlock and chain on the door. I peered in and saw just a few scattered boxes, light coming in through a hole in the roof.

Next door, just past the end of the boardwalk, was the still functioning Park Theater which offered both heterosexual and gay sex films but reassured its patrons 'Separate entrance for all male films, separate entrance for all girl films'. It was the only place open the length of the boardwalk. As I walked back to the far end, where I had parked, a dozen snatches of Springsteen's songs came into my head, evoked by the places I passed. Even a sudden bitter wind that chilled my cheeks right through could not dispel the feeling that I had found another place which gave me the key to a star.

There were other landmarks to take in. I drove further south on Ocean Boulevard to Belmar, where I found E Street, on which the band used to have a rehearsal hall, and from which it took its name. It was a quiet suburban cul de sac. Belmar was a lot less tatty than Asbury Park. Its boardwalk was intact, and uncluttered with buildings, except for a smart pale blue and white pavilion which turned out to be a McDonald's. People were scurrying to it through the rain, to sit inside eating their burgers in their overcoats, the wind whistling through. A whole restaurant full of people chewing and silently watching the white horses on the threatening grey sea.

A couple of years ago I might have seen Bruce Springsteen jog past on the sands. Until, that is, he finally left his home for Los Angeles. I sat there wondering why he did, if Asbury Park was so important to him, a place that – by his own admission – reminded him who he was, that gave him an anchor to reality when stardom, fame, and wealth threatened to set him adrift in a world of empty praise and hollow friendships.

By all accounts he went because he had lost his privacy. The fans pestered him when he was out jogging, or shopping at the Delicious Orchards grocery store at Colts Neck, and hunted him down in the mansion he'd bought just inland at Rumson. If that was the case he had paid a potentially perilous price for fame. If the place you were born and the way you lived as a young man are so important to what you create, being cut off from them could be fatal, I would have thought. It was interesting to contrast Springsteen with Dylan, who loathed his home town and had to flee it. Hibbing can't have offered much less than Asbury Park, and yet Springsteen had stayed, written of it with affection, and still become hugely successful.

And what about R.E.M. and Athens, Georgia, where my journey began in the spring? Michael Stipe and the rest of the band had managed to remain at the centre of small-town life, to put up with the attentions of fans and, instead of shutting themselves away, had remained completely visible and become more and more involved. They were as famous as Springsteen; the pressures cannot have been any less. It struck me that, of all the different ways I had discovered different stars coping with their stardom and trying to live relatively normal lives, R.E.M. had the best approach. They, almost alone, had pulled it off. Of course, they had not been as overpoweringly famous for as long as Springsteen has, and he had managed to remain in Asbury Park for a number of years. Maybe they too would be forced to flee at some point.

Or maybe there comes a time when you have to move on. Could Springsteen really have kept writing about boy racers for ever? He wrote and recorded 'Tunnel Of Love' in the Rumson house, a $1m white-columned colonial mansion, in the mid-eighties, and hints in the lyrics that he knew how much he had changed since seventies albums like *Greetings From Asbury Park NJ*, *The Wild, The Innocent and The E Street Shuffle*, and *Born To Run*. He sang there not of beat-up Chevys but of having a fancy foreign car. At one point a character looks at the open highway and rather than feeling a sense of release, of freedom, all he sees is road. Is that growing up, or losing sight of something fundamental? Probably it is simply moving on, as Springsteen himself did physically a couple of years later.

Although Asbury Park was Springsteen's chosen stamping ground, and the place where he came to live when he left home, he was born in Freehold, a minor industrial town fifteen miles inland. I took a drive out there, prepared to find it as portrayed in 'My Hometown' on *Born In The USA*, in which Springsteen sings of a man driving around town with his young son, recalling doing the same with his father when he was a boy. It is a song of decline, of race riots and redundancy, of empty stores and windows whitewashed over.

I found Freehold nothing like I had expected. The song had more relevance to Asbury. Its main street had a pleasant, Victorian, brick solidity. Banks, the Dunkin' Donuts and the pizza parlours were in old buildings rather than, as is so often the case, having moved out to malls around the edge of town which leave the centre empty and dead. The air was filled with the aroma of coffee from a huge Nescafé factory.

Springsteen lived here for eighteen years, first in Institute Street, then on South Street. I found them both just off Main Street, their gutters blocked with fallen leaves. There was the house next to the gas station and the little flat roof on to which Bruce would drag his mattress on summer nights. Here he listened to the comings and goings on the gas station forecourt, which was about the closest thing to a social centre that the town possessed. He found the place narrow-minded and restrictive. In the late sixties he could hardly walk the streets without being hassled because of his hippy clothes. But it was here, aged fourteen,

211

that he first heard Elvis, and craved a guitar of his own. Compared to Freehold, Asbury was relatively glamorous and liberated, but New York City, fifty-three miles north, was the real honeypot. Springsteen was drawn up the New Jersey Turnpike like so many thousands of other kids out for adventure.

Manhattan was drawing me too: going there seemed the natural progression. Many of the stories I was following led me to New York City. It was time to take the Turnpike, the road on which Paul Simon counted the cars in his song 'America'. Chuck Berry wrote 'You Can't Catch Me' after a late-night race on the Turnpike between his Buick and a bunch of kids in a souped-up car who challenged him. He won, but was stopped by the police. Springsteen has called the Turnpike the 'golden road of the east', and it does have a powerful resonance in the American psyche, almost as strong as that created by Route 66.

Simon's song tells the story of two young lovers taking a Greyhound bus to find the real America, and themselves. He wrote it in the late sixties when voyages of self-discovery were all the rage, and rebellion was being replaced by a concern for rediscovering older values and an older, simpler America. Mobility was central to that dream too, hence the appeal of the song – and hence the problem. Everyone is searching for the same dream; the Turnpike is clogged with cars, which makes counting them an impossibility. And what they are looking for may be long gone.

Coincidentally, the New Jersey Turnpike was the place where Jack Kerouac began his crazy, zigzagging trips across America, trips which provided the inspiration for his most famous book, *On the Road*. Kerouac was the supreme poet of America's love affair with the car and the road. He styled himself a lonesome traveller, a man for whom travelling was (don't cringe) a metaphor for the road of life. *On the Road,* published

212

in 1957, inspired the postwar generation for whom cheap, fast travel over vast distances was an everyday reality. The book remains a powerful evocation of the joys of free movement across the American continent, saying much about the way Americans see themselves and their country.

For Springsteen, unlike Simon and Kerouac, the Turnpike was magical not because it led out into the vast continent of America but because, from the New Jersey hinterland, it led to New York City: the centre of his universe, the place that meant excitement, danger, and fame. As a teenager he would escape there at night whenever he could. In 'Meeting Across The River' on *Born To Run* he tells the story of a kid from Jersey convinced that he can pull a scam in the city, that if he can only get the loan of a few bucks for a ride through the Lincoln Tunnel to Manhattan he can pick up two grand.

This time the road I travelled did not disappoint me. Maybe it was the fact that it led me to Manhattan, on a journey which so many of the people I was following had taken before me, that captured my imagination. New York was the antithesis of the small towns, poverty, or plain ordinariness that many, from Bob Dylan down, were fleeing.

The Turnpike took me through a grimy landscape that felt like New York's back yard, full of the messy machinery that kept the city humming with life. There were refineries, dozens of white-painted oil-storage tanks, power stations covered with white pinpricks of light and squeezing white columns of steam into the grey sky. It was Veterans' Day and quiet on the road. Counting the cars was no problem. I passed through a forest of electricity pylons, their power lines so numerous they made a black web overhead. Above them at intervals the bellies of planes appeared, swooping low on their approach to Newark airport.

213

Then Manhattan filled the horizon. The tower-block skyline was dark grey against the lighter grey of the sky. The city hung like a painted backdrop to the mess I was travelling through. Then I was sliding into the Lincoln Tunnel, the grimy glazed tiles along its walls making it feel like a long, antique urinal. I emerged into a new world. I had travelled from the east right across the south of the country, up the west coast, looped back through the north and now I was on the east coast, in what was undoubtedly the most important place on the journey of a lifetime.

Chapter Twelve

I remember you well in the Chelsea Hotel

'Sid Vicious! I mean, Sid Vicious? Is that all you came here to talk about? When you could ask me about Bob Dylan, Leonard Cohen, Buffy Saint Marie, Janis Joplin, the Grateful Dead? I mean the list goes on and on and on. John Lennon and his wife – they were thinking about an apartment here before they went to the Dakota. There is almost no-one in the music scene or in the cultural movement that didn't at one time have the Chelsea be part of their life, it affected them in some way, they wrote a song about it. And you keep on at me about the night some junkie wasted a broad.'

Stanley Bard threw his hands in the air and let them slap down on his cluttered desk in the little office that looked as if it hadn't been decorated since 1930. Two little billows of dust rose in the shafts of yellow autumn sunlight slanting through the room, up towards the cherubs painted on the ceiling.

Stanley had a point. When Sid killed Nancy Spungen in their room here in 1978 it was just another in a line of deaths, one more act of weirdness in the bizarre life of Manhattan's rock and roll hotel, the Chelsea. The poet Dylan Thomas went into a fatal coma in room 206 after a marathon session at the White Horse Tavern in Greenwich Village. The woman who shot and almost killed the pop artist Andy Warhol in 1968 lived here. Delmore Schwartz, teacher and mentor of Lou Reed, died here of an excess of drugs and debauchery. Sid and Nancy were by no means the strangest residents the hotel had seen, nor the most destructive. When they set fire to their room it was not the first blaze Stanley had had to cope with. Odine, one of the stars of Andy Warhol's series of sixties experimental movies, caused at least two fires when she lived here. Sid and Nancy never brought in lions and tigers from the Bronx Zoo for a full rehearsal of the grand march from *Aida* as Katherine Dunham did. The pair look positively straight when compared with Sarah Bernhardt, who slept in a coffin on the seventh floor. No-one thought she was weird, either.

But Stanley did admit I was not the first to show an interest in punk's unhappy couple. Indeed, he had allowed Alex Cox to film his movie, *Sid and Nancy*, in which the pair's sordid decline to junkie death is mercilessly chronicled, on the premises. In the film, their room is identified as number 100.

'We get thousands of people call up and try to book room 100,' said Stanley. 'We have no room 100.'

I had watched the film a couple of weeks before. It portrays the hotel as a freak show, with drug-pushers prowling the corridors. While Sid gets hurled downstairs by Nancy, Stanley is shown coming up with a preppy young couple in Burberrys. He is intoning the litany that he had spouted for me and a million others: 'A lot of famous artists stay here . . .' breaking off as the punks tumble, screeching, past to explain, 'it's a couple of my foreign exchange students.' After Sid and Nancy, in a doped stupor, set fire to their room Stanley is shown moving them to a new one, telling them Dylan Thomas and Andy Warhol stayed here, and that 'This is not a place where people set light to their rooms.' An aged retainer in a green uniform who looks the colour of death and as if covered in cobwebs follows them, carrying a guitar. 'He wants you to like this room,' he says to Sid, of Stanley. 'Bob Dylan was born here.'

Stanley shook his head over my morbid curiosity. 'I mean,' he said, 'didn't you notice the plaques outside?' I had: they commemorated the likes of Mark Twain and Dylan Thomas. Didn't I know how much great literature had come out of this twelve-storey Victorian pile, the tallest edifice in Manhattan when it was built, at 222 West 23rd Street, in 1884? He gestured to a glass-fronted bookcase behind a stack of cardboard boxes filled with junk. It was crammed with volumes written here and inscribed with things like 'A perfect place to write (Eugene O'Neill)'.

'We have had some of the most prominent, Mark Twain, O. Henry, Eugene O'Neill, you are talking about the most renowned people in their respective fields. There is no aspect of creativity in which the Chelsea didn't attract the cream. It's like a Mecca, it's unreal, it's almost mind-boggling that so much creativity should be under one roof in one building in this big city.'

Stanley sighed again, giving me up as a lost cause, and then relented a little. Weren't there, he asked, any great musicians he could tell me about?

Yes, there were. Did he remember Leonard Cohen, Bob Dylan?

'Sure I recall Bob Dylan. I rented him an apartment, I remember when he came he was married and he had a baby here and then he moved to Woodstock. Maybe for about a two-year period in the 1960s he was here. I talked to him, he was a quiet person.'

And Leonard Cohen?

'Sure I remember him too, but not so well, a quiet guy.'

I sensed I wasn't going to get very far with musicians, so I asked him about Andy Warhol.

'Andy Warhol was a very quiet person. All quiet people.'

Clearly, to Stanley, some of the biggest noises

around were quiet people. No doubt to him Sid Vicious was a *very* quiet person. Had all his residents always been nice quiet people? Not quite all. Brendan Behan was not a nice quiet guy and was thrown out for rowdiness with his sailor friends. Valerie Solanas was not a nice quiet woman. When she shot Andy Warhol in 1967 she had been a resident for two years. Arthur Miller, who wrote *After the Fall* here, had complained to Stanley about her, about the way she would stand in the lobby handing out literature in which men were viciously attacked. She was the founding president and only member of SCUM, the Society for Cutting Up Men. Miller warned Bard, 'She's dangerous. She's going to wind up killing somebody.' This was a bit rich coming from the man who, in *Timebends*, had lauded the Chelsea as a place with 'no rules, no taste, no shame'. Stanley made Valerie move out. Shortly afterwards she emptied a gun into Warhol's lungs, stomach and liver. During five hours of surgery he clinically died twice before pulling through.

But it wasn't Sid, former bass guitarist with the seminal punk band the Sex Pistols, who had brought me here; it was the fact that two of my favourite songs were composed in the Chelsea.

Leonard Cohen lived here in the late sixties when he first came to New York from his native Montreal to put his poetry to music. He came back to write *New Skin For The Old Ceremony*, which includes the song 'Chelsea Hotel II' about Janis Joplin, a fellow resident. It has the lines:

'I remember you well at the Chelsea Hotel
You were famous, your face was a legend.
Giving me head on an unmade bed
While the limousines wait in the street.'

Bob Dylan wrote 'Sad-Eyed Lady Of The Lowlands' here, a song which fills up a whole side of the 1966 double album *Blonde on Blonde.* In another song,

'Sara', on the *Desire* album, he sings:

    'I'd taken the cure and just gotten through
    Staying up for days in the Chelsea Hotel
    Writing "Sad-Eyed Lady Of The Lowlands" for
    you.'

Bob Dylan was married to Sara on 22 November 1965, and he wrote 'Sad-Eyed Lady Of The Lowlands' virtually as a wedding song for her. While doing everything he could to keep his wife out of the public gaze, he revealed her in this song. She was his equivalent of Shakespeare's Dark Lady. Those who know her say there are many specifics of her appearance and personality which ring true, from her 'hollow face', 'flesh like silk, and your face like glass' to her sad eyes. He gives details of her past, mentioning her 'magazine husband who one day just had to go'. Sara had had a relationship with Victor Lowndes, who was prominent in the *Playboy* organization, but was not married to him. When she met Dylan she already had a little girl called Maria. One line talks of her 'with the child of a hoodlum wrapped up in your arms'.

I needed no other persuaders that this was the place to stay in New York while I went on the trails of Dylan, Cohen, John Lennon, Lou Reed and Paul Simon. But I confess to having been apprehensive about staying here. I had expected a circus freak show, a cross between a madhouse and a geriatric home, with Stanley as a kind of officiating crabby maiden aunt. In fact it was cosy and comfortable in a dusty, slightly decrepit way, but it *was* certainly weirder than the Sheraton where I had stayed for a week in New Jersey. Thank God.

From the minute you arrive you realize no other hotel in the world resembles the Chelsea. To enter the lobby is like walking into an art gallery that doubles as a soup kitchen. There are large colourful works on the

219

walls: a portrait of Warhol, a parody of 'Déjeuner sur l'herbe' and a white plaster girl on a swing hanging from the ceiling. Oblivious to this, there was a dog asleep in the fireplace and a bag lady sorting through her finds on one of the plastic benches. Men in black bomber jackets inscribed FBI on the back were carrying circular saws, sanders and other tools out of the lift. Anywhere else their presence might have been alarming, but here they could just as easily be a firm of hip maintenance men, or a bunch of roadies, as a team of agents taking the place apart looking for drugs.

Alice Cooper once ran into an FBI raid in this lobby, dropping his pet python in panic as he fled. Maybe it was maintenance men that time too. It would not have been the first misunderstanding to occur here, where Jimi Hendrix was once mistaken by a white southern lady for a bellboy: 'Boy, I need some help with my bags here.'

My room was pretty different, too. It was like the worst bedsit I ever had as a student, only that had never cost me $85 a night. Behind a curtain were a gas cooker, a sink and a fridge, and there was an aged bathroom with no plug in either tub or basin. The twin beds had threadbare candlewick covers. A desk with a chair too large to fit under it faced five mirror tiles, the sixth having fallen off, leaving a brown square of wall showing through. There was a chest, a chipboard job, and a newish TV with the word Blitz scratched into it, on which I never managed to get a picture. A length of coaxial cable had been poked through a recently drilled hole above the door and was hanging in midair. One day it and the TV would be united. But not, I felt, for some time.

At least my room was at the front of the building. I had a cast-iron balcony on which sat two rust red chairs. I climbed out and stood looking down at the street, and the rusty Hotel Chelsea sign. I could see little neighbourhood shops, with signs that said: 1hr Photo, Dorothy's Dress Shop and Professional Tax Services. While I was looking out, a limo pulled up, a blue stretch number with a fin on the rear boot like a boomerang mounted on a plinth. It waited in the street, just to complete the picture for me.

Leonard Cohen found the Chelsea Hotel, when he hit town from Montreal, by asking around for the place where the musicians stayed. He booked into a room not unlike mine, a narrow affair filled up with two single beds, and it became his home and launching pad. His big break came because Judy Collins recorded 'Suzanne' and 'Dress Rehearsal Rag' for her album *My Life* in 1967. John Hammond, the CBS man who signed Bob Dylan, and later Bruce Springsteen, heard him and signed him up to make his own records. One of his finest early songs, 'Marianne', was completed here. At one time he numbered Bob Dylan, Joan Baez, Jimi Hendrix and Janis Joplin among his fellow residents.

It was the ready availability of drugs that drove Cohen away. In the sixties you couldn't eat anything prepared on the gas cookers behind the curtains with safety. Everything was spiked with LSD – even fried potatoes could send you on a trip you hadn't been planning to make.

Stanley had told me about the episode that occurred on Leonard Cohen's floor when he was in residence, which may have hastened his departure. 'Katherine Dunham was to appear in *Aida* at the Metropolitan Opera House,' he said. 'She told me she was having a rehearsal up on the sixth floor where she had an apartment and I said fine. I think nothing of it until I get a strange call at home about seven o'clock. The clerk was terrified. He said, "Mr Bard, you have to see, there are tigers." I thought he was kidding . . . he was drunk. I asked to speak to Katherine and she said, "Don't worry, there are trainers here." She guaranteed it was all under control but I said, "The people in the hotel will be very disturbed," but she said no and she was right. Chelsea-ites are a very strange breed, they loved it that she was doing it here. So it worked out, but I didn't sleep that night.'

As I clambered back into the room the racket the central heating was making brought Joni Mitchell to mind, and her song 'Chelsea Morning', also written here:

'The song outside my window
And the traffic wrote the words
It came ringing up like Christmas bells
And rapping like pipes and drums.'

The song could easily have started life as a complaint to Stanley about the lousy plumbing and the din in the street. There was a banging in the pipes as if someone was taking the heating system apart. And when the banging stopped it was replaced by a jangling sound like that of a Hare Krishna troupe shaking their bells. I awoke more than once to find myself chanting Krishna Krishna, Krishna Krishna, Hare Rama, Hare Rama in my head. More than a week of this and I would wake up in saffron pyjamas with my head shaved.

'How do you like the room?' Stanley asked me when I met up with him again later in the lobby.

'Fine.'

'Good,' he said, adding conspiratorially, 'I gave you an upgrade.'

Stanley seemed to spend most of his time in the lobby, talking to his tenants ('I don't think of them as tenants, they're my friends'). He was a little skinny guy, his hair gummed over the bald patch on his crown, his skin a grey one shade lighter than his suit. He looked as if he inhabited a world of nicotine and grime, just like his hotel. He didn't need to tell me that the Chelsea was his life, but he did anyway. Just as it

222

had been his father's life right from 1930 when David Bard, a Hungarian Jewish refugee, rescued the place from bankruptcy and began building its reputation. Just as it would be Stanley's son's life when Stanley retired.

The art in the lobby is from Stanley's collection: all are works either given by artists who lived here, or handed over in lieu of rent when times were hard. It is rumoured that he keeps the really good stuff, the Jackson Pollocks and the Warhols, at home. 'I think it's very fitting that the Chelsea should have a gallery in the lobby,' he said. 'When other people get ordinary presents for Christmas I get art. I learned a lot about art from my tenants, they took me in hand and taught me about it. It's a mutual admiration society.'

I took his picture leaning against the grand Gothic fireplace, another gift from an impoverished but talented tenant. The flash freaked the bag lady. 'Hey, how come you point it at him, you take my picture,' she demanded, gathering herself angrily. 'Don't you take my picture, I don't say you can.' Stanley calmed her down before going on to tell me the secret of his success.

'It is all to do with management,' he said. 'My father was a person of compassion and understanding. He understood what artists' needs are and he made them feel very good and very comfortable, and an artist more than anyone else needs that to create. They are a strange breed – they are very much apart from the mainstream. They are unusual people and they need that something which sets them apart to be really creative. My father understood this and I hope I have inherited his quality of understanding.

'I befriended people like Arthur Miller, Peter Brook, Larry Rivers and Jasper Johns. They were very appreciative that they were in a place where somebody had their best interests in mind.'

The question was, is it still like this? Nobody could doubt that in the forties and fifties the Chelsea was chock-full of literary giants, or that in the sixties the beautiful people piled in, but is it still a Mecca for the creative? Stanley insists that it is. He told me of musicians, composers, film makers, dancers who all lived here, and sent me off to ask them. Meeting them was not exactly a walk on the wild side. Typical was Doris Chase, a film maker currently working on a documentary about the hotel. She and an assistant had taken a break from interviewing tenants and were eating some very right-on looking concoction of vegetables and nuts from little ethnic bowls.

'I've lived here twenty years,' she said. 'And I feel in truth that it is like a model or a microcosm of what could be the ideal world. There is a tremendous amount of tolerance here, we leave space for people to do what they do or try what they want to try as long as they don't hurt someone. There is probably something as well, maybe a magnetic thrust in the earth or a ley line or whatever because artists continually come here, though of course not everybody becomes a Janis Joplin or a Jimi Hendrix.'

She showed me to the door, insisting that the place was just as creative as it had ever been. I'd just missed the Grateful Dead, she said, and a Japanese rock band had come to stay a couple of days ago. At Tokyo University they probably agree with her. The modern history degree course includes an option on the Chelsea Hotel. But it was hardly like the old days.

I did not, for instance, see anyone like Candy Darling, the transvestite immortalized in Lou Reed's 'Walk On The Wild Side', floating around and being filmed by Andy Warhol for his movie *Chelsea Girls*. And I didn't find someone like Sandy Daley organizing little performance art events, such as the one filmed as *Robert Getting his Nipple Pierced*. In this the photographer Robert Mapplethorpe undergoes the operation while Patti Smith, who used to live at the Chelsea with Sam Shepherd, recites poetry in the corner. Patti, incidentally, now lives very quietly in one of the nicer suburbs of Detroit, with her husband John Sinclair, one-time manager of the group MC5. Maybe if I had gone beyond the downtown decay to places such as Grosse Pointe I would have found the avant-garde alive and well in Detroit. Or maybe not.

In case I was missing something I wandered around the gloomy cream and chocolate brown corridors, looking for any sign of craziness or creativity. The nearest I got to it was being invited in for coffee by a jazz musician, and the graffiti on the fire-escape notice by the lift. The map of the hotel had a pink 'You are Here' dot. Beside it some wild and wacky creative type had written: 'I am the legendary pink dot.' Clearly this had got the creative juices of the whole place flowing, because underneath someone had added: 'How does one become a legendary pink dot?' And under that: 'One does not become a legendary pink dot. One simply is.' Finally came the one-word rejoinder: 'Bullshit.'

Should I try and meet up with these crazy, brilliant graffitists? I'd rather have my nipples pierced.

Chapter Thirteen

Some Time in New York City

Once there were three superstars living in Greenwich Village: Bob Dylan, John Lennon and David Peel. I know this because David Peel told me.

The time was 1971, when Dylan had come to live in the village for a second time. He had been chased out by fans once, and gone to live in Woodstock, a hundred miles north of the city. But now he was back, in a smart house on Lower MacDougal Street. Lennon had his little place a mile away at 105 Bank Street. David Peel lived in a poky room in East Fifth Street on the Lower East Side.

Peel had three places to take me that, he said, would make this story come alive. The first was Washington Square Gardens. One day David Peel was singing his composition 'The Pope Smokes Dope' on this oblong of rough grass, crisscrossed with paths like a Union Jack, where New Yorkers traditionally come to demonstrate, get high or simply doze in the sun. Suddenly he became aware of John Lennon and Yoko Ono standing at the back of the crowd. They got talking, and became close friends.

The second place he wanted to show me was 94 MacDougal Street, Dylan's house at the time. Peel remembered being outside with A. J. Weberman, self-styled Dylanologist, and a party of his students. They were on a field trip, planning to further their studies by going through Dylan's rubbish to check whether it was peanut butter or strawberry jelly, heroin or acid which was colouring his inspiration that particular week, when Peel spotted Dylan coming round the corner. He yelled to Weberman that their prey was sighted and they ran across to confront him. A big row ensued.

The third place Peel said I had to see was his own apartment, where Bob Dylan once visited, and where superstar Peel keeps the memorabilia from his relationships with the two other superstars. Among his possessions are copies of his LP, also called *The Pope Smokes Dope*, that John Lennon produced and released on Apple Records, and the lyrics to the song Lennon wrote about Peel on his *Some Time In New York City* album, which include the lines: 'His name was David Peel/And we found that he was real'.

Walking through the Village with Peel is an experience. The former Best Known Hippy in the Village is quite a character. He has been singing on the streets for over twenty years and everybody knows him. He talks in the most strangled New York accent I have ever heard, trying to make up for his incomprehensibility by bellowing, and failing. Once he looked like a young Stevie Winwood, now, in middle age, he looks like an old Freddie Garretty, but there are those who used to think him a dead ringer for John Lennon.

'Dylan was once looking at a picture of me and John,' he told me as we strolled through the park, past the benches on which the dope dealers huddled together against the cold, and the fenced-off triangle in which dogs are brought to shit, Peel stopping every ten steps when he got caught up in his recollections. 'Bob said, "Man, you look great like that." I said, "Thanks a lot, Bob, that's not me, that's John Lennon." If he can confuse me, and the FBI can confuse me – that's another story which we better not get into now – I guess all is one, maybe we are finally getting a metamorphosis of lookalikes.' He paused to savour what he had just said before yelling at a couple walking past under umbrellas, 'It ain't raining.'

Peel still sports the wire-rimmed glasses, straggly hair and shoulder bag from his Lennon lookalike days in 1971. He had with him a quiet kid wearing a blue anorak, with thin sideburns and a weedy moustache. He introduced him as Gregg, his assistant. Gregg followed us around, silently, except when muttering a correction to something Peel said, which would be acknowledged with a quiet 'thank you brudder'. Peel showed me the place, a low wall beside a tree, where he was playing his guitar when Lennon saw him, and told me that because of the cops, who stopped performances after complaints from residents, he had been unable to play in the park since 1985.

Lennon included his account of the meeting with Peel on *The Pope Smokes Dope*, talking of how he was at the back of the crowd and Peel was shouting questions about why it was necessary to pay to see stars. Lennon was thinking, he must be talking about me, he must know I'm here, but he discovered later that Peel was unaware of this.

Lennon and Ono escaped to the Village from a lifestyle of rich seclusion at Tittenhurst Park, their mansion in Surrey, and from the public's disapproval of their relationship – the one that was supposed to have broken up the Beatles. There they were prisoners of fame and loathing, here Lennon was free for the first time since he became a Beatle. They could ride round the village on bicycles, buy newspapers in Sheridan Square, eat soul food at the Pink Tea Cup in Grove Street, walk about without being hassled. And someone like David Peel – uninhibited, irreverent and radical – was a perfect foil. John and Yoko's eighteen months in Greenwich Village was their breaking-out, and David Peel is convinced it was the happiest time of their lives.

Peel has no false modesty about his impact on Lennon. 'I was his alter ego,' he says. 'When he looked at me he saw himself without all the shackles that his fame and his wealth had locked him into.'

Indeed, David Peel has absolutely no sense of modesty whatever. He hands out maps of Manhattan inscribed 'The Wonderful World of David Peel', and biographies headlined 'David Peel – Rock and Roll Outlaw' in which he describes himself as 'Musician, writer, radical leftist . . . one of the best underground street-rock singers in the world . . . a survivor from a time when political anarchists were considered heroes . . . from a period when people were interested in fighting the system instead of joining it . . . There are many people who weren't around during the Sixties Renaissance. They now want to know who David Peel is.'

'I got to know Lennon really well after that meeting here,' he said, returning to his story. 'A little while after that, John heard I was going on a walkabout and he said he wanted to come along. I said sure and we went around the village singing, we stood on Second Avenue and Seventh Street singing "The Pope Smokes Dope". We drew a big crowd but the police got nervous for Lennon's safety, and they broke it up.'

David Peel helped free Lennon, and he decided Bob Dylan needed freeing, too. But he was less successful here, as he explained to me as we walked south from the park for a block or so on MacDougal. Peel broke off his explanation to yell 'Beggars can't be choosers' into the open doorway of a chi-chi clothes shop in which well-groomed ladies were riffling through the racks.

We came to No. 94, a substantial, four-storey, double-fronted place where Dylan had lived on the lower two floors and had tenants on the upper two. There was a brown historic marker on a post outside the house which said: 'This block was a pioneering

229

effort at urban renewal by William Sloane Coffin . . . to attract middle-class professionals he renovated brick row houses built in the 1840s and 50s.' In attracting Dylan, Coffin probably did better than he expected.

Peel had brought me here to tell me about the day he met Dylan. He pointed out the great view of the Empire State Building Dylan had enjoyed up the street to the north, and showed me the places on either side of the front door behind black wrought-iron railings where Dylan kept his rubbish.

'A. J. Weberman had this thing called the Dylan Liberation Front,' said Peel. 'He used to run classes in Dylanology at the Alternative University which we had up on Fourteenth Street and this particular day was a field trip. He brought about thirty, forty people along and they were going to go through his garbage cans and analyse his trash. There were people climbing up to the windows to see if he was inside. He wasn't but his kids were. They seemed to be a little scared and surprised.

'I saw Bob across the street here and I grabbed Weberman and pointed him out. Weberman was like freeze-frame for a moment, but I pushed him over to Bob so's they could meet. They started having this encounter of the worst kind. Weberman wanted to know if he shot up heroin and this and that, all these different accusations came out against each other.'

I asked him what they had expected, given that Bob Dylan had come back to the Village to escape the attentions of fans in Woodstock, and that this was his second attempt to live in peace in the only other place where he felt really at home. By the late sixties there were tours being run up to his Woodstock house and people were digging up the lawn as souvenirs. Weren't Peel and Weberman persecuting Dylan even more than these people?

'No man, we were fans,' said Peel. 'This guy is

extreme, this guy is interesting. You have a guy like this, I don't care, you do anything, you analyse his blood. If you hate a guy you don't go through his garbage, you ignore him. Weberman was the greatest fan of Dylan. But the thing is, when rock stars get so big, they ignore you. We wanted to get him to communicate.'

He wrote a song about the episode, called 'The Ballad Of A. J. Weberman', and there on the pavement he sang me a snatch about how that day in his garbage trawl:

'He found a letter Bob Dylan wrote to Johnny Cash
   and other things for rock interpretation'

He reminds Weberman in the chorus:

'Bob Dylan's not your enemy, he's just your friend.
You are just a Dylanologist'

and describes the point when Dylan appeared:

'Weberman had finally met his God.'

At this point he was put off by a tramp who pushed between us muttering, 'Hungry hungry.' Maybe the dustbins were on his patch. Peel broke off to yell at him, 'Yeah yeah [imitating him] money for fooood money for fooood. I seen you today already. I recognize you from before.'

David Peel's reason for being with Weberman was not to go through Dylan's rubbish. 'I wanted Dylan to be in alliance with John and Yoko and also to be reborn again into the scene. I wasn't here because I hated Bob Dylan, let's get that straight.'

But the attentions of people like Peel and, in particular, Weberman, made Dylan regret moving back to the Village. His first period here, when he had a flat on West Fourth Street from '61 to '64, also ended unhappily. Earlier that day I had walked down that street, just a mile or so west of MacDougal, past No 161 where Dylan and his girlfriend Suze Rotolo lived. The ground floor is now a sex shop called the Pink

231

Pussycat Boutique. 'Erotic novelities' promises a sign below Dylan's window. This street was familiar. I recognized it from the cover of Dylan's second album, *The Freewheelin' Bob Dylan*. On the sleeve a very young-looking Dylan is walking, hands jammed in jeans pockets, shoulders hunched against the cold in his leather jacket. Suze has her arm through his. She is slim and pretty with long, light brown hair, a dark coat and boots. Their heads are close together and they are smiling, walking in the middle of the street through dirty snow.

The fans chased him away that time too. The second time around, the period when he worked on *Self Portrait, Nashville Skyline* and *New Morning*, he was persecuted by those who thought this material was politically incorrect. The Dylan Liberation Front wanted Dylan to go back to the protest songs he had not written for eight years, to become a radical again and to stop living like a fat cat. In the end he had to negotiate with his persecutors, and Peel was to return to MacDougal Street by invitation.

'I was going into his house,' said David. 'He had a little white dog and the dog nipped at my hand. Wait! Dylan's dog bit David Peel! The dog had no rabies, I know 'cos I'm still alive and I'm not mad. He had black nannies in his household and this was a guy talking about revolution! Anyway, I was about to get talking with him when along come the Dylan Liberation Front people. That blew the whole thing. I was out of there!'

We walked east through the village, Peel punctuating our conversation with bellowed asides such as 'Where's the fire?' to firemen clambering into their engines, sirens already wailing, outside a fire station, and stopping to berate Gator, an ageing hippy with long grey hair, for not being at the Halloween Smoke-In in Washington Square Park.

When we got to his apartment on East Fifth Street, I

could see the truth in another of the statements in the biography he had handed me: 'Unlike other rockers, David Peel chose NOT to live life as a typical rock star, preferring to direct his profits into the good of his community.' We walked through a passage beneath the building that fronted on to the street, across a tiny courtyard to another building boxed behind the first. We climbed the narrow stairs to the fifth floor, Peel telling me how when Dylan called he came in disguise, in hat, scarf and dark glasses.

Inside the flat it was as if a sixties student revolutionary's apartment had been left to compost down. There were huge Union Jack scatter cushions everywhere and flags on the wall and ceiling, covered with badges portraying Dylan, Lennon, marijuana leaves and slogans of an anti-war and pro-drug tendency. David and Gregg make and sell them. Peel gave me a badge of Dylan, *circa* 1966, when I think he looked his best. There were pictures of Lennon and Ono with David Peel, which illustrated the problem of identification Dylan came up against. But you can tell them apart. Peel is the one with his mouth open.

The place was in a state of casual decay, the walls more lath than plaster and improvised curtains taking the place of doors. A fat steam-pipe running up the wall had a safety valve on it which gurgled and whistled with an insistent rhythm. There were filing cabinets and shelves stacked with tapes, records, leaflets and documents, all the paraphernalia needed to market David Peel worldwide. Through one curtain was Gregg's room, and across a waist-high partition some sort of tiny kitchen. We drank water out of jam jars while David directed Gregg on how to dull the sound from the safety valve with wet washcloths, at the same time telling me about giving Dylan copies of two of his records, *American Revolution* and *Have A Marijuana*. He sold me copies of *The Pope Smokes*

Dope and *Bob Dylan vs A. J. Weberman*, which consisted mainly of taped phone conversations in which Dylan tried to get Weberman to change things in an article he had written about him. They cost me $6, but then I'm not Bob Dylan.

'It was me told Dylan John Lennon was living on Bank Street,' said Peel when it was at last possible to talk over the deadened hissing of the steam. 'He didn't know. Dylan says, "That's good. It's good to have more superstars around me." I rendezvoused 'em. Dylan went to Bank Street and they had a rap for a few hours. The two giants put together by David-who-stoned-Goliath-Peel.'

The meeting with Bob Dylan coincided with Peel's writing the songs for *The Pope Smokes Dope* album, and he was inspired by this meeting to write one called 'The Ballad Of Bob Dylan'. He remembers auditioning it at Bank Street before Lennon, his producer.

'John was on his bed with a drawing pad, and I was singing the chorus which goes "Bob Dylan, Robert Zimmerman, Bob Dylan, Robert Zimmerman" etc etc, and Lennon is singing along with me. I go "Bob Dylan" and he goes "Superzimmerman", "Bob Dylan", "Superzimmerman" and while we were singing he drew this picture of Dylan with a Z across his chest with muscles, bare naked, with Yoko in the corner of the paper smirking and smiling, and it says in the caption, "It's Zimmerman". I have the original. Not only did I get John to sing along with me on my audition of "The Ballad of Bob Dylan" but I got a drawing as well. Lennon was a big fan of Dylan, and a jealous one too,'

Peel's influence on Lennon is shown more than anything by the album *Some Time In New York City*, which in its radical politics, musical style and format draws on Peel's approach, his belief that music is there to aid fast mass communication, like a singing newspaper. The title song is about Peel, and David described to me the first time he heard it. 'Lennon called me up here and said he'd written about me and did I want to hear it. He sang it for me down the phone, playing an acoustic. I felt very flattered, this is the highest honour. And then he put my picture on the cover of the album and the lyrics on the back cover.' He sat back, smiling, and added: 'It's hard to choose between Lennon and Dylan and Peel. Dylan dropped in to listen to the recording of "The Ballad Of Bob Dylan". I thought, my God, there's John and Yoko producing it, there's Bob Dylan listening to it and there's David Peel. The Four Horsemen. Or the Four Musketeers. Or, wait! The Four Rocketeers!'

Peel's time in the limelight did not last long. When Lennon moved uptown to the Dakota on Central Park West he was left behind. He felt like Cinderella at the ball when the clock struck midnight. Within a year Dylan had got sick of the attentions of the Dylan Liberation Front and had escaped from the Village once more, this time to Malibu. Here he could hide up in the woods and gaze out over the Pacific, forced, like Bruce Springsteen would be, to live in rich-man's anonymity, cut off from the worlds that sustained them. David Peel's carriage turned back into a pumpkin, the horses into mice, and the belle of the ball was in his rags again.

I was thinking about John Lennon next day, in the cab taking me uptown from the Chelsea. The one thing everyone knows about him and New York is that this is where he was murdered, outside a mansion block called the Dakota on Central Park West where he and Yoko moved after their time in the Village. This was ironic, because the most important thing about this period, as far as I could see, was that it was a very happy one. Unlike Dylan, Lennon had found a place in

235

which he could be at peace, where he could handle the attentions of fans, where he needed neither to run nor to hide.

A coachload of Japanese tourists were videoing the building where Lennon lived from April 1973 until his death, on 8 December 1980. 'One of the world's great rock and roll landmarks,' their tour guide was telling them. To me it seemed redolent of death. I felt like a ghoul just being here, but I stood for a while, looking up at the building. It was screened in scaffolding, there to enable workmen to remove the thick grime from this giant Gothic monstrosity. Up on the scaffolding walkway at first-floor level, a builder in a hard hat was showing a group of schoolkids the work that was being done. By the entrance arch where Lennon was gunned down there is a security booth manned twenty-four hours a day by a blue uniformed guard, and iron security gates. On the pavement a blue sign placed by the builders carried one word in red: 'Danger'.

Yoko Ono still lives here, in a sixth-floor apartment overlooking the park. There is still an all-white room with the white piano on which Lennon composed 'Imagine', one of his best songs. John gave the instrument to Yoko on her birthday in 1971, and it bears the inscription: 'This morning, a white piano for Yoko'. On the ground floor are the offices from which the Lennon estate is administered. After John and Yoko's son, Sean, was born in 1975, Lennon spent five years as a house husband, looking after him, while Yoko became a businesswoman, managing their investments from the ground-floor offices and building up their stake in the Dakota to five apartments.

I didn't like standing here alone, staring up at Yoko Ono's windows as the man who murdered her husband must have done, so I walked down West 71st Street, to the Fortuna café, for coffee and cheesecake.

John Lennon came to this quiet, dark Italian café most days to drink a cappuccino, smoke Gitanes, buy bars of Luisa chocolate, and read the papers. Virtually from the day Vincent Urwand opened it in 1976 John Lennon adopted it: a quiet, simple place in a residential street where he would be left in peace. I read the *New York Times*, listened to New York conversations at the tables around me, and thought about John Lennon.

I had read that, like Elvis Presley, Lennon had a thing about numbers. He believed the number nine dominated his life. And I remembered how, back in Memphis, Dolores Cunningham, who had been Elvis's parapsychologist, had told me that numerologists consider nine to be a very unlucky number. Lennon was born on 9 October 1940, his son Sean was born on 9 October, Brian Epstein, the Beatles manager, first saw them in the Cavern on 9 November. The group's first record contract was signed on the ninth and their first release, 'Love Me Do', had the catalogue number 4949. When Lennon died, at 10.50 p.m. on 8 December 1980, the time difference meant it was already 9 December in England. Well, I don't know. I was staying in room 509 at the Chelsea, but I couldn't see that this would make it any more likely that I would get shot there. The house I lived in for the first ten years of my life was No. 9. Of course, I'm not as old yet as Lennon was when he was killed. Perhaps that number is stalking me still.

I walked back, past the Dakota, and crossed the street to an area of Central Park where Lennon used to walk every day. After John's death, Yoko paid $1m to have the two and a half acres landscaped and maintained for ever as a memorial to him. It was named Strawberry Fields after the Utopia evoked in his song 'Strawberry Fields Forever'. I passed two carts selling pretzels and Strawberry Fields Forever

T-shirts, and a wisteria-covered arbour under which sheltered two tramps, each with a pair of supermarket trolleys loaded with rubbish in black plastic bags. I walked into a grassy, undulating area thick with trees, to a ring of benches around a marble mosaic circle, in the centre of which was the single word IMAGINE. Further on, set into a rock, was a plaque reading 'Strawberry Fields. Imagine all the people, living life in peace'.

The day Lennon died was a clear, warm, sunny day, just like today. Although it was November, the leaves were still on the trees, giving a fragmented view of the Dakota from the benches around the IMAGINE mosaic.

That day in December 1980, John and Yoko were busy. Lennon had returned to recording after his five-year sabbatical and the new John and Yoko album, *Double Fantasy*, was at number 12 in the charts. They had a photographic session with Annie Leibovitz for the cover of *Rolling Stone*, and gave a long interview for a San Francisco radio station from their ground-floor office.

Meanwhile, a twenty-five-year-old married man from Honolulu called Mark Chapman got up at 10.30 in his room, 2730, at the Sheraton Centre, twenty blocks south of the Dakota at 811 Seventh Avenue. He adjusted a display of items including a Bible inscribed Holden Caulfield, who is the hero of J. D. Salinger's classic novel of teenage angst, *The Catcher in the Rye*. He had altered one heading to read 'The Gospel According to St John Lennon'. He walked to the Dakota with a copy of *Double Fantasy* under his arm and a gun in his pocket, and hung around all day with the clutch of fans gathered outside the gates and the security booth at the side entrance.

During the afternoon he saw Paul Simon, Mia Farrow and Lauren Bacall go in and out of the building, but no Lennon. Then Sean arrived with his nanny and Mark shook the little boy's hand. Just after 5 p.m. John and Yoko came out, to find their car was not waiting. While they stood around on the pavement Mark Chapman got Lennon's autograph on the album he had brought along, and was captured in a photograph facing the man he had come to shoot. But for some reason he did not kill him then. Perhaps there was too thick a crowd for Chapman to be sure of success. After the couple had gone he hung around again as the rest of the fans drifted off, telling the doorman he would wait for them to return from the Record Plant near Times Square where they had gone to work on the tapes that would make up the *Milk and Honey* album. He wanted Yoko's autograph too, he said.

At the Record Plant John heard *Double Fantasy* had gone Gold in England. Just before 11 p.m. he and Yoko left for home, their car taking them up Eighth Avenue, around Columbus Circle, up Central Park West and left to pull up at the Dakota's side entrance. Yoko got out first, followed by John, carrying the tapes they had been working on that day. When Mark called his name Lennon turned, and was shot four times at point-blank range. Mark Chapman was famous.

When Elvis died in June 1977, and John Lennon was given the news, he retorted, 'Elvis died when he went into the Army'. Sitting in Strawberry Fields I considered when Lennon died artistically. It was certainly long before 1980. His last albums, *Double Fantasy* and the posthumously released *Milk and Honey*, strike me as nothing more than sentimental dross. What had he done that was good in his time in New York? *Some Time In New York City* was trite sloganeering. 'Happy Xmas (War Is over)' fits seamlessly with the other terrible Christmas songs that were already being played in New York's stores. *Mind Games*? Nothing there of note. *Walls and Bridges*? The track on that album called 'Whatever Gets You Thru The Night' just about makes it.

Musically, nothing good came out of New York. What was the last good thing he did? 'Imagine', probably, or 'Instant Karma', or 'Cold Turkey'. Trying to remember John Lennon at his best, it was these three songs that ran through my mind as I sat in Strawberry Fields. I vowed to end my journey somewhere I could picture Lennon alive rather than dead.

Chapter Fourteen

The wild side and the safe side

In Harlem, at the junction of Lexington Avenue and
125th Street, they don't ask a white boy what he is
doing uptown any more, as they used to ask Lou Reed.
Today they think they know why you're here.

In 'I'm Waiting For The Man', which Reed recorded
with the Velvet Underground in 1967, the white boy is
uptown at Lexington/125 for heroin. He is waiting for
his dealer, $26 in his hand, 'feeling sick and dirty more
dead than alive'. He knows he will have to wait well
past the appointed time before the dude dressed in
black with New York shoes and a big straw hat shows
up, takes him up three flights of stairs in a brownstone
and sells him what he needs to get through another
day.

That's what everyone assumed I was uptown for, the
concept of rock tourism – or indeed tourism of any
kind – not exactly having caught on in Harlem. And I
hardly felt I could explain. What would I say: 'I'm just
looking, thanks'?

It hadn't been easy getting here. It was only by luck
that I found a Yellow Cab prepared to bring me. Few
whites, the driver told me, would venture here. If
anyone needed confirmation that an unofficial but
very real apartheid exists in America they need only
compare the principal streets to the south of Central
Park, with 125th Street. Travelling up here was like
moving into another, startlingly different country:
from West into East Germany, say, the day after the

Berlin Wall was breached and before capitalism flooded through and started to lessen the distinction. Here there was no wall. America's system of depriving the have-nots and rewarding the haves runs so quietly, so efficiently, that any physical barrier would be superfluous. But the segregation was as sharp as if one had been erected. For whites, Harlem hardly exists. My tourist street map was cut off halfway up Central Park, yet still claimed to be a map of Manhattan.

At first, as we drove around Harlem, it was hard to put my finger on the most notable difference between these two cities within a city. It wasn't that the buildings were so different, although they were. It wasn't that I felt as if I had moved instantly fifty or sixty years into the past, to the days before the tower blocks ousted the handsome five-storey brownstone terraces. It wasn't even that the streets were not jammed with new cars. The real difference, I realized at last, was that there were none of the products of modern corporate America that are posted over every other main street in the country. There were no McDonald's, no Burger Kings, no Dunkin Donuts, no Colonel Sanders. And without their bright reds and yellows and blues and golds, this place felt like a backwoods American town stripped of its identity. All the badges and epaulettes that identify modern American popular culture were missing.

Instead of the chain stores there were second-hand furniture outfits with faded painted signs, thrift stores piled with old clothes, places selling reconditioned TVs and domestic appliances, lots of grand funeral homes, and plenty of churches. We drove past Sylvia's, which the cabby, who told me his name was John Newlin, said was the finest restaurant in Harlem. It was a neighbourhoody kind of place, like a Greek or Italian district in London that had remained one generation out of date. John Newlin pointed out the

Canaan Baptist Church, its spire lopped off. 'Go to a church like that as a white person,' he said, 'and they'll make a hell of a fuss of you. They'll shake your hand, someone will stand up and officially welcome you.'

It was Lou Reed who had brought me to Harlem. Reed has been the foremost chronicler of New York's seamy side through songs about pimps, prostitutes, transvestites and drug dealers, songs about the pleasures of heroin and of sex involving whips, zips and chains. All are sung with a casual, cool menace. Perhaps the most famous is 'Walk On The Wild Side', about his transvestite friends, which is on his 1972 solo album, *Transformer*.

I got out of the cab at Lexington/125, the point at which the song 'I'm Waiting For The Man' is set. There were three cops, white kids with pasty faces, standing legs apart, hands behind their backs, in a row. Beside them was a newsstand, but it was nothing like the extensive, red-painted stands to the south, which are piled with every conceivable publication. This one was modest and dark green, lacking the advertisement for *Time* or *Newsweek* that I had got used to seeing, and with just a handful of newspapers and magazines on sale, as if even access to information was severely restricted up here in Harlem. But, hey, not by decree. This is a free country, after all.

There were a couple of dozen people around, lounging against the wire mesh fence surrounding an empty lot or sitting on the steps of the faded brownstones. Every few steps someone hissed at me, 'Hey dude, crack? Coke? Crack? What choo lookin' for?' Others were hanging round the subway entrance on the corner, a glass-brick tower beside a store called Nobel Cash and Credit. Several buildings were boarded up, but it was not as bad as Detroit.

I walked to the east, where a wrecked car was resting, wheel-less, on the wide pavement. It had no doors or glass in its windows, but blankets had been draped as curtains and there were two sleeping forms on the ripped-up seats. A girl came up to me. 'You wanna blow job?' she asked. I told her not now and walked round her to where John was waiting in the cab. 'I want your white body!' she yelled after me, and the guys lounging around all laughed.

OK, that was enough of the wild side, how about a walk on the safe side?

Lou Reed and Paul Simon came from similar Jewish middle-class backgrounds. Reed was from Brooklyn, Simon from Forest Hills, both went to university, Simon to study Law and Reed to study English. While Reed the rebel went on to graduate with honours, Simon dropped out and went to England to play the folk clubs. But his upbringing had missed one harrowing experience that Reed's had contained. At the age of seventeen, Reed's parents decided to try and cure him of his homosexuality with twenty-four treatments of electric shock therapy. While Simon was getting into hippiedom, Reed was a part of the Chelsea Hotel set, which included Andy Warhol. To look at them both in 1967 is to see them at opposite ends of the musical spectrum. While Paul Simon and Art Garfunkel were playing the Monterey Pop Festival as stalwart supporters of the Summer of Love, the Velvet Underground released their first album. It came complete with an album sleeve designed by Andy Warhol, featuring a banana which could be peeled to reveal pink fruit, and containing songs which lauded hard drugs and sadomasochism.

Paul Simon's safe side was the East Side. In 1967 he had an apartment just to the north of the 59th Street Bridge, overlooking Carl Schurz Park, a little patch of green on the riverside. I paid off my cab there and walked between the half-bare trees, past the inevitable dog-shit corral and up a set of sweeping stone steps to the riverside, where one or two old people were sitting huddled on benches, well wrapped against the cold.

I could see the bridge to my right, a bridge that became a Paul Simon landmark through the song '59th Street Bridge Song (Feelin' Groovy)'. The song, an uplifting burst of pure joy at being alive in New York City, must have sounded like a foreign language to Lou Reed. The 59th Street Bridge was Paul Simon's route into Manhattan from his surburban home, and must have had the same symbolism for Simon as the Lincoln Tunnel, Bruce Springsteen's way to the city and all it promised, did for him. While Simon was writing this, Reed was working on 'Waiting For The Man'. Talk about light and shade.

Simon and Garfunkel played the song at the Monterey Pop Festival in June 1967, an event that would have been totally alien to Lou Reed but which filled Simon with the joys of peace, love and understanding. Simon's ten-minute version of '59th Street Bridge Song' was a highlight of the show. He called Monterey a jubilee, an occasion of innocence, openness and discovery. I had come to the park to meet a friend of Paul Simon's from the late sixties, Monica Boscia. She had a story to tell me of Monterey and this park, and we leant against the black railings watching the river flow as she talked.

'When Paul got back from Monterey he came down to my apartment on Fourth Street in the Village,' she said. 'He was totally afire. He said, "Oh my God it was incredible, music is changing," and we sat talking and talking, about the festival and the music and his thoughts, and then he took these little tablets out and put them on the table.'

It was acid, which he had been given at the festival.

'He said, "Monica, I feel that as an artist I have a

responsibility to tell people about the experience." So I said, "Paul, look, make sure if you do this be really careful." He knew my thoughts on drugs. Well, he must 'a left my house two-thirty, three in the morning. I go to sleep. About seven the phone rings. It's Paul, and he asked me if I could come up right away. I said, "Paul. You took it!" I jumped in a cab. By the time I got there he was with his manager, an older man sitting there as if he's thinking, like, what is this? I told him he could leave and I stayed with Paul all day. Paul was talking and talking. This is a very talented, bright person and he was tripping on probably the strongest, best acid you could get.

'A person totally exposes themselves on acid, all their inner emotions come out, and I saw Paul like that on that day. We used to talk about therapy a lot because I had been in therapy and he was very curious about it. I was always very pro looking inward and he was always kind of questioning, but I could see the acid was making him look inward that day. He was tripping for twenty-four hours until, early the next morning, he was finally coming down and I decided to take him out for a walk.

'We crossed over here to Carl Schurz Park. It was a very bright, sunny day and he was saying Wow! and looking at everything like he had never seen it before. Then he got an idea for a song. So he called CBS and told them to bring an engineer with portable equipment. We met the guy back at Paul's apartment and he sat down and wrote 'Old Friends', which is on the *Bookends* album. He got the idea while we were walking. We had seen some old guys and we stood there and we really watched these old people, you know how they sit in the park and talk, and I can picture that scene very clearly still if I listen to the song. So, he got the idea on tape and finally, about midnight, I got him to go to sleep.'

I liked Monica. She resembled Joni Mitchell but had a laugh like Joan Rivers. She was slight, with high-lighted blonde hair, and looked lost inside her fur coat as she huddled against the cold, chainsmoking as she talked. We got in a cab and went to a Mexican restaurant across on Broadway, where we started knocking back frozen margueritas. She could really talk, but it was fascinating, and I kept delaying ordering anything to eat so as not to interrupt her flow of stories about Paul. She told me about herself, too. About how she was the oldest of nine kids, her father died when she was fourteen, and she went out to work at sixteen as a secretary at CBS Radio to bring some money in.

She told me she first bumped into Simon and Garfunkel when she was showing some friends around the studios, and soon afterwards met them in a café across the street. They invited her back to hear what they were doing. 'They had me do hand claps and so on. I can't remember the songs they were recording, but from then on we hung out a lot. One time I was at Paul's apartment and I said, "Look, the only songs I know of yours are your hits." And he said, "Monica, I'm going to play you everything we have recorded and I want to know what you think."

'I'll never forget it, I listened to it all and then I said to him, "I think they are really good but I'll tell you the truth. There is only one positive song in the lot and that's the '59th Street Bridge Song'. The song that's most like you is 'I Am A Rock'."'

And she laughed 'Hah!' Just like Joan Rivers.

'Paul and I used to debate all the time. He had been president of the debating team in high school and he was really very good. There would be a group of people all pitching in but Paul and I were always at odds intellectually. He was always questioning me. It was great being with him. We never had a romance or

247

anything, but he was a good friend, good company. I liked just hanging out with him at his apartment or mine when he had his guitar and we would sing and I'd see songs taking shape. I remember when *Sergeant Pepper's Lonely Hearts Club Band* came out, Paul called me up and said, "You gotta come over and listen to this." He had a wonderful sound system and we both put on headphones and it was fantastic, really amazing. This was around the time of Monterey and I could see that he saw this record as part of the new thing, and he wanted desperately to be a part of it.

'It was hard being friends because he lived in a different world. He was famous even then and it was very difficult. He would come down to my apartment on Fourth Street and we'd try to go out. Once his brother was playing somewhere and we went over but people came up to us all the time. Paul is like a regular guy, you know, and it was awkward because you couldn't just go some place.

'He got bothered a lot and complained to me that he couldn't write, "I gotta get away", so I said, "Why don't you get a place in the country, don't give me the phone number then when you want to have friends out, get them out." Of course, he got this great mansion at Stockbridge, upstate near Woodstock. I went out there for a weekend and it was nice but I kinda decided I liked Paul but he just argued with me too much. He would take exception to everything I said and I told him I was tired of it and we drifted apart. I didn't see him again until years later. He was in his car outside a record store and I said hi and got in. He told me he'd gone into therapy and was getting married, to Peggy Harper, and he was like, oh boy, Mr Women's Lib [Joan Rivers laugh], and I'm thinking to myself it was good in a way but this ain't going to work. It didn't.

'I haven't seen him in years and years. I've no idea where he lives or anything. I'm sure if I ran into him it would be nice. It would be interesting to see where he's at.'

We left the restaurant and Monica took me uptown to a little Irish bar she knew. On the way we called in at the Power Station recording studio. It was run by Tony Bongiovi, cousin of the rock singer John Bon Jovi, whom she wanted me to meet. I had been telling Monica about my journey and where I had been, and when I mentioned Detroit she said I just had to meet Tony.

We sat in Reception waiting for him, around a table bearing a huge bowl of fruit which anyone who passed through picked at. High on the wall a screen showed MTV. Tony runs one of the most successful recording studios in America. Springsteen has recorded here, Tony has produced the Ramones, Talking Heads, Gloria Gaynor. Fifteen years ago when he opened the Power Station he worked with Chic, very successfully. 'In fact,' he said, 'they are downstairs recording right now.'

Tony was a tubby little Italian guy with a heavy cold. He punctuated the conversation with angry snorts to try and keep his nose clear. He wanted to go home and nurse his cold, he said, not go drinking with us, but he did tell me about him and Motown before we went our separate ways.

'When I was in high school I called them up,' he said. 'I said I think I've worked out how you get your sound. I had a little recording studio I had built in a shed at home, and I used to listen to Motown records and try to enhance them. Completely by accident I worked out how they got their sound. I discovered that they had a reverberation room with an extremely short decay time.' This meant nothing to me, so he explained, 'Instead of adding an echo like we would know it, it was adding a shimmer to the sound.

'They flew to New York on the Monday to talk to me

and the following Thursday I was producing at Hitsville. One week I was buying records by the Supremes and the Four Tops, the next week I was right in there with the stars. I got like a graduate course in producing there, they really had a science to how they did it, the creativity within the company was just incredible.

'They would fly me out for two weeks at a time, put me in a hotel. I'd never been in a hotel before, except down at the beach. I couldn't read the menu. It was all Chicken Kiev, Chateaubriand. I was a little Italian kid, I'd never had this stuff before. So I called my mother, I said, "What do I eat?"'

We said goodbye to Tony and walked on to the bar, where we sat at the counter and talked about ourselves. Monica filled me in on her and Tony. She had just broken up with him, she said, and moved back into her flat in the Village. While she was living with Tony she had been renting her apartment to a guy who had contracted AIDS. He had only recently died, and Monica had nursed him in the final few weeks. So we talked about death, she about her father, who died when she was so young, me about mine, she about her brother who was asphyxiated in his Volkswagen Beetle as a teenager. A few months before this I would have found it the gloomiest, most depressing conversation imaginable, and gone quite a way to avoid it. Now I could handle it, in fact I welcomed it.

Chapter Fifteen

By the time I got to Woodstock

I felt out of place in Woodstock. I didn't have a dead
deer on the roof of the car.

Everyone had one except me. It was the start of the
hunting season, and the men who live in the woods
take their right to kill one animal a year very seriously.
Some hunters go crazy, shooting anything that moves,
so people put fluorescent coats on their dogs, and
bright headbands on themselves, to ensure they cannot
be mistaken for Bambi. At the Woodstock exit from the
New York Thruway, which had brought me a hundred
miles up the Hudson river valley from the city, men in
uniforms with clipboards were clambering up on the
cars to look into the mouths of the dead creatures.
'Yup,' they were presumably concluding each time,
'that's a deer and it's a dead one.' As I drove the last
eight wooded miles on winding country roads into the
Catskill mountains and Woodstock, I passed a string of
further fatalities. I started longing for one car, just one,
with a deer driving and a dead hunter on top.

Everyone has heard of Woodstock, because of the
festival that took the village's name. These 'Three days
of peace, love and music' in 1969 were seen by
enthusiasts as the greatest flowering of the hippy
culture. Woodstock was Eden. It was a birth. Or, if you
think it marked the commercialized end of a brave
experiment, it was a death. Take your pick.

In fact, as locals feel they must point out as soon as
you raise the subject of the festival in the village, it

didn't take place here at all, but on Max Yasgur's dairy farm in Bethel, seventy-odd miles away. Local worthies stopped it taking place on their patch, and even tried to prevent use of the name Woodstock.

The organizers wanted to use the name because of Bob Dylan, when you come right down to it. If he hadn't made Woodstock his retreat and then his home, and if the cream of sixties music – the Band, Van Morrison, Frank Zappa, Tim Hardin, Paul Butterfield – hadn't followed him, Woodstock would not have got the reputation that it did as the hippest place on God's earth. But enough about art, let's eat.

I chose the Tinker Street Café, not because I wanted a Yasgur's Farm Salad for lunch, or because I thought the chilli and beer here would be any better than in the other half-dozen joints on Tinker Street, which winds through Woodstock trailing a string of bijou little craft shops with it.

I chose it because, upstairs, Bob Dylan wrote two albums: *Another Side Of Bob Dylan* and *Bringing It All Back Home*. That gave me something to think about while I ate. In the sixties it was called the Expresso and was run by Bernard and Marylou Paturel as a French café. The porch had rows of tables with red and white check cloths, where people would play chess. Dylan did that, and he sat inside in the evenings, at one of the tables close to the low stage to the right of the room. Here he listened to the folk singers Bernard and Marylou introduced in 1962 to try and boost trade after Labor Day, when the tourists had gone, and they faced a long dull winter.

Not that Bernard or Marylou had much idea who Dylan was in those days. But then one night, Tom Paxton was appearing and he introduced 'Blowin' In The Wind' by saying, 'I'd like to dedicate this to Bob Dylan who happens to be sitting here tonight.'

'That was when we met him,' said Marylou when I

caught up with her later. 'Tom Paxton introduced him to us and we became good friends.' She and Bernard remained friends with Dylan throughout the sixties but it was in 1964–5 that they knew him best, and when they helped him the most. 'One night,' she remembers, 'Bob had had quite a bit to drink and he was in really no fit state to make it back to his manager, Albert Grossman's house where he had a room. So we put him to bed upstairs, in what we called the white room. And from then on he used that room whenever he wanted to.

'He had his typewriter and his guitar up there – nothing else – and, really, it was an honour to have him here. I liked having him around, he was a gentleman, and I enjoyed his humour, he always had a smile. If he wrote a song and he wanted to play it to someone for the first time he'd ask if you'd care to listen. As if we might say, "No, we don't really want to hear this, Bob. Please come back later." One song in particular I remember him playing for me was "If You Gotta Go, Go Now" which has a line in it about if you don't leave now you'll have to stay all night. I don't know why but that one sticks in my memory.'

'If You Gotta Go' was written in 1964 at the time of the other songs on *Another Side Of*, but did not make it on to the album. Those that did include 'All I Really Want To Do', 'Chimes Of Freedom', 'Motorpsycho Nightmare', 'I Don't Believe You (She Acts Like We Never Have Met)', 'Ballad In Plain D', and 'It Ain't Me Babe'. Some of my very favourite early Dylan, and he wrote them all here! And not just them, but tracks on *Bringing It All Back Home* that I love even more, including 'She Belongs To Me', 'Subterranean Home-sick Blues', 'Maggie's Farm', 'Mr Tambourine Man', 'Gates Of Eden', and 'It's All Over Now, Baby Blue'.

'He dedicated *Another Side Of Bob Dylan* to us,' Marylou went on. 'That was a real honour, the sleeve has "Thank you to Bernard, Marylou, Jean Pierre, Gerard Philip and Monique for the use of their house". My second daughter Nichole wasn't born then and she was really mad when she was old enough to realize that the album was not dedicated to her, so I have to ask Bob would he please dedicate one to her now.

'I don't know how important it was having the white room, and the fact that nobody knew about it. We never discussed it. He was just around. I suppose he knew he could have privacy here. And the café was a fun place to be. If there were fifteen people in the café they would be fifteen interesting people, so each evening was an incredible, wonderful time, you just never knew what would happen next, or who would do what.'

Dylan's room really *was* a secret. To this day Sally Grossman, widow of Dylan's former manager, cannot believe that he spent more than an odd afternoon there, and Billy Faier, a local folk singer who was Bernard Paturel's best friend at the time, told me Bernard never once mentioned it to him. It is a measure, perhaps, of Dylan's intense need for privacy and of the strong protective instincts he aroused in those close to him. Today the white room is used by a photographer, and there is nothing in the café to tell you that *Another Side Of* and *Bringing It All Back Home* were written there.

It was a bitterly cold day, and the café was almost empty, just me, a fat barman with a ponytail, and three guys in baseball caps and lumberjack jackets talking about the band that had played here last night. 'Sure,' the barman told me, 'everyone knows the Dylan connection. The history is here, we just don't see why we should exploit it.'

The bar displayed posters celebrating the twentieth aniversary of 'Woodstock: The summer of our lives'.

There were also posters advertising future appearances of bands at the café: live music six nights a week, and comedy on the seventh. 'Come out of the woods and laugh' was the suggestion. That's unless you're Bambi, in which case you hide.

I took a stroll around the village, which is little more than one street winding through the woods in a narrow valley enclosed to north and south by mountains. Woodstock is a mixture of the hip and the homely. The numerous trinket shops, the Not Fade Away Tie-Dye store and Crabtree and Evelyn have not pushed out the hardware emporia. Certainly you can buy a Woodstock T-shirt, or consult the 'Genuine Welsh Palm Reader', but you can also choose a chainsaw from a wide selection or buy a pick-up load of timber for your fire. Woodstock is the sort of place where cars stop when they see you waiting to cross the road.

The smell in the air was of woodsmoke rather than marijuana, but half the people on the street could have come straight from the festival. Fashion has not moved on in Woodstock since 1969. Long hair, star-spangled T-shirts, loon pants and tasselled shoulder bags are still in. Every so often an acid casualty comes shambling past, still hallucinating after all these years.

Since the turn of the century Woodstock has been a home to artists, an oasis of enlightenment in a redneck desert. Drive up the road a little way and they really do come out of the woods and laugh at you. The tourists who come to see where it all happened can raise a chuckle in Woodstock, though. In 1989, the twentieth anniversary of the event, the village had a lot of visitors. The locals started sporting their own T-shirts which had on them 'You are here' and then a long wiggly black line with, at the other end of it, 'Festival was here'. When the tourists asked kids for directions they would be sent up to a field above the village. The kids would follow them up and snigger while they stood there wide-eyed, going 'Like, wow!'

The festival was the fullest flowering of the peace and love movement that came out of San Francisco a couple of years earlier. Swamped by hundreds of thousands more visitors than had been expected, it was declared a free event. Even torrential rain on the second day, a dangerous shortage of food and the declaration that it was a national disaster area did not dampen the fans' enthusiasm.

Among the stars who still mean something were Jimi Hendrix, Santana, the Who, Crosby, Stills, Nash and Young and the Band. John Sebastian, who had come to watch, went on stage for an acoustic set when a power cut put the amplified bands out of action, and Joni Mitchell, who wasn't even there, wrote the song 'Woodstock'. CSN and Y recorded it on their album *Déjà Vu*: it was about us all being stardust and golden and having to get back to the garden.

The name Woodstock, having been swiped from a village by a pop festival, became hugely portentous when twinned with the words Nation and Generation. The Woodstock Nation was a new, idealistic community to which almost everyone under thirty wanted to belong. The Woodstock Generation was anti war, pro peace, anti hate, pro love, pro drugs, pro self-expression, pro freedom of every kind. Since then some opinions have been revised. Sure, many who were around at the time still see it as the dawning of a new age which, perhaps, we have not tried hard enough to realize. Others saw it as the hugely bloated ritual of the hippy subculture going under. It was followed swiftly by the ugliness of the Isle of Wight festival and murder at Altamont, where Hells Angels killed a fan while the Rolling Stones were on stage.

At Yasgur's Farm there is a memorial stone bearing

the festival's dove and guitar symbol on a red background. Max Yasgur has retired to Florida, but the organizer, Michael Lang, still lives in Woodstock and now manages Joe Cocker.

By the time of the festival, Woodstock had been wrecked for Dylan. It was no longer a retreat and he was planning his escape back to Greenwich Village. For seven years Woodstock had been a hugely important place for him. He first came in 1962, to a cabin on Broadview Avenue on the hills of Ohayo Mountain to the south of the village. The cabin was owned by the family of Peter Yarrow of the Peter Paul and Mary folk group. (Remember 'Leaving On A Jet Plane'?) Dylan spent the summer there with Suze Rotolo. She painted, he wrote, and was completely at peace with himself. By 1964, his relationship with Suze over, he spent more time up here and less in his drab flat on West Fourth Street in Greenwich Village. That year, Dylan's then manager Albert Grossman and his wife Sally came to town, buying a substantial mix of property and land two miles west of Woodstock in Bearsville.

They set about creating a complex with a recording studio, a 250-seat theatre, two restaurants, a bar and video-recording hall. Albert died in 1986 of a heart attack while on a plane to London, and is buried here, in a plot marked out with a white picket fence down by the stream. It is covered in a carpet of wild flowers. Sally has continued to realize his dream.

The studio is hidden away up an unmarked dirt track at the top of a wooded hill. Ian Kimmet, a Scot whom Albert brought from London to manage the place in 1978, showed me around the two studios, rehearsal room, accommodation and related facilities. 'We have everything up here the bands could want,' said Ian, 'so they can forget about everything else and concentrate on the music. You get people, they walk in

257

the door wired, but after a couple of days they relax and get in a groove.'

As I arrived a group of people were eating spaghetti round a big table in the studio kitchen. Among them were the Indigo Girls, who were recording an album, and Budgie, Siouxsie's drummer, who was over from England for two days to play with them. Up a pine spiral staircase was the TV lounge and on the wall a selection of the studio's recent greatest hits. The framed album covers included R.E.M.'s *Green*, Robbie Robertson's *Storeyville*, and records from TESLA, Metallica, Psychedelic Furs, and Paul McCartney's *Tripping the Live Fantastic*, which was mixed here.

That night, in the Bear Café, Ian introduced me to Sally Grossman. I had seen her before, but only on the cover of Bob Dylan's *Bringing It All Back Home*. She sat with a glass of red wine, which she hardly touched, and a series of cups of cappuccino sprinkled with cinnamon. Her black hair was fuller than in the cover picture. She wore a black coat and squashy black Paddington Bear hat, and a grey Bearsville sweatshirt. She was tall, close to six feet.

I could remember every detail of that album cover. Dylan is in the foreground, hunched forward on the foot of a chaise longue, with a magazine promoting a Jean Harlow movie and a fluffy grey cat on his lap. At the other end of the chaise longue, in a stylish red suit, her black hair parted at the side, is Sally, holding a cigarette aloft. The photograph, taken in Sally's living room in her house just up the hill from this restaurant, is a part of rock history.

I remember the cover so well because I must have stared at it a thousand times as a teenager while I played the record. The photographer, Daniel Kramer, wanted to fill the picture with objects which related to Dylan and reflected the mood of the music on the record. There was a sign from a fallout shelter, a copy

of *Time* with Lyndon B. Johnson on the cover and LPs
by the Impressions and Robert Johnston. Most of the
props were gathered by Dylan, Sally and the photographer from around the house. Just visible on the
wall above the mantelpiece is a clown's face which
Dylan made by glueing pieces of coloured glass to a
plain glass background. It looks rather like the picture
of himself he painted for the cover of *Self Portrait*. He
gave the clown to Bernard Paturel, who kept it in the
Expresso, and loaned it to them for the picture.

Behind Sally's left arm is the cover to *Another Side
Of Bob Dylan*. There used to be a rumour that the
woman on the record sleeve was Dylan in drag, hence
the placing of *Another Side Of*. But then, they used to
say that if you looked at the cover of the 1968 album
John Wesley Harding upside down you could see the
faces of the Beatles formed in the bark. The previous
year the Beatles had released the psychedelic *Sergeant
Pepper's Lonely Hearts Club Band*. Dylan had produced nothing in 1967 and his contribution to the new
consciousness was eagerly awaited. But there was
nothing psychedelic about *John Wesley Harding*, a
stark collection of songs which Robert Shelton,
Dylan's biographer, called: 'Studies in allegory, psalm,
parable, symbol, metaphor, and moral tale'. Dylan had
certainly turned the Beatles on their heads musically, if
not on his album sleeve.

Sally could demythologize both the album covers.
She was on *Bringing It All Back Home*, she said,
because Columbia wanted a woman on Dylan's next
sleeve. Suze must have helped sales of the second
album, *The Freewheelin' Bob Dylan*. But the *John
Wesley Harding* picture was spontaneous. It was taken
behind Sally's house at the edge of the woods. Dylan,
in battered suede coat and black hat, is flanked by two
men I had imagined were Red Indians. An elderly gent
in glasses stands behind his left shoulder, squinting

against the sun. Who were these people, if they weren't the backing band? The guy at the back, it turns out, was a local carpenter and stonemason called Charlie Joy who happened to be working around the place that day. The other two were members of an Indian group called the Bauls of Bengal, who were staying with the Grossmans.

Sally often gets calls from people asking whether she has kept her living room the way it is on *Bringing It All Back Home.* She has, but is surprised that such things can still mean so much to people.

She arrived at the restaurant with a grey-haired black guy called William, who works at the complex. They were having fun, holding hands, joking and laughing a lot, and their enjoyment was infectious. At one point Sally was enthusing about a new type of candy she had discovered and asked for a box to be brought. They were growths of sugar crystals on sticks, called Rock Candy. She handed them round and we dipped them in our coffee and sucked on them.

As we talked, the restaurant filled up with New Yorkers here for the weekend. It was a cleanly modern, high-ceilinged room with plate-glass windows over-looking trees and a stream, the stream beside which Albert is buried. The background music was 'Blood On The Tracks' and later on 'Desire'. It occurred to me that for Sally, Dylan's music had been a constant background to her life. She was close friends with Sara, whom Dylan married in 1965, and throughout that decade Dylan was never far away. She and William joked about Dylan, the music reminding Sally of funny little things, like Dylan's mother struggling to understand one of his lyrics. William was shaking his head at 'Isis'; what a boring song, he was saying. I remarked that *Desire* had been my favourite album in college. Sally looked surprised. 'Was it?' she said, in a way that made me think she was a tough woman.

I started to moan about immigration officials in the United States, how they seemed to have arrived on the plane before yours. Tell them you are in Detroit to write about Motown, or in Texas on the trail of Buddy Holly, I said, and they will not have heard of either of them. Sally took exception, asking if I thought everyone was ignorant who did not know about Shakespeare. Wooh! Let's leave this woman on the LP sleeve, I was thinking. But she cooled down and started to tell a story about Dylan taking his parents to New York City from Woodstock for his mother's first visit. 'His mother had never been but all he did, he took them down, drove straight down, pointed out the Statue of Liberty, and brought her back for lunch at the Skyways. And that was it, that was her trip to New York.'

Sally asked me about my journey, where I had been, whom I had met, where I was going, and said it sounded interesting, but I doubt that it did. It was embarrassing telling her about it. How could a fan's journey like mine appeal to a woman who had known one of the main people I was writing about for years, been a part of the most exciting of times, in the most central of places? It must have seemed to her like an exercise in rock-tourist rubbernecking.

Next morning I was awoken by a wailing siren. I found the guest house was opposite the Woodstock Volunteer Fire Station, and that at this time of year there were many chimney fires as people started burning wood again. I went into the village for breakfast, and sat reading the local paper, the *Woodstock Times.*

It told me about a place that was a long way from New York, even if geographically it was just up the road. The news was reassuringly local in its concerns. The front-page lead warned of a possible 44 per cent rise in property taxes and there was a pic of the Veteran's Day parade at the Woodstock War Memorial. A fight on Halloween between the town's two newest cops was headlined 'Police Pugilist Punches Parked Policeman' and there was a court case about the Corner Cupboard Deli which had been prosecuted for selling beer to someone under twenty-one. The case was dismissed because it was 'a sale to a twenty-year-old deputy sheriff in a questionable sting operation'. There were ads for more live music venues than you get in most medium-sized American towns, including one for the Skyways, the place Dylan took his mum: 'Entrees Cup of soup/Salad. Steaks. Saturday Night entertainment for your listening and dancing pleasure NIGHTSHIFT featuring Donna Ducker'. Yep, I decided, I could live here. At the back of the paper were property ads for 'Gorgeous contemporary ranch, $190,000; Farmhouse charm, $109,000; Mansion on the hill, $129,000'.

After breakfast I went on a Dylan tour of Woodstock, heading north for a mile on a road through the woods that climbed the foothills of Mount Guardian. Here, in the last house on the right, where Camelot Road petered out into a track, was the house Dylan bought in 1965. It was the family home, where three of the four children Dylan and Sara had together, Jesse, Anna, and Samuel (Jacob followed in 1971) were born. Sara already had a daughter, Maria. It was a big turn-of-the-century cedarwood, ranchlike place with blue window frames, built on a four-acre plot and with a swimming pool fashioned out of an old quarry. Dylan lived here until the spring of 1969, when he was driven to move because of the constant attention of fans. It had a huge living room with a high, dark panelled ceiling. In the study, when Dylan was writing *John Wesley Harding*, a large Bible stood open on a lectern and the albums of Hank Williams were at hand.

The house was part of the Byrdcliffe Estate. An historic marker I had passed explained: 'On the hill above in 1902 P. R. Whitehead led workers in many arts and crafts to try an experiment in utopian living.' Just down from the house was the Byrdcliffe Theater which is open in the summer, when the wooden cottages among the trees are let to artists. Dylan's old house is called the Webster Place after Ben Webster, an architect and stage director, who built it. Dylan began to paint while he lived here, a neighbour teaching him, and he produced the paintings which appear on the covers of the Band's *Big Pink* and his own *Self Portrait*.

It was from this house Dylan set out on his motor-bike on 29 July 1966 for the garage at Bearsville where the machine was to be repaired. I followed his route down Camelot Road, turning into Upper Byrdcliffe and down to the Glascoe Turnpike. I went right at a Stop sign which had been adapted to read 'Stop Homophobia' and left into Striebel Road, a narrow lane running steeply downhill to Bearsville. There are crash barriers to the right where the ground drops sharply to the River Sawkill and the main road, Route 212. Dylan was riding down here when, as he explained later, he hit an oil slick and went over the handlebars. No-one knows how seriously he was hurt, he and Albert Grossman always refused to talk about it, but Dylan seems to have used the accident as an excuse to retreat, which he did for two and a half years.

The time was not unproductive, however. He spent some of it at a substantial pink-painted house at 2188 Stoll Road in West Saugerties, a few miles north-west of Woodstock. I drove over there. The house was lived in at that time by the Band, with whom Dylan had recently been on a world tour; they followed him to the country. They called it Big Pink and named their album after it. It looks exactly as it did then, when it appeared on the original gatefold sleeve of the record. It was in the basement during 1967 that the series of informal recording sessions, which were much bootlegged and eventually gained legitimate release as *The Basement Tapes*, took place.

This was Dylan and the Band getting into the Woodstock groove Ian had talked about, getting laid back, taking the pressure off and enjoying themselves. I felt like I was in the groove too. I spent a couple of days wandering around the place talking to people, and found almost everyone had memories of Dylan and the Band.

In a cabin in the woods near a lake on the west of town I talked to Billy Faier, a folk singer since the fifties. He was a close friend of Bernard Paturel, who moved away from Woodstock in the early seventies when he and Marylou divorced, and helped get the folk music off the ground at the Expresso.

We started chatting outside, where Billy was working on an extension to his home. 'I'm racing the winter,' he explained 'trying to get this sub floor down and covered over before the snows come.'

A sleek black kitten with sawdust on its nose and wood shavings on his fur scampered between us. Billy told me he wanted to preface everything he said about Dylan with the statement that he was a giant. A genius. But he could be a very nasty piece of work.

'I was a victim of one of his truth attacks, once,' he said. 'I was running for local office and we were upstairs at Bernard's, talking, when Dylan started letting me have it. This was a technique he had where he rounds on a person and tries to take them apart, destroy them. Ask them who they think they are, tell them their opinions are worthless, they are worthless. It was strong and it made me feel really bad. I never got to where I hated him for it, but it was a devastating thing to do. Having a very powerful personality, a very well-known personality, turning on you, focusing a lot of negative energy on you is very, very hard to cope with.'

Talking to me was slowing Billy down and the cold was getting to him, so we went inside. The little house was beautiful, light and airy, with south-facing windows high up in the wall of the living room, and steps up to a sleeping area above the kitchen. He told me he had built it himself, thirty years ago.

Many of the people who came to live in Woodstock, the Band, Van Morrison, John Sebastian, grew up on Billy. They would seek him out.

'When someone famous comes here and tells me how much my music meant to them years ago, it's a good feeling,' he said. 'One day the Band sat right here on the chairs, I sat on the step playing to them. I played Woody Guthrie songs with Van Morrison. Every time he got drunk he wanted me to sit down and play Woody. The first couple of times it was OK but after that it got a little old. But I loved playing with all the people who came out here, all of them.'

While he liked the people, he had less enthusiasm for the concept of the Woodstock Nation. 'Horseshit!' he said. 'That's just stuff they sell in shops. It's a commodity, there is no reality to it. The Aquarian airheads, the hip capitalists, are selling it. "Ooh [he mimicked] the spirit of brotherly love." I suppose there are totally naive people who believe in the spirit of the Woodstock Nation. OK, I wish I was one. It's not real, it's not happening.

'Woodstock was like any small town with good people in it. Dylan coming here was a beautiful beginning but then money destroyed it. You got big houses up on the mountain where there were no houses ten years ago, they got all the little shoppy-poos in the town for the tourists. Woodstock has sold out its heritage for money.'

I moved on, to the south of the village up Ohayo Mountain Road. I was going to visit Elliott Landy, an official photographer at the festival. In spring 1969, Dylan moved this way too, having been hounded out of Byrdcliffe by the tourists peering through his windows and taking bits of his lawn as souvenirs. He sought seclusion on a lonely hundred-acre farm known as the Walter Weyl place. But it didn't work, and by the time of the festival Dylan had already decided to move back to Greenwich Village. Coincidentally, the first place he stayed in Woodstock, the Yarrow cabin, was up here too. I found it on the corner of Broadview Avenue and Hill 99, just down from Elliott Landy's place.

The cabin was derelict, the roof half caved in. I scrambled down a steep bank to get to it. Inside it was deep with the fallen leaves that the holes in the roof had let in, an eerie place.

Elliott had supplied photographs for *Big Pink* and *The Band* albums, and went up to Byrdcliffe to take the picture of Dylan that appears on the front of *Nashville Skyline*. Shot from below, Dylan is silhouetted against a blue sky, holding a glossy acoustic guitar and raising his hat.

One of Elliott's most memorable festival pictures is a panorama of the crowd, which he shot from the stage. This picture was the most widely used during the twentieth anniversary of Woodstock, and another made the cover of *Life*.

He gave me a copy of a poster on which the crowd scene was used, together with a text by him from which you will gather he thinks it was a pretty important event:

'The mystical teachings tell us that with the birth of each age there is a sign, a teacher, which appears, to lead the way. As Christ was the example for a world two thousand years ago, so the experience at Woodstock can be an example for our world today. Just as the birth of Jesus could find no place, so too, Woodstock was without welcome – but both found their place to be: one in Bethlehem, the other in Bethel; the similarity of names whispering to us of a cosmic declaration, an intelligence beyond our own.'

My journey was nearly over, Montreal the last stop. I drove north again on the New York Thruway on a beautiful, bright winter's day. The road snaked gently through the Adirondack mountains, through forests of pine and silver birch. Once north of Albany the traffic thinned rapidly, and so did the radio stations, that other reliable indicator of the density of the local population. Each time a station went out of the radio's range the seeker mechanism would tumble through more green digits to find another signal.

As I drove I ran through the whole of my journey in my mind. It had been incredible: I had been to so many places, discovered so much about the rock stars who meant the most to me, stepped into their lives, talked to their friends.

The closer I got to the Canadian border the thinner the traffic and the fewer the radio stations, until in the very northernmost reaches of America mine was the only car on the road and just one radio station was within reach. It was not like travelling between two major cities, more like journeying to the edge of the world. I was driving the only car going to Canada, and no-one was coming the other way. It was a beautiful, lonely road, forty miles or so between intersections, with occasional glimpses of still lakes through the trees, and of little timber-built towns. Somehow I felt more isolated on this drive than on any other. Once I pulled off for gas although I didn't need any, just to talk to someone. I found myself prolonging the conversation, asking for directions when I knew exactly where I was, just to delay for a few minutes getting back in that car and going out on that road, alone.

I began to worry that the radio stations would peter out all together, that I'd be left watching the green digits on the radio tumbling through empty air, with nothing to listen to, not even the Rolling Stones and Beatles greatest hits which I had always been able to find before. There is so much of their music on American radio that I believe you could travel right across the continent and, by spinning the dial, listen to nothing but 'Get Back', 'Hey Jude', 'Brown Sugar', 'Jumping Jack Flash' and the rest, all the way.

The radio stations that I could pick up came from places way off my route, from Connecticut and Vermont. Several ran nostalgia trivia quizzes. If I could say who sang 'Mrs Brown You've Got A Lovely Daughter' I could win a free hot-dog dinner at Carl's, the home of the hot dog. Another station kept going over to a reporter standing outside a courtroom waiting for the arraignment of a woman accused of a triple murder in the small town. There was little to say before she arrived, so he would give an update on how many television crews had set up their equipment on the sidewalk in this sleepy town, and interview more locals. This consisted of asking them all the same question about how surprised they were to hear of a triple murder in this little place; their replies were invariably well, gee, they were sure surprised, they sure were *very* surprised that it should happen here. Eventually the woman arrived, and the reporter described the alleged triple murderer's red suit and sleek hair as she was bundled inside.

Then I started picking up French stations and knew Canada was near.

Chapter Sixteen

John, Yoko and Suzanne

Down by Montreal harbour, guided by the words of a song, I went looking for Suzanne. In 1965 Leonard Cohen wrote about a woman who took him to her place near the river and who fed him tea and oranges.

He has often said that the song is journalism, that it is completely accurate, which may or may not be true. Certainly there are clues to the place within its words, and he has furnished other hints about the woman in a way uncharacteristic of a man with an intense sense of his own privacy.

The river referred to is the St Lawrence, on which Montreal is a large island, an amalgam of fifty villages. From Suzanne's apartment he can hear the boats go by, which indeed you can from the area south of Notre Dame, a place of steep and narrow cobbled streets in the most French-seeming corner of a very French city. He has told interviewers that the tea and oranges were actually a tea with orange peel in it, called Constant Comment. He sings of Suzanne wearing Salvation Army rags and feathers, of her showing him where to look among the garbage and the flowers, and of the sun pouring down on Our Lady of the Harbour.

The latter is easily identified. He is referring to the Église de Notre Dame de Bonsecourse, which has towering above it a huge statue of the Blessed Virgin, arms outstretched, looking over the harbour. There was no sun pouring down on my early-morning visit, rather a freezing fog rolling in off the river. Tramps were forming a long queue at a side door of the church. Later I saw them drifting off with plastic carrier bags stuffed with winter clothes, a curious echo of the line in the song about Suzanne's charity-store garments. There was a Bonsecourse market too, which might explain the garbage and the flowers.

The place was not particularly picturesque. Workmen were ripping the street apart alongside the harbour quays. The harbour itself looked neglected, an area of ugly waste ground which blocked my view of the St Lawrence. I walked the cobbled streets of what could easily be a quiet corner of Paris. There were cafés, clubs, and a few tacky gift shops outnumbered by art galleries. From the upper floors of the tall, narrow stone buildings there must be a good view of the harbour.

Leonard Cohen has said that Suzanne was a real woman, the wife of a friend. This is why, in the song, though he spends the night beside her he touches her only with his mind. He has said she is a ballerina, hence the perfect body he refers to, and that her husband was a sculptor. According to him, she is still in Montreal.

Coming to this place was the closest I got to her, however. This is probably what Cohen has intended for those who want to nose around in his life. Those who know him well suspect that this is a cover-up, to put snoopers off the true scent. Clive Rawlings, Cohen's biographer, told me: 'I think it is a red herring. I said to Leonard I don't believe the stories he puts about. In the latest interview I have read he again emphasizes she was the wife of a friend. I have my doubts as to the precise nature of that story. Read between the lines, look to Paris, not Montreal, for Suzanne.'

That was all he would say on the subject, but it sounded plausible. Leonard Cohen is an intensely private man, as people kept telling me, and it is unlikely that he would draw people to an old friend quite so readily. He is so secretive that he has sold all his personal papers, his personal archive, to Toronto University and put a sixty-year embargo on them. This makes him twice as paranoid as the British government, which imposes a thirty-year delay on the disclosure of sensitive information. Cohen's addresses, even the names of his favourite restaurants, are guarded like state secrets. So I didn't find Suzanne, but I did find a place that brought the song vividly to life for me. Of course, Leonard Cohen has written other wonderful songs about women, but 'Suzanne' is my favourite and the one that seems rooted in his home city of Montreal.

Cohen was born into an upper-middle-class Jewish family in 1934, and by the mid-sixties was an established poet and novelist. He started to set his poems to music and when Judy Collins recorded 'Suzanne' in 1966 he came to the attention of CBS. They signed him as a performer. He was an unlikely-looking rock star, a quiet academic type much given to black leather sports jackets, woolly pullies and knitted ties. He was not conventionally good-looking. Photographs from the period reveal a forehead too low, a mouth too big, teeth too brown, and hair as moulded as Barbie's boyfriend Ken's. Despite it all this poet of romantic despair possessed a sexual magnetism that made him the thinking woman's Tom Jones. Now in his lean and leathery late fifties, he is still rated as a pretty tasty bit of older man.

His career is also going strong still. After a bit of a dip following the early albums – Songs Of Leonard Cohen, Songs From A Room, Songs Of Love and Hate and New Skin For The Old Ceremony – he came back with the wonderfully witty and sexy I'm Your Man in 1988. Seventeen of his younger pop admirers including R.E.M., the Pixies, Ian McCulloch, John Cale and Lloyd Cole got together in 1991 to record an album of their interpretations of Cohen songs. His mix of melancholy desperation and humour is very much to contemporary tastes.

From 1959 he spent much of his time on the Greek island of Hydra, and he now has a permanent base in mid-town Los Angeles. But Montreal, which he has called the Jerusalem of the north. is a place that he belongs to more than any other, and it regularly draws him back.

Cohen and his sister Esther have kept the family home after the deaths of their parents: perhaps this is some measure of the importance to him of his roots. The house is maintained as it was when Leonard was in college, but neither he nor his sister use it, it seems. She lives in Manhattan and he has another house in Montreal to stay in during his visits. The addresses of both homes are supposed to be top secret. If you are allowed to visit one, several people told me, Cohen puts you on oath not to reveal where it is. I may not have found Suzanne, but I did find the houses.

I went to his family home first. It is in Belmont Avenue, in the Westmount area of the city, backing on to the King George VI Park. The ground here rises steeply towards the hilltop Parc Mont Royal after which the city is named, and upon which it looks down. Leonard and Esther were brought up here, with a nanny and a maid, in a substantial semi-detached house with a white-painted porch and white steps running down to the garden. Across the park is the family's synagogue, and the two schools Cohen attended, Roslyn Junior and Westmount High, are just a few minutes' walk away.

The park was his childhood stamping ground, and the scene of a friendship that has all the pathos of Cohen's songs. One day, walking through, he met a young man playing a guitar. Cohen got talking to him and asked him to teach him how to play. Three lessons took place and Leonard was doing well, but at the next the man did not appear. Cohen phoned his home, and found that he had hanged himself.

I walked around the steeply sloping park. There are tennis courts, a children's playground and a pavilion, locked up for the winter. There were fine views, down over the St Lawrence and south towards America. Across to my left was downtown, its huge shiny skyscrapers clustered like a mutant growth.

The early-morning fog had cleared and the day was warm and sunny, in the 60s instead of the 40s as it should have been for the time of year. I sat on a bench and thought about the stories I had heard of Leonard Cohen as I had been travelling. In Manhattan, I had been told, I would find Cohen's unofficial archivist, the person who probably knows more about him than anyone. Just go to the largest newsstand in Time Square and ask for Robert Bowers. I did, and he was there, and about to go on his break. So we stepped outside, steering round the derelicts and into a café, where over a tuna-fish sandwich he told me about the time Leonard let him stay in the family home.

'I spent four days there,' said Robert. 'Esther invited me. She lives in Manhattan and she dropped the keys off at the store. I checked with Leonard to see that it was OK with him, and I got the message back that it was. It was fun being in his home, his books are pretty much intact, his bedroom is the way it was when he was in college, the rest of the house was pretty conventional.

'For twenty-two years Leonard has been an integral part of my life. I have followed him on tour, on a twenty-five-date tour of Europe and a forty-five city tour of North America. I have collected everything I can about him, read everything that has been written, and I have eighty boxes of material. I'm very fortunate to have gotten this close to him. He is a hero. Years ago it would have been Fitzgerald or Hemingway, but they are both dead. I don't live vicariously through him but he is one of the most important things in my life, and my collecting is compulsive behaviour. I am single, I live alone, I don't date girls and my life revolves around Leonard.'

The stay at Belmont Avenue was a reward for the support Robert had given Cohen over the years.

'I do various things which help Leonard. I clip articles and sent them to Esther. She is a lady in her sixties and she doesn't have access to a lot of the publications that feature Leonard. But I see them all at the newsstand. We carry a large number of foreign publications. My father had this business for years and I've carried it on. Recently Kelly Lynch, Leonard's assistant, called me up and asked if I had a copy of a 1956 poetry book of Leonard's called *Parasites of Heaven*. His books are very hard to find. Now, I don't know why he can't have Hazel, who is a close friend of Leonard and lives at the back of his other house in Montreal, go round to the family home and get it. I know he has a copy there, but no, Kelly asks me. I was moving apartments at the time and although I went through all eighty boxes I couldn't find it. Then finally at 4.30 a.m. it came to me where it was. I woke up and went right to it.

'For myself I feel incredibly close to Leonard but he keeps himself at a distance. He won't call me on the phone, he has other people do it. He sends me books, faxes, badges with notes saying thanks for your help. He needs barriers and space, he retreats to monasteries for six weeks at a time.'

On my travels I had collected other stories about Leonard Cohen. Monica Boscia talked about meeting him in Manhattan when he was recording *Songs Of Leonard Cohen*, his first album.

'I was leaving CBS one day and I went to grab the door and it was like a monsoon. Wild. And this man was standing there, so we looked at each other and said, "Oh my God, what are we going to do?" And it didn't stop. So we finally decided let's brave it. We ran to the corner and got absolutely drenched. There was a café and he said, "Come on, let's go in and have a cup of coffee." So I had coffee with this man. I had no idea who he was, but we got chitty-chatting and he's telling me he was really tired, he had just come from Greece. I said, "Are you a musician?" He said, "No, actually I'm a poet. They've put some music to my poems and now they want me to make a record." So I said, "Do you sing?" and he said, "No, not really." Then he mentioned Judy Collins had recorded one of his songs. I asked him which and he spoke a few words from "Suzanne", I said, "I absolutely love that song." Then he told me some of his poems, just kind of said them. And we sat there for hours, long after it had stopped raining. Finally we left, I was living in the Village on Fourth Street, he was staying in the Henry Hudson Hotel on Ninth Avenue, and we walked together and we just kept talking and talking. I told a friend later I had met a lovely interesting man, but I never saw him again.'

And then she asked me: 'Is he still alive?'

Someone else told me a story about their sister, who was staying at a hotel in Geneva. One night she went to see Leonard Cohen in concert and afterwards, coming back to her hotel, she saw him going into the building. So she went up to her room, thinking about him, and then rang Reception and got put through to his room. She wanted to tell him how wonderful the concert had been and how he had made her feel. They talked and Leonard said, 'Why not come up to my room?' She said

275

she would, but once she had put the phone down she changed her mind, and never went.

Tough luck, Len, I thought, sitting in the park behind his house.

I headed back across town, making for Cohen's other home, and stopping off at one of his favourite restaurants, on Boulevard de Maisonneuve, for lunch. Ben's Delux Restaurant and Deli is a big corner place dating from the early years of the century. It has high ceilings and a chrome sign with huge red lettering outside, and tubular metal chairs and tables of a certain age. In the window were pasted pictures and recommendations from stars, most of whom meant nothing to me. Johnny Halliday was one of the few I recognized. They said things like 'Sincerely, a great meal'. There was nothing from Leonard Cohen, though in his youth this was his prime late-night hang-out. In the sixties the Canadian Broadcasting Corporation made a film called *Ladies and Gentlemen: Leonard Cohen* in which they followed him around the city and into Ben's. Cohen talks about the appeal of rare late-night centres like this, where disparate groups whose only link is that they have to be, or choose to be, up late, are pressed together. He enthuses about the 'urgent conversation' that results and says that staying up late, refusing to sleep, is the first real rebellion.

Leonard Cohen's other Montreal home is on a small square called Vallieres off the Boulevard St Laurent, just to the west of Parc Mont Royal. Number 28 is a three-storey stone-fronted Victorian house, painted grey and shuttered in the French style. It overlooks a small park, complete with a tiny bandstand on which a young couple in black were clowning and photographing each other. Squirrels were burying nuts under the close-cropped grass, fussily patting the turf down over their treasure.

This is where Cohen stays on his visits to Montreal. Like everywhere else he lives, the house is sparse, the walls plain white and the furniture simple. In his bedroom is a single bed with a small television at the foot. This sounds as you would expect if you have listened to 'Tonight Will Be Fine' from the *Songs From A Room* album, in which he talks of choosing the room he lives in with care, with small windows and bare walls, one bed and one chair.

The house is linked to a smaller unit where Cohen's lifelong friend, the sculptor Morton Rosengarten, has his atelier. It backs on to another building in which Hazel lives.

I took a walk around. On the Boulevard St Laurent, which sweeps uphill from Sherbrooke, the stores are old-fashioned; the street has the feel of a large provincial French city. At the hardware store on the corner they were putting up their Christmas decorations. Opposite the square were two clubs offering music and dancing and a bar with a generous Happy Hour running from 4 to 8 p.m., when drinks were two for the price of one. There were a couple of lingerie stores catering for the older woman. Just down the hill is El Gaucho Empanadas, a Portuguese restaurant where Cohen breakfasts on *café au lait*.

He bought the house in 1969 and lived there for a while with Suzanne Elrod who, by all accounts – though one can never be too sure with Cohen – is not the woman in the song. With this Suzanne he had two children, Adam and Lorca, and for a while enjoyed family life for the first time since his childhood. But they drifted apart and his children are now in Paris. Suzanne Elrod is a record-sleeve star, too. She is the beautiful dark-haired woman pictured to Cohen's right on the cover of the *Death Of A Ladies' Man* album.

I drove out west, to the cheap hotel I had found by the Olympic stadium, which looks like a giant modern electric kettle, on Sherbrooke. It was a depressing place, even as cheap hotels go, and as I drove Cohen's thoughts on hotel rooms from the *Ladies and Gentlemen* film came back to me. He talks of them being 'temples of refuge', oases, sanctuaries: places that are comfortable, anonymous and subtly hostile. 'You have found a place in the grass, the hounds are going to go by, you can have a drink, light a cigarette and take a long time shaving.'

OK, for tonight I would try and endure it in that spirit, but tomorrow I was going somewhere grander, and going there with a lofty purpose.

The desk clerk was impressed when he called up my reservation on the computer and found I was in the John Lennon Suite. 'Oh,' he said, 'you have the nicest room in the hotel. I'll come up and show it to you.'

In 1969 John and Yoko had a week in bed in room 1742 of the Queen Elizabeth Hotel on Boulevard René Levesque. It was a bed-in, they did it for peace, and spent the week being interviewed by TV, radio and the press, and receiving supporters and others who needed persuading of the seriousness of their intent. They also recorded 'Give Peace a Chance' here.

'How long are you staying?' the clerk asked as we ascended in the lift. When I told him just the one night he said, 'Yes, of course. It is a very expensive room.'

I smiled, but started to worry. I hadn't asked the price. It was an extremely expensive-looking hotel – the long lobby was so full of glass and marble it was like navigating a maze just getting from the door to the front desk. The people browsing round the designer shops in the lobby looked exceedingly well-heeled. How much was it going to cost?

Of course, I could have just asked, but I knew that even if it was really, *really* expensive I would still have to stay here. I had to stay in the room to write about the bed-in. It was better to put the cost out of my head. After all, this was the end of my journey. Surely I could splash out on my last night? But what if it was a thousand pounds? What if it was two thousand?

'And how many of you are staying here?' the clerk asked as the lift stopped at the seventeenth floor.

'All of me,' I said, 'but nobody else.'

He looked surprised. When he opened the door and ushered me into the suite I could see why. It was the size of a small house. There was a lobby with a black marble floor, a kitchen complete with fridge and microwave, a bathroom, a dining room with a table set for six, a sitting room, a master bedroom and a second bathroom. The clerk beetled round on a tour of inspection.

'I don't get to see the John Lennon Suite very often,' he said as he looked to see if there was a second minibar.

A second minibar? I told him one was plenty. Two televisions were enough, too.

'I like these,' he said, reaching up and tickling the glass beads on one of the chandeliers.

After he had gone I went on my own tour of inspection. In the fridge I found a flower arrangement which I stuck on the dining-room table. In the lobby there were three framed photographs of John and Yoko in bed in this suite. In one they were sitting up with hand-drawn posters reading 'Hair Peace' and 'Bed Peace' on the windows behind them, the bedhead against the window and the followers and reporters sitting at the end of the bed. As I wandered around it became clear that they had rearranged the apartment for the purposes of the bed-in, moving the bed into the living room, presumably because the bedroom was too small to receive the world's press in.

On a table by the bed was a basket piled with snacks, hand-made crisps, pretzels, cashew nuts and a very large Toblerone. In an envelope I found the key to the minibar. It was stacked with a vast array of bottles. I chose lemon, lime and mineral water which I drank with the Toblerone. This was really living.

Then I saw the price of the things and started to worry again about what the room would cost. $3 for the Toblerone, $2.90 for the drink! Well, I thought, I could cut costs by going to a grocery to buy food and using the kitchen's microwave, and not watch a movie, but that might save me $20 or so, a drop in the ocean.

I looked at the views. The best was from the living room west along Boulevard René Levesque. Directly below me was the cathedral-basilica of Mary Queen of the World. The clerk had told me it was a half-size copy of St Peter's in Rome. How very Canadian, I thought. Even when they steal an idea they can only reproduce it half as effectively as the original. A clutch of four tower blocks at least twice as high as the hotel took great bites out of my view of Montreal, though one was rather handsome, like a giant green bottle. I could still see the St Lawrence river, hazy in the winter gloom, to the south.

John and Yoko sat with their backs to this view for a week. I couldn't manage that, but I could have a sort of mini bed-in, for twelve hours or so. Or maybe, failing that, a minibar-in. Because if there is one thing that interests me as much as world peace it is a well-stocked minibar. I had a copy of a video called *John and Yoko: The Bed-in*, and I watched it to get some tips on how to proceed. I stood there thinking maybe I should get the hotel staff in to move the bed through into the living room, for authenticity's sake, but it seemed like a lot of bother just for one day. When John and Yoko arrived they set about writing slogans on white card with black marker pens. I had a block of Post-it notes and a biro, so I improvised. I wrote G - I - V - E, one letter to a sheet, until I had written Give

Peace a Chance, and stuck the sheets up across the window.

I have to confess the video was pretty boring. It was full of people asking, 'Is there not a more positive way of demonstrating for peace than sitting in bed for a week?' and Lennon saying, maybe, but this is our way and if you can think of a better way you go out and do it. Someone came in and told them how to stop capital punishment in America instantly. They should take their film crew and film an execution. Then they should say there is going to be a Beatles special at 2, and tell people not to eat before it. Then instead of the special you run the capital punishment film. People will be (a) so disgusted at the spectacle of someone frying in the chair and (b) so angry that they did not eat earlier and feel too nauseated to do so now, that they will rise up and call for an end to capital punishment.

'Beautiful,' said John. 'It's a beautiful idea.'

They were told about a lot of hare-brained schemes, all of which they adjudged 'Beautiful, really beautiful'. Clearly these were days of hope, a month before the Woodstock Festival. John and Yoko seemed convinced they had the Establishment on the run. They were unapologetic about their series of stunts to publicize the cause of peace. In fact their campaign was quite a clever one. They saw the stunts as a series of commercials for a product called peace. It was like selling to housewives, said John, ever the sexist. You had to get them to feel that there were two products on offer. War, and Peace. When they realized that, they would surely buy peace.

All sorts of people visited them apart from journalists: radicals, revolutionaries, nervous-looking girls who were giving out flowers for peace. They were beautiful. A man arrived who had walked from Toronto to Montreal for peace. 'Well done, that's a beautiful thing you did,' said John. Did he want to eat?

Well, no, he had been fasting since Wednesday. 'Walking and fasting for peace. That's fantastic. Beautiful.'

The video showed John washing his hair in one of my baths, using my hairdryer, Yoko putting her numerous white outfits in my closet, and John lying in my bed with his dirty feet and skinny ankles poking out.

There were plenty of phones in the room, three in the living area alone, so I decided to use them. I opened a can of Molson, one of the five types of beer in the minibar, and ordered a Fellini's Pizza from the video snack menu on the card above the TV ('Twin a first-run movie with a first-class armchair snack with the stars'). Then I got out the phone book, put on one of the complimentary bathrobes and started dialling. I looked up all the TV and radio stations and newspapers I could find.

The phone book was in French, which was a problem. What was the French for newspapers. Journaux? I ran down the list . . . *Canadian Jewish News, Corriere Italiano* . . . no, I don't think so. *Gazette Journal*? I rang and asked for the news desk.

'Hello,' I said, 'I'm in the John Lennon Suite of the Queen Elizabeth Hotel and I'm having a bed-in for peace.'

'Uh huh?'

'I wondered if you would like to come and interview me?'

'Well. Let me get this straight. You are having a what?'

'A bed-in, like John Lennon did here in 1969 in this room. I'm having another one. Can you cover it?'

He would get back to me.

I rang the *Globe and Mail*. They didn't think they could make it at such short notice. Could I fax them a press release? The *Journal de Montreal* was unimpressed too.

I tried television next, beginning with CBC. I got a girl who couldn't stop giggling. I tried others. CBMT English TV, CBFT French TV, CBM English Radio, CBF French Radio and CBF FM. I told them all that the *Globe and Mail* were coming, that I had only a few slots left in my busy itinerary but could just fit them in. How soon could they get here?

They would ring me back. It was beginning to look pretty hopeless. What was the matter with them? John and Yoko were fighting the press from their door! It looked as if I would get no-one. And then all my phones rang. It was the hotel's public affairs office. They had had some calls from the media. Was I organizing a media event? Because they could help if they had some prior notice.

I said I was having a bed-in for peace.

'For peace?'

'Yes. In what was Yugoslavia, in the former Soviet republics, in South Africa. I'm following the tradition of launching great peace initiatives from the Queen Elizabeth Hotel, Montreal. Surely there's not a problem with any of this?'

There was a silence. Well, they said, let us know if we can be of any help.

I was getting bored. My bed-in would be a wash out. I wandered out into my lobby and looked at the pictures of John and Yoko. Suddenly I realized something was not quite right. In the picture of them sitting in the bed in my living room, the windows were different. There were more panes. What was this? Had they called just any old room the John Lennon Suite? Would it be $2,000 or whatever for a room John and Yoko never even stayed in? I was trying to get the photograph off the wall to take it into the living room for a closer examination when the doorbell rang. It was my pizza. I pointed out the discrepancy between window styles to the guy who brought it. They replaced the windows, he said, a few years back.

I took a slice of pizza and went back to the phone book. The pizza tasted like you might expect a pizza made in Canada to taste, like a meat and mushroom pie. It was to pizza what the church next door was to St Peter's.

I decided to try the Hare Krishna organization. There was an entry for Hare Krishna Geetha. I tried it, not sure whether I was calling an organization or a man. There was no answer. So I ate some more pizza and tried another can from the minibar selection of beers.

Who next? I looked under Peace and found the Peace Bridge Brokerage, Peace, George, Peace, John, Peace, Larry and Peace Maintenance Ltd. This might just be a right-on organization still carrying the flame Lennon ignited here in 1969, but was probably not. I was disheartened.

I had finished the pizza, too. Should I have the minibar cashews? They were in a dinky glass jar, but cost $10.15, so I had the hand-made crisps instead, and the quarter-bottle of champagne.

No-one was calling, no-one was coming to my bed-in, and it was getting dark. I put a tape in my Walkman and sat on the windowsill behind the curtains, watching night fall.

I could look right into dozens of offices. There were spruce-looking blokes sitting in swivel chairs with their hands clasped behind their heads, or standing with phones crooked between neck and shoulder. They looked as if they could buy a $10.15 jar of cashews without even blinking. What the hell. I had the cashews, and a double gin and tonic. The minibar was looking a little depleted.

Maybe I'd get up at 2 a.m., when they shove the bills under the doors, to see what the damage was.

On the roof of the cathedral below me, Christ and the twelve apostles stood in a row on the very edge of the south face, their arms raised, toes just peeping over the edge. Lit from below, with their long hair and sandals, they resembled a sixties band standing in the white glare of the footlights, receiving the applause at the end of a gig.

They looked as if they were taking a final bow. 'Thanks for coming. You've been a great audience. Thank you and good night.'

Yep, it was just me, the band and the minibar at the end of the road. I sat on the windowsill, knocking back the remaining contents of the minibar, listening to tapes of all the people I had been following around America. R.E.M., Elvis, Roy Orbison, Buddy Holly, the Beach Boys, the Doors, Dylan, Motown, Lennon, Paul Simon, Lou Reed and Leonard Cohen. Maybe I should trash the room, as is traditional at the end of a gruelling tour. I'd been on the road so damn long. I'd paid my dues. Rock an' Rrroowl! Just then my bill came under the door. It was for $800. But it was beautiful, really beautiful.

The Lady and the Monk
by Pico Iyer

'A beautifully written book about someone looking for
ancient dreams in a strange, modern place'
Los Angeles Times

In *The Lady and the Monk*, Pico Iyer, the author of *Video
Night in Kathmandu*, returns to Japan to spend a year in
the beautiful city of Kyoto. A place of temples, monks and
ancient ritual, Kyoto is somewhere to seek tranquil
contemplation and perhaps to gain insight into the source
of Zen Buddhism. But even living in a monastery, Iyer
finds distractions and unsettling contradictions. The
monks wear Nike shoes, ride motorcycles and spend their
evenings watching TV game shows, while out on the
streets, the traditional Japan of lily-ponds and lanterns
clashes uneasily with the high-tech commercialism of
modern city life.

Then he meets Sachiko. Locked into an arranged marriage
with a corporate executive on a twelve-hour day,
dreaming of America and in love with Western rock stars,
she is in her way the essence of modern Japan. Through
her, Iyer's affair with the idea of her country blossoms
delicately into a romance of a special and very different
kind.

'Sachiko's presence illuminates a narrative that, in its
richness, its complexity, its elegance and its vast
contradictions, accurately reflects the culture that
inspired it'
Sunday Telegraph

'Iyer combines an acute sense of place with a mordant
irony . . . a *Madame Butterfly* for the 90s'
Time

'The first travel book on Japan I can remember that's
actually made me want to go there'
Time Out

0 552 99507 X

BLACK SWAN

A SELECTED LIST OF NON-FICTION TITLES
AVAILABLE FROM BLACK SWAN AND BANTAM BOOKS

THE PRICES SHOWN BELOW WERE CORRECT AT THE TIME OF GOING TO PRESS. HOWEVER TRANSWORLD PUBLISHERS RESERVE THE RIGHT TO SHOW NEW RETAIL PRICES ON COVERS WHICH MAY DIFFER FROM THOSE PREVIOUSLY ADVERTISED IN THE TEXT OR ELSEWHERE.

☐ 17542 4	THE LIVES OF JOHN LENNON		*Albert Goldman*	£4.99
☐ 99364 6	VIDEO NIGHT IN KATHMANDU		*Pico Iyer*	£5.99
☐ 99507 X	THE LADY AND THE MONK		*Pico Iyer*	£5.99
☐ 40445 8	PETER LAWFORD: THE MAN WHO KEPT THE SECRETS			
			James Spada	£5.99
☐ 13058 3	THE MARILYN CONSPIRACY		*Milo Speriglio*	£3.99
☐ 99433 2	SHOCK! HORROR! THE TABLOIDS IN ACTION		*S.J. Taylor*	£6.99
☐ 99366 2	THE ELECTRIC KOOL-AID ACID TEST		*Tom Wolfe*	£6.99
☐ 99370 0	THE PAINTED WORD		*Tom Wolfe*	£3.99
☐ 99371 9	THE PUMP HOUSE GANG		*Tom Wolfe*	£5.99

All Black Swan and Bantam Books are available at your bookshop or newsagent, or can be ordered from the following address:

Corgi/Bantam Books,
Cash Sales Department
P.O. Box 11, Falmouth, Cornwall TR10 9EN

UK and B.F.P.O. customers please send a cheque or postal order (no currency) and allow £1.00 for postage and packing for the first book plus 50p for the second book and 30p for each additional book to a maximum charge of £3.00 (7 books plus).

Overseas customers, including Eire, please allow £2.00 for postage and packing for the first book plus £1.00 for the second book and 50p for each subsequent title ordered.

NAME (Block Letters) ....

ADDRESS ....

....